KT-387-127

438125

303.
5

ZERO-SUM WORLD

Politics, Power and Prosperity
After the Crash

Gideon Rachman

Atlantic Books
LONDON

First published in hardback in Great Britain in 2010 by Atlantic Books,
an imprint of Atlantic Books Ltd.

This paperbck edition published in Great Britain in 2011 by Altantic Books.

10 9 8 7 6 5 4 3 2 1

A CIP catalogue record for this book is available from the British Library.

ISBN: 978 1 84887 704 7

Printed in Great Britain by CPI Bookmarque, Croydon

Atlantic Books
An imprint of Atlantic Books Ltd
Ormond House
26–27 Boswell Street
London WC1N 3JZ

To Olivia, my companion in Cambridge, Washington,
Bangkok and Brussels

CONTENTS

Part Three: The Age of Anxiety

Introduction

ZERO-SUM WORLD

FOREWORD

Writing a book on contemporary politics is a hazardous exercise. All such works are vulnerable to unexpected shifts in world affairs that can make wise-sounding predictions suddenly seem foolish. I finished the first draft of *Zero-Sum World* in January 2010. In the following year, however, the central arguments of the book seem to me to have gained in strength.

What I call the 'rise of zero-sum logic' in international politics has become more visible in three vital areas: US-Chinese relations, the crisis inside the European Union, and global governance. Meanwhile, in early 2011 popular revolts across the Arab world – above all, in Egypt – have injected new uncertainties into global politics. These events, foreshadowed in my book, are still unfolding. Depending on how they turn out, they could end up either re-energizing the liberal narrative of the Age of Optimism or further heightening the uncertainties of the Age of Anxiety.

An increase in tensions between America and China was one of the most striking political developments of 2010. In the background was the growing sense that the financial crisis had marked an important shift in economic and political power from West to East. The US is still the world's largest economy and its dominant power. But on both sides of the Pacific there is now a realization that China's challenge is becoming much more real. The much-touted Goldman Sachs prediction that China would become the world's largest economy by 2027 was made before the collapse of Lehman Brothers in 2008. In the aftermath of the Great Recession, new calculations moved the date forward. Projections by *The Economist* suggested that China might be the world's largest economy by 2019.[1]

American anxiety about the rise of China was increased in 2010 by the knowledge that the US budget deficit was out of control. Towards the end of that year, Admiral Michael Mullen, the head of the Joint Chiefs of Staff, argued that America's burgeoning national debt was now the single biggest threat to national security. He pointed out that some 50 per cent of the discretionary spending in the US budget goes on the military. Observing the deep cuts in military spending being made by cash-strapped European governments (including Britain), the admiral remarked, 'I do worry that it won't be too long before these kind of cuts will be part of our future as well, and that would be very dangerous.'[2]

The perception of an emerging threat to America's military dominance of the Pacific was strengthened by China's military build-up. Shortly before a trip to Beijing in January 2011, Robert Gates, the US defence secretary, expressed concern at China's latest weapons developments. On arriving in Beijing, Mr Gates was greeted with the spectacle of the maiden flight of China's first ever stealth fighter. To many observers, it looked like a deliberate and bellicose message from Beijing to Washington.[3]

1   'Dating game', *The Economist*, 16 December 2010.
2   Edward Luce and Daniel Dombey, 'US military chief warns on spending', *Financial Times*, 15 September 2010.
3   Kathrin Hille and Daniel Dombey, 'Stealth test flight overshadows Gates trip', *Financial Times*, 11 January 2011.

It is not just the United States that worries about a more assertive China. Possibly emboldened by a sense that power was moving their way in the aftermath of the economic crisis, the Chinese government took a noticeably tougher line with its neighbours during the course of 2010. Talking to Indian officials, I found mounting alarm about what the government in New Delhi claimed was increasing Chinese pressure over the two countries' unsettled territorial dispute over the Indian province of Arunchal Pradesh. The Indians also looked with alarm at China's close strategic and economic ties with India's neighbours – Sri Lanka, Pakistan and Burma.

China's assertion that its territorial claims in the South China Sea were now a 'core national interest' alarmed many of its South-East Asian neighbours, in particular Vietnam. That led Hillary Clinton, the US secretary of state, to assert that America too has a national interest in developments in the South China Sea – a statement that was received with some hostility in Beijing.[4] Japan was yet another Asian power to take fright at the spectacle of a more assertive China. A clash over a Chinese fishing boat that strayed into waters claimed by Japan became a major diplomatic incident in the second half of 2010 – and sent Japan hurtling back into the arms of Uncle Sam. Indeed, one of the biggest geopolitical shifts since I completed the first draft of this book has been Japan's abandonment of its flirtation with a rapprochement with China. Following the fall of the Hatoyama government in June 2010, Naoto Kan, the new Japanese prime minister, shifted his country's policy back in a more pro-American direction.

Inept and overassertive Chinese diplomacy during the course of 2010 handed the US a diplomatic opportunity in the emerging struggle for power and influence between the two nations. Increasingly disillusioned by its relationship with China, the US began to cultivate much warmer military and diplomatic ties with China's neighbours – in particular

4 Geoff Dyer, 'Power play in the South China Sea', *Financial Times*, 9 August 2010.

India. In November 2010 President Obama visited India and lavished praise on the country, hailing its emergence as a great power.[5] Indeed, just as the Indians worried about encirclement by allies of China, so China began to look anxiously at a network of powerful American allies surrounding the Middle Kingdom – including Japan, India, South Korea and Australia.

A battle to win friends and influence allies is clearly under way between the US and China. Some American strategists have argued that their country's budgetary problems could be compensated for by the construction of a network of Asian alliances, in a policy of 'soft containment' of China. And yet many countries in the region face a strategic dilemma as their economic and security interests increasingly diverge. China is now the major trading partner of Japan, South Korea and Australia. But these countries' key military relationship is with the United States. Unless China massively overplays its hand, these economic ties may end up mattering more in the long run, particularly amidst lingering questions about America's staying power in the Asia-Pacific region. As Kishore Mahbubani, the Singaporean academic, put it to me in early 2011, 'The countries of the region have to be careful. We know China will still be here in a thousand years, time. We don't know if the United States will still be here in a hundred years' time.'[6] By the end of 2010 tensions between China and the US were so overt that President Hu Jintao, shortly before visiting Washington in January 2011, took it upon himself to warn against those promoting 'zero-sum cold war thinking'.[7] (I decided not to take this reproof personally.)

While security and strategic tensions between the US and China soared over the course of 2010, economic tensions continued to simmer.

5 James Lamont and Edward Luce, 'Obama calls for top India role at UN', *Financial Times*, 8 November 2010.

6 Conversation with the author, Davos, 26 January 2011.

7 'Hu, China US must give up zero-sum cold war thinking', *Times of India*, 18 January 2011.

Shortly before the US mid-term elections of November 2010, the House of Representatives passed a law that would allow the US to raise tariffs in response to Chinese currency manipulation. Mike Rogers, a Republican from Michigan, put academic economists' concerns into blunt political language, when he complained of the Chinese: 'They cheat to steal our jobs.'[8] But the Senate failed to pass the tariffs bill and – after the mid-terms – the steam seemed to go out of the drive for anti-Chinese tariffs. The fact that China's currency was allowed to rise a little, in advance of President Hu Jintao's visit to Washington in January 2011, helped to cool protectionist sentiment.

Yet it would be complacent to write off the chances of a resurgence in protectionism. With American unemployment still very high and the US trade deficit with China at near-record levels, the conditions for a rise in protectionist sentiment remain. In a worrying sign for the relationship, American business leaders are beginning to complain of an increasingly hostile investment climate in China. Jeff Immelt, the head of General Electric, questioned the very idea of a win-win economic relationship between the US and China, when he grumbled at a private dinner in 2010, 'I'm not sure in the end they [the Chinese] want any of us to be successful.'[9]

While the US bemoaned Chinese currency manipulation, China made its own complaints about the American policy of 'quantative easing' (otherwise known as printing money), which China argued was a deliberate effort to drive down the value of the dollar. Third parties complained that they were being damaged by both Chinese and US currency policies that were making other countries' goods uncompetitive. Guido Mantega, Brazil's finance minister, charged that, 'This is a

8 James Politi and Daniel Dombey, 'US Congress backs action on renminbi', *Financial Times*, 30 September 2010.

9 Geoff Dyer and Guy Dinmore, 'GE chief gives vent to frustration over China', *Financial Times*, 15 July 2010.

currency war that is turning into a trade war.'[10] But Brazil's response – to impose controls on the free movement of capital – was seen by some as eating away at the fabric of a globalized world. It was a telling example of how the rise of zero-sum logic in the relationship between America and China – the world's two largest economies – could infect international relations as a whole.

The crisis within the European Union that unfolded over the course of 2010 looked more like an internal European affair. Except that, with the EU as a whole ranking as the world's largest economy and with troubled European banks plugged into the global financial system, the rest of the world knows that it is implicated in the continuing European drama.

As the crisis rolled from Greece to Ireland and then on to the Iberian Peninsula, so political tensions rose between EU nations and within individual European countries. There was immense bitterness in Ireland at what was regarded as high-handed pressure from Germany and the European Central Bank as the country's banking system tottered. Many Irish commentators, as well as influential outsiders, regarded the terms of the bail-out forced on Ireland in 2010 as unfair and unsustainable. And yet German politicians were also under enormous political pressure at home, from a public and a judicial system that were deeply hostile to the idea of further bail-outs. Senior German and French politicians seemed to be united on the need for new rules and policies to pull Europe back together again. But the details remained dangerously vague and elusive.

Meanwhile, as the countries at the cutting edge of the European debt crisis struggled to cut back spending, so social and political tensions mounted. In Greece, Spain, Ireland and even Britain, unemployment shot up – with youth unemployment particularly high. Speaking at the

10 Jonathan Wheatley and Joe Leahy, 'Trade war looming, warns Brazil', *Financial Times*, 9 January 2011.

World Economic Forum in Davos in January 2011, George Papandreou, the Greek prime minister, expressed worry that in Europe the rich continued to prosper, while the middle and working classes were being squeezed. This, he warned, was a formula for the rise of racist and nationalist political movements.

A troubled European Union is less and less able to promote the European model at a global level through the development of the G20. By the autumn of 2010 it was apparent that the G20 was becoming increasingly troubled. Approaching a new G20 summit in Seoul, arguments between China and the US over currency and trade were threatening to destroy the façade of big-power unity. Manmohan Singh, the Indian prime minister, spoke for many when he warned that, 'We've lost consensus about how to tackle the situation... The G20 is in serious difficulties.'[11] Those who bothered to check up on what had happened to previous promises made at G20 summits could only agree. The pledge to 'take strong action to address the threat of climate change' had not been acted upon. The promise to avoid 'competitive devaluation' was being ignored. Financial regulation was one area where there had been some progress. But, even there, the major issues – in particular tackling the problems of banks that were thought 'too big to fail' – had yet to be properly addressed.

Skilful diplomacy prevented an open row breaking out at the G20 summit in Seoul. But even the most ardent advocates of global governance were beginning to despair. Mark Malloch-Brown, once the number two at the United Nations and the author of a book arguing passionately for more global governance,[12] was nonetheless bleakly realistic about where the world had got to. In a co-authored article, he

11 Lionel Barber and James Lamont, 'India warns on damage from G20 tension', *Financial Times*, 19 October 2010.
12 Mark Malloch-Brown, *The Unfinished Global Revolution* (London: Allen Lane, 2011).

lamented that, 'International co-operation has stalled. From climate change and trade to nuclear proliferation and UN reform, macroeconomic rebalancing and development funding – and the list could go on – nearly every major initiative to solve the new century's most pressing problems has ground to a standstill.'[13]

Amidst all this gloom and stagnation, the spread of revolutionary fervour across the Middle East in early 2011 is transforming the atmosphere of international politics. It took just six weeks for the arrest of a vegetable seller in Tunisia to spark a chain of events that led to the fall of a president in Egypt. As I write (in February 2011), unrest has spread to the Gulf states and across North Africa to Libya and Algeria.

Although it is fashionable to say that nobody could have predicted the uprising in Egypt, in fact, that was not the case. Many experts on North Africa and the Arab world had written that Egypt and its neighbours were potentially unstable countries. In the hardback of *Zero-Sum World* (published in late 2010), I wrote of Egypt that 'there are clearly social and political pressures that make the country a pressure cooker', and floated the possibility that 'Egypt's autocracy will be swept away by an Islamist-influenced revolution'. I also wrote that 'the pressures visible in Egypt are replicated across North Africa'.

In the event, the early stages of the Egyptian revolution were not dominated or even strongly influenced by Islamists. On the contrary, the image of middle-class, English-speaking Egyptians – organizing a rebellion through Facebook and Twitter – could have been designed to appeal to a western audience.

Two rival narratives could now emerge from the turmoil of the Middle East. If the revolutions in Egypt and elsewhere in the Arab world succeed in establishing working democracies, it will be a triumphant re-assertion of many of the ideas of the Age of Optimism. The democ-

---

13 Richard Samans, Klaus Schwab and Mark Malloch-Brown, 'Running the World, After the Crash', *Foreign Policy*, January–February 2011, 80.

ratization of the Middle East will come to be seen as the latest example of the global advance of democracy, chronicled by Francis Fukuyama and others. The spread of political liberty in Western Europe in the 1970s was followed by the democratization of Latin America in the 1980s and of Eastern Europe, after the fall of the Berlin Wall in 1989. If democracy now takes root in the Middle East, the 'Arab exception' will have ended – which will seriously dent the confidence of the 'axis of authoritarianism' I describe in my book. The role of new technologies in spreading the revolutionary virus would also bolster the beliefs, expressed by Bill Clinton and others, that new technologies combined with globalization, will bring about political freedom.

There are, however, a great many 'ifs' in the preceding paragraph. It is entirely possible – probably likely – that the emergence of a new political order in the Middle East will be much more turbulent and unstable than the relatively smooth spread of democracy experienced in most of the former Soviet bloc.

A second story that could emerge from the turmoil in the Middle East would involve a long period of social and political instability, punctuated by violence and economic dislocation. From a western point of view, this would be accompanied by a loss of American power and influence in a strategically crucial part of the world. Just across the ocean from North Africa, the European Union would have the flow of immigrants to worry about and potential radicalization of Muslim immigrants in mainland Europe.

Ending this foreword perched precariously between optimism and pessimism about the Middle East is, perhaps, appropriate for a book that has struck some readers as excessively gloomy – and others as far too hopeful. In truth, there are elements of both optimism and pessimism in *Zero-Sum World*. My prognosis for the future of international politics over the next decade is undoubtedly bleak. The faith in the power of liberal political and economic values ultimately to prevail is a positive message.

At various seminars and talks that I gave in the weeks after the hard-back was published, I found that I was frequently asked whether I was optimistic or pessimistic about the future of the world. The answer that I came up with is that I am 'a medium-term pessimist and a long-term optimist'. That still seems to me about right.

Gideon Rachman
London, 18 February 2011

PROLOGUE

Davos, 2009

Every January political leaders from all over the world gather in a Swiss mountain valley. At the World Economic Forum in Davos, the assembled politicians agree to set aside their differences and to speak a common language. Closeted together in a ski resort, they restate their commitment to a single, global economy. They mingle cheerfully with the same multinational executives and investment bankers. They campaign to attract foreign investment and trade. For five days, the world's leaders seem to agree on a narrative about how the world works. At Davos, even the most intractable political differences are temporarily smothered by the globalization consensus.

But at the Davos forum in 2009, it was clear that something had gone badly wrong. The meeting took place just four months after the collapse of Lehman Brothers had tipped the world into the biggest financial crisis since 1929. The international bankers, who normally strutted proudly around the Davos cocktail circuit, were in hiding, as their institutions reeled and public opprobrium mounted. The Obama administration – locked in desperate economic negotiations at home – was conspicuous by its absence. With the Americans out of the way,

Wen Jiabao, the prime minister of China, was the star of the Davos show.

One late afternoon, an audience of the world's leading businessmen crowded into a seminar room to hear his views on the gathering economic storm. With China now the world's largest exporter and the biggest single buyer of American government debt, the audience had every reason to listen intently. There was nothing overtly charismatic about Wen. A slight man in a suit and spectacles, his style was that of a senior manager, reporting to the board. But towards the end of his talk, the Chinese premier dropped his bureaucratic manner and grew philosophical. In an effort to understand the crisis better, he said, he had been 're-reading Adam Smith'. Perhaps showing off a little, Wen made the point that the book he was consulting was the eighteenth-century economist's *The Theory of Moral Sentiments*, rather than the much better-known *Wealth of Nations*. For anyone with a sense of history, it was a bizarre moment. A leader of the Chinese Communist Party was openly turning to the founding father of free-market economics for guidance.

But while a communist leader was coming to the support of capitalism in Davos, some of the leaders of the major capitalist powers seemed to be flirting with communism. In the immediate aftermath of the collapse of Lehmans, Nicolas Sarkozy, the president of France, had allowed himself to be photographed reading Marx's *Das Kapital*, while Peer Steinbruck, Germany's finance minister, observed that 'certain parts of Marx's thinking are not so bad'.[1]

This political and ideological confusion was understandable. The financial and economic crisis unleashed by the Wall Street crash of September 2008 threatened the globalization consensus that the leaders of the world's major powers had all accepted. It created something close to panic in prime ministers' offices and presidential palaces across the world.

Faced with the most serious economic upheaval since the thirties, politicians fearfully looked back to the politics of the interwar period. Ed Balls, a British cabinet minister and the closest ally of Gordon Brown, the country's then prime minister, observed gloomily just after the Davos meeting of 2009 that the world was facing a financial crisis that was even more serious than that of the thirties, adding 'and we all remember how the politics of that era were shaped by the economy'.[2]

Over the next twelve months the world suffered its deepest recession since the thirties. Yet fears of a return to a world of soup kitchens, political extremism and fascist marches did not materialize.

So was it all a bad dream? A scare story? Might it be possible to go back to international business as it was conducted before the crash of 2008?

It would be a mistake to believe that. It is the argument of this book that the international political system has indeed entered a period of dangerous instability and profound change.

Over the past thirty years the world's major powers have all embraced 'globalization' – an economic system that promised rising living standards across the world and created common interests between the world's most powerful nations. In the aftermath of the Cold War, America was obviously the dominant global power, which added to the stability of the international system by discouraging challenges from other nations.

But the economic crisis that struck the world in 2008 has changed the logic of international relations. It is no longer obvious that globalization benefits all the world's major powers. It is no longer clear that the United States faces no serious international rivals. And it is increasingly apparent that the world is facing an array of truly global problems – such as climate change and nuclear proliferation – that are causing rivalry and division between nations. After a long period of international co-operation, competition and rivalry are returning to the international system. A win-win world is giving way to a zero-sum world.

Both as individuals and as a nation, Americans have begun to question whether the 'new world order' that emerged after the Cold War still favours the US. The rise of Asia is increasingly associated with job losses for ordinary Americans and with a challenge to American power from an increasingly confident China. The crash has heightened awareness of American economic vulnerability and the country's reliance on continued Chinese and Middle Eastern lending. Of course, even after the crash, the United States remains the most powerful country in the world – with its largest economy, its most powerful military and its leading universities. But the US will never recover the unchallenged superiority of the 'unipolar moment' that began with the collapse of the Soviet Union in 1991.

Meanwhile, the European Union, the other main pillar of the western world, is going through its most serious crisis since its foundation in 1957. The steady progress towards 'ever closer union' in Europe over the past fifty years was built on a win-win logic. The nations of Europe felt that they were growing stronger and more prosperous by merging their fates. The creation of a single currency and the near doubling in the size of the Union between 2000 and 2007 fitted perfectly with the logic of globalization. Economic and political barriers between nations were being torn down. But the threat of contagious debt crises across Europe has provoked bitter recriminations within the Union, as countries like Germany worry that they will be dragged down by their neighbours. The process of European integration is threatening to unravel.

Zero-sum logic, in which one country's gain looks like another's loss, has led to a sharp rise in tensions between China and the United States. Zero-sum logic is threatening the future of the European Union, as countries squabble over the costs of managing a single currency. Zero-sum logic has prevented the world from reaching a meaningful agreement to combat global warming. The US, China, the EU and the major developing economies all hesitate to move first – for fear of crippling their domestic economies, and so boosting the relative power and wealth of rivals. A similar competitive rivalry blocks the world's ability to find co-operative solutions to nuclear proliferation, as the major powers manoeuvre for advantage rather than acting decisively to combat a common threat. Zero-sum logic hovers over other big international challenges – such as shortages of energy, food and water, as the world's biggest powers struggle to secure resources.

The emergence of a zero-sum world undermines the key assumptions of US foreign policy since the end of the Cold War. Both Bill Clinton and George W. Bush believed that it was in America's interests to encourage the rise of major new powers, such as China, because globalization was bending history in America's direction. In 1999 Bush captured the conventional wisdom of the age when he observed, 'Economic freedom creates habits of liberty. And habits of liberty create expectations of democracy… Trade freely with the Chinese and time is on our side.'[3] Clinton even came to believe that globalization was changing one of the oldest rules of international relations, the notion that rising and established powers would clash with each other as they jostled for power. His aide James Steinberg later recalled that the president 'didn't see that there had to be inherent competition among nations. The success of some was not threatening to others. It was their failure that was threatening.'[4]

Clinton's belief in the possibility of a win-win world was not a personal eccentricity. One of the most influential political ideas of the thirty years between 1978 and 2008 was the theory of the 'democratic peace'. The idea was that capitalism, democracy and technology would advance simultaneously – and global peace would be the end-product. In a world in which all the major powers embraced democracy and market economics – and globalization and high technology drew people together – war might become a thing of the past. Consumerism and connectivity would trump conflict. People would visit McDonald's rather than fight each other. They would surf the internet rather than riot in the streets.

The notion of a win-win world did not seem incredible in the heyday of globalization, for this was also an Age of Optimism in much of Asia and in the European Union. Predictions that the Chinese miracle would be ended by the Tiananmen Square massacre of 1989 proved wide of the mark. Instead, Chinese growth was relaunched at an even faster pace after Deng Xiaoping's 'southern tour' of the country's manufacturing heartlands in 1992. Almost two more decades of rapid economic growth led the Chinese cheerfully to embrace the idea of a win-win world. Hu Jintao, China's president, even used the phrase when he toured a Boeing plant near Seattle in 2006, saying that 'Boeing's co-operation with China is a vivid example of mutually beneficial co-operation and a win-win outcome.'[5]

By the mid-nineties it was clear that India too was growing rapidly, and the rise of the Indian IT industry became one of the clichés of globalization. Even the Asian economic crisis of 1997–8 – which temporarily devastated the economies of Thailand, Indonesia and South Korea – could not alter the sense that the rise of Asia was inexorable. The emerging Asian middle classes had reason to feel optimistic on a personal level for, as Kishore Mahbubani, a Singaporean intellectual, put it, Asia's rise involved 'the empowerment of hundreds of millions of individuals who previously had felt a total sense of powerlessness in their lives'.[6]

The years from 1991 until 2008 were also years of hope in Europe. The stability and prosperity of the EU proved a magnetic attraction to its neighbours. Between 1994 and 2007 the Union more than doubled in size – going from twelve to twenty-seven members, as it incorporated most of the countries of the old Soviet bloc, as well as some that had remained neutral during the Cold War. By the time of the crash of 2008, the European Union had almost 500 million citizens and – taken as a whole – was the largest economy in the world.

In 2007, the year before the crisis struck, optimism about the global economy hit new heights among the Davos crowd. Steve Forbes, a publisher and former US presidential candidate, exulted that 'This is the richest year in human history. The best way to create wealth is to have free markets and free people, and more and more of the world is realizing it.'[7] That same year, David Hale, an international economist (and, like Forbes, a fixture on the Davos circuit), wrote that 'The world economy is currently experiencing a level of growth unsurpassed in human history.' Better still, as Hale pointed out, this new global boom was far more inclusive than previous long expansions because 'During the past twenty years, China, India, the former Soviet Union, Eastern Europe and Africa have rejoined the global economy.'[8]

The global economic crisis unleashed in 2008 ended this period of heady optimism. During the heyday of globalization – from 1978 until 2008 – successive American administrations were committed to the idea that globalization was good for America, good for China and good for the world in general. But when American unemployment rose sharply in the wake of the Great Recession, that belief began to crumble in the US. By the beginning of 2010, the basic rate of American unemployment stood at around 10 per cent – but it rose to 17 per cent once 'discouraged' workers and part-timers who would prefer full-time work were included. At the Davos meeting in January 2010, Larry Summers, President Obama's chief economic adviser, told the assembled plutocrats that one-in-five American male workers aged between twenty-five and fifty-five was now unemployed. In the sixties, 95 per cent of the same group had been in work. Summers strongly implied that Chinese trade policies were partly to blame – and he was not alone in his diagnosis.[9] Even mainstream American economists were beginning to blame Chinese 'mercantilism' for financial instability and job losses in America.

The return of economic growth to the United States in 2010 could not take the edge off these fears. It had been bought at the expense of a huge and unsustainable increase in deficit spending by the government. The surge in America's national debt sharpened fears about the future, even as it softened the immediate economic crisis.

Rising economic tensions between America and China may well lead to a serious increase in trade protectionism in America. That, in turn, will feed Beijing's paranoid fear that America is ultimately intent on blocking China's rise – poisoning political relations between the world's two most important powers, and so destabilizing the global system.

Europeans are also questioning the merits of the 'new world order' ushered in by globalization. Leaders like President Nicolas Sarkozy call for the EU to protect Europeans from 'unfair competition' from Asia. The European Union, as an institution, is also losing confidence. The whole construction of the EU was based on an effort to replace the ruinous and bloody rivalries of European history, with a new logic based around mutual economic interests. But in the aftermath of the crash of 2008, rising public debts in countries like Greece and Spain have cast doubt on the future of one of a united Europe's proudest achievements – the single European currency that came into being at the beginning of the twenty-first century. Greek leaders, under pressure from Germany to cut spending, made dark references to the Nazis' occupation of Greece during the Second World War – precisely the sort of terrible memories that European unity was meant to banish.[10]

Europe's leaders have also taken to agonizing publicly about the continent's declining importance in a world that looks set to be dominated by Asia and the Americas. European voters are reflecting this defensive new mood. They have turned against further enlargement of the Union and are increasingly voting for radical, anti-immigration parties.

The risks of new international tensions and conflict are heightened by the emergence of a new set of dangerous global political and economic problems that, if they remain unsolved, could provoke wars, environmental disaster and debilitating new economic shocks.

What are these dangers? President Obama gave a succinct summary in his first major address to the United Nations in September 2009: 'Extremists sowing terror in pockets of the world. Prolonged conflicts that drag on and on. Genocide and mass atrocities. More and more nations with nuclear weapons. Melting ice caps and ravaged populations. Persistent poverty and pandemic disease.'[11] President Obama's list was alarming – but by no means comprehensive. To his list can be added a further set of perplexing global problems: the threat of new trade wars and the international political tensions they will foster; a rising number of failing states and the cross-border problems they spawn; the struggle between nations to gain control of natural resources, in particular oil and food; the renewed strength of authoritarian regimes and ideologies that threaten to clash with the democratic world; cross-border flows of refugees and illegal immigrants; the growing power of international organized crime in places such as Mexico and the Balkans.

Even if tensions between a wounded West and a rising Asia can be contained, the relative weakening of the United States makes it significantly less likely that the world will be able to find solutions to these festering international problems. In the aftermath of the financial crisis, there was much talk of the need for a 'new Bretton Woods' – a reference to the conference in 1944 that laid the foundations for the international architecture of the post-war period. But in the aftermath of the Second World War, America was powerful enough to design the world's new institutions – and then to ensure that they were accepted. In today's world, the US does not have the power to impose solutions to international political problems. Without a dominant power, multi-polar, multinational forums for negotiation and debate are liable to get bogged down and to fail – as the international climate-change talks have amply demonstrated. In this new world, the international problems referred to by President Obama are more likely to worsen than to be solved.

Phrases like 'global economic imbalances', 'failed states' and even 'nuclear proliferation' can sound abstract and even a little dull. But failure to deal with these problems effectively over the next decade could cause global political turmoil. Among the biggest risks is the danger of a major new war in the Middle East, provoked by a failure to rein in Iran's nuclear programme. The debt crisis in Europe or trade wars, triggered by American anger at Chinese mercantilism, could plunge the world economy into a severe new downturn. The inability to stabilize failing states could see countries like Afghanistan and Pakistan slipping further into violent anarchy, with dangerous consequences for the rest of the world. Over the longer-term, a failure to deal with climate change could provoke the most serious international crises of all – leading to flooding, famine, mass migration and even war.

Crises such as these ultimately threaten the future of the whole world. Yet the world's major powers are unable to deal with them co-operatively. That is because a damaged and dysfunctional world economy and the growth of new international rivalries – in particular, between the US and China – are increasingly trapping the world in a zero-sum logic, in which one country's gain looks like another's loss.

This dark new international mood contrasts sharply with the liberal dream of the past thirty years of a more prosperous and peaceful world, pulled together by the ineluctable forces of globalization, and regulated by markets and American power.

To understand the dilemmas facing today's world's leaders we need to understand this recent past. That is why the first two sections of this book are devoted to the international and intellectual history of the past thirty years.

Starting the narrative in 1978 may not seem obvious to all readers. Americans, in particular, have tended to regard the defining moments of recent history as the end of the Cold War and the al-Qaeda attacks on the United States. One of the best recent histories of US foreign policy is subtitled *From 11/9 to 9/11* – the two dates in question marking the fall of the Berlin Wall and the start of the 'war on terror'.[12] But the collapse of the Soviet system and 9/11 were part of an even bigger story – the creation of a globalized world economic and political system. The two key events framing that story were the opening of China in 1978 and the 2008 crash.

I have divided this thirty-year epoch into two distinct periods. The first part of this book deals with the Age of Transformation that began in 1978 and explains how and why the world's major powers all embraced globalization – and how this sparked the rise of China and India. Part Two is about the Age of Optimism, from the collapse of the Soviet Union in 1991, through to the near collapse of the international financial system in 2008. This explains how globalization created a win-win world that stabilized relations between the world's most powerful nations. The final part is called 'The Age of Anxiety'. It explains why international politics are about to get more dangerous and unstable – and what can be done to break away from the perilous logic of a zero-sum world.

PART ONE

The Age of Transformation
1978–91

INTRODUCTION

'No power on earth can stop an idea whose
time has come.'

MANMOHAN SINGH, INDIA'S
FINANCE MINISTER, JULY 1991

The Age of Transformation began in December 1978 in Beijing at the third plenary session of the Eleventh Central Committee meeting of the Chinese Communist Party. It ended on Christmas Eve 1991, when the flag of the Soviet Union was lowered for the last time over the Kremlin.

In late 1978 Deng Xiaoping laid the foundations for the opening of China and his country's emergence as an economic superpower. By contrast, the economic and political reforms initiated by Mikhail Gorbachev in the mid-eighties brought about the break-up of the Soviet Union. But while the domestic political effects of Russian and Chinese economic reforms were very different, their global significance was similar. At the beginning of the eighties it still made sense to speak of a socialist and a capitalist world. The Cold War was the defining principle of international politics, as it had been since 1949. By the end of the Age of Transformation, the world was no longer divided into two rival political and economic camps. The celebration of capitalism and wealth creation seemed all but universal. In the United States, Ronald Reagan insisted that 'What I want to see above all is that this country remains a country where someone can always get rich.' In China, Deng Xiaoping agreed: 'To get rich is glorious,' he famously proclaimed.

While the period was book-ended by events in the Soviet Union and the People's Republic of China, it was not just the communist world that was transformed between 1978 and 1991. In the United States and Britain, the Reagan revolution and Margaret Thatcher's radical reforms heralded a resurgence of free-market ideas and private enterprise, and a rethinking of the role of the state. The European Union also took a marked turn towards liberal economics, with the decision to create a single European market in 1986. The free-market wave also swept over Latin America and India – two parts of the world that had long been suspicious of liberal economics and American-style capitalism.

By the middle of the eighties it was clear that these events were beginning to form a global pattern. Initially, however, each country had its own specific and local reasons for launching into free-market reforms. Deng Xiaoping was reacting against the destructive madness of Maoism. Margaret Thatcher was driven by a desire to reverse decades of British economic decline and to take on trades-union militancy at home. Ronald Reagan wanted to reverse the 'malaise' of the Carter years and the growth of the American welfare state. Mikhail Gorbachev was intent on reviving the indebted and ossified Soviet economy. The opening and democratization of Latin America was spurred on by a continent-wide economic crisis in 1982. In 1991 India's reforms were sparked by a foreign-exchange crisis at home.

The United States and Britain initially experienced deep recessions in the early eighties. But by the middle of the decade these had given way to spectacular economic booms. The obvious and ostentatious wealth being created in London and New York served as an advertisement for the power and benefits of free-market reforms – and for the financial industry that served as a handmaiden for globalization. Thatcherite policies like privatization, deregulation and tax-cutting began to be wide-ly emulated across the world. The collapse of communism in Eastern

Europe in 1989 also provided a vital negative lesson. By 1991 there simply was no Soviet model to look to. The opening of the Indian economy in that year meant that the last major world power to resist globalization had joined the system.

Ronald Reagan and Margaret Thatcher could draw upon exuberant domestic traditions to support free-market ideas. Adam Smith was a Scot; Milton Friedman was American. But, in much of the rest of the world, the embrace of capitalist economics and globalization involved dramatic political, ideological and even psychological shifts. This was particularly true for the major communist powers, which had defined themselves through opposition to international capitalism. But in large parts of the developing world, the ideas of free trade and international investment were also deeply suspect – and tainted by memories of colonialism.

For China to embrace free trade with the West meant overcoming the lingering suspicions dating back to the Opium Wars of 1839–42 – a conflict provoked by Chinese efforts to crack down on British opium traders, which had ended in humiliating defeat and the forced Chinese concession of trading privileges to the British. Latin American and Indian attitudes to western multinationals were also weighed down by the baggage of history. India had once been colonized by a multinational – Britain's East India Company. In much of Latin America, US multinationals were often seen as little more than agents of imperialism. But the free-market tide was so strong in the eighties that it swept many of these historic suspicions aside.

The Age of Transformation was not just about economics. It was also a period of dramatic change in politics and in the international balance of power. The eighties saw remarkable advances for democracy across the world. There was a contagious wave of democratization in Latin America, which took in Argentina in 1983, Brazil in 1985 and Chile in 1989. All told, sixteen Latin and Central American countries established democracies during the Age of Transformation. Democracy also made

significant gains in western client-states in Asia. The Marcos regime
was overthrown in the Philippines in 1986. South Korea moved away
from authoritarianism when it staged direct presidential elections in
1987. The most extraordinary democratic breakthrough of all came
in Central and Eastern Europe in 1989, with the collapse of the Soviet
bloc and a series of revolutions from Poland to East Germany, Hungary
to Czechoslovakia.

China stood out dramatically against the global democratic tide, with
its bloody suppression of the student movement in Tiananmen Square
in June 1989. Were it not for events in China, the global move towards
democracy during the Age of Transformation would have seemed just
as all-encompassing as the move towards free markets. And in 1991,
with the memories of Tiananmen and of the revolutions in Eastern
Europe still fresh, it seemed reasonable to assume that it would only be
a matter of time before democracy triumphed in China as well.

At the start of the Age of Transformation, the US was experiencing
a crisis of confidence. By the end of the period, American optimism was
back. This change of mood was partly due to the resurgence of the US
economy and the long boom of the Reagan years. But it was also about
the transformation of the international environment.

The most obvious confidence-boosters were the collapse of the Soviet
bloc and the global spread of liberal political and economic ideas. But
events in Japan and the Middle East in 1990 and 1991 provided a further
boost to the new mood of American triumphalism.

As US anxiety about the Soviet challenge had waned in the second
half of the eighties, so concerns about a new challenge from Japan
had grown. The fearful mood was captured by books such as Michael
Crichton's paranoid novel *Rising Sun* and symbolic events such as the
purchase of Rockefeller Center by Japanese investors in 1989. But the
Japanese stock market peaked in December of that year – and crashed
in 1990. As the country's economy entered a long, painful slump during
the nineties, so talk of an alternative Japanese model gradually dwin-

dled away. The new challenger to American dominance, Japan, entered a long period of economic stagnation, just as the old challenger – the Soviet Union – began to break up.

The year 1991 completed the Age of Transformation. A victorious war against Saddam Hussein's Iraq restored America's faith in the power and utility of its military and 'kicked the Vietnam syndrome', in the exultant words of President George H. W. Bush. And on Christmas Eve 1991 the Soviet Union was finally buried. The United States was now the world's sole superpower.

CHINA, 1978:

Deng's Counter-Revolution

The opening of China to the outside world was the first, the most significant and the least-noticed event of the Age of Transformation.

The policy of reform and opening initiated by Deng Xiaoping in late 1978 brought China – one-fifth of humanity – back into the mainstream of international politics and economics. It transformed first the Chinese and then the global economy. In creating a new economic superpower, Deng also shifted the global balance of power. For Americans and Europeans living at the time, the defining event of the Age of Transformation was the collapse of the Soviet Union. But the simultaneous transformation of China was also stealthily setting the stage for the rise of a new potential rival to the United States. As the most populous nation on earth, China was more than just another Asian Tiger. Lee Kuan Yew, the creator of modern Singapore, put it in awed terms in 1993: 'It's not possible to pretend that this is just another big player. This is the biggest player in the history of man.'[13]

And yet the transformation of China into a mainstay of the global capitalist system was scarcely imaginable in 1978. At that time, the rise

of Deng seemed just another twist in the operatic political struggles in
China that followed the end of the Cultural Revolution in 1976 and the
death of Mao Tse-Tung that same year.

Deng took power at a time of life when most western politicians are
well into retirement, and after experiences that would have broken many
people. He was born in 1904 in Sichuan province and so was well into
his seventies when his moment came. A diminutive figure who stood a
little under five feet tall, he had lived in Paris for six years as a young
man and had taken away a knowledge of French and an enthusiasm for
soccer. Deng also joined the Chinese Communist Party while living in
France – and the rest of his life was devoted to the turbulent and bloody
political struggles of China in the twentieth century.

On his return to China in the mid-twenties, Deng got involved in
revolutionary politics and the burgeoning Chinese civil war. He participated in the Long March and fought against the nationalists in the
run-up to the communist victory of 1948. For much of his career Deng
was associated with the more pragmatic and practical wing of the party
– and for that reason he often fell out of favour during periods of revolutionary zeal. During the Cultural Revolution in 1967, he was sidelined
and humiliated by Maoist radicals, who denounced him as a 'capitalist
roader'. In 1973 he was rehabilitated by Mao, who praised him publicly,
allowed him to chair Politburo meetings and to press ahead with the
'four modernizations' of the Chinese economy. But by 1975 Deng was
again being accused of unwonted pragmatism. Mao turned against him
once more. The party newspaper, the *People's Daily*, quoted Mao as
complaining that Deng 'knows nothing of Marxism-Leninism'.[14] In 1976
Deng was once again stripped of all his official positions.

Deng survived personal as well as political tragedies. His first wife
died while giving birth in 1930. During the Cultural Revolution his
younger brother was driven to suicide and his eldest son was thrown
from a roof by radical Red Guards and paralysed from the waist down.[15]

By 1978 he had emerged, in the words of Jonathan Fenby, a journalist and historian, as 'the ultimate survivor, a loyalist who...had delivered grovelling self-criticism when necessary, a man whose loyalties and abilities could not be seriously doubted, but who knew, in times of trouble, how to sway with the tide like a rocking doll'.[16]

Mao's death in September 1976 provided Deng and his supporters with the political opening they needed. Deng stood for reform, modernization and an end to revolutionary upheaval, so his supporters in the party pressed for his rehabilitation. In July 1977 he was restored to the five-man standing committee of the Politburo.[17]

Handed his opportunity, Deng manoeuvred throughout 1978 to rehabilitate other party members who, like him, had fallen out of favour during the Cultural Revolution and to advance his policies of 'modernization'. During 1978 Deng pressed to allow more Chinese students to study overseas. By the end of the year, he was in a position to win the political and ideological argument at the now-celebrated Third Plenum of the Eleventh Central Committee of the Chinese Communist Party.

The plenum officially adopted the policy of 'socialist modernization'. But behind this bland-sounding policy lay some changes with revolutionary potential. Jonathan Spence, a leading western historian, identifies three crucial shifts.[18] First, there was the application of the 'four modernizations' to industry. Crucially, the plenum recommended that authority should be 'shifted from the leadership to the lower levels'. Local managers were to be given much more initiative to run their businesses. This was what might be called 'deregulation with Chinese characteristics'. Second, the plenum gave more latitude to Chinese peasants to break free from the system of collective farms and to cultivate crops on individual plots through 'side-occupations' like growing fruit and vegetables and raising livestock.[19] Finally, the plenum made a nod in the direction of the need for a more independent judicial system, to arbitrate the kind of disputes that would arise in a 'new world of local commercial initiatives'.[20]

On paper, this was a very modest and tentative beginning to market-based reforms. Most of the measures that were to transform China into a powerhouse of the global capitalist system were to come later. The setting up of Special Economic Zones for foreign investors, which drove the manufacturing boom in southern China, was already being considered in 1979. But the zones were not mentioned at the plenum and did not really get going until the early eighties. Other far-reaching reforms – such as the privatization of housing and the reform of state-owned industries – were still more than a decade away.[21]

Nonetheless, 1978 was still the critical turning point. It was the true start of the Deng era and of China's path to modernization and integration in the global economy.

Economic progress was remarkably rapid. By 1985 China's income from exports had reached $25 billion, up from $10 billion in 1978.[22] As farmers were allowed more freedom, the countryside grew richer. It was claimed that in 1978 around 270 million people or 28 per cent of the population lived in poverty;[23] by 1985 that number had fallen to 97 million or less than 10 per cent of the population.[24] The Special Economic Zones along the coast provided employment and higher incomes for millions of migrant workers, as China sucked in manufacturing activity from the rest of Asia. By the early nineties China's share of world trade had quadrupled since the beginning of the reform era. By 1993 China was receiving more foreign direct investment than any other country in the world.[25] By 2008 – when the global financial crisis struck – China was the undisputed workshop of the world, about to become the world's largest exporter and sitting on top of the world's largest foreign reserves.

Given the importance of what was afoot in the late seventies and early eighties, foreign observers were – in retrospect – a little slow on the uptake. Christopher Hum, who was, at the time, a young British diplomat in Beijing (he later returned as ambassador), says that in 1978 and 1979 the diplomatic community was much more preoccupied with the brief upsurge in political freedom and freedom of speech in China, associated with the 'Democracy Wall' in Beijing.[26] The trial of the Gang of Four in 1980 and the downfall of Mao's wife, Jiang Qing, provided further distractions. *Time* magazine was prescient enough to make Deng its 'Man of the Year' for 1978, remarking that some of the reforms he was advocating 'sometimes look suspiciously like a capitalist road'. Still, the magazine concluded, 'It will be a long time before Peking joins Washington and Moscow as the capital of a first-rank global power.'[27]

As part of his policy of opening to the outside world, Deng was intent on transforming relations with the West. The economic reforms of 1978 coincided with the normalization of Chinese diplomatic relations with the USA. In early 1979 Deng visited the US, amusing the crowds by donning a giant Stetson in Houston. Rather less amusingly, China invaded Vietnam at the end of 1979.

These political and international events were more dramatic and eye-catching than technical-sounding reforms to agriculture and foreign investment. Perhaps as a result, western leaders were very slow to understand the speed and scale of the transformation of China. The memoirs of Margaret Thatcher and Ronald Reagan demonstrate an instant and passionate interest in Mikhail Gorbachev's reforms in the Soviet Union. But the economic transformation of China barely registers. All Thatcher's references to China concern the tortuous negotiations to hand back the British colony of Hong Kong. Writing in 1990, Reagan noted that in 1984, Don Regan, his Treasury secretary, had 'come back from a trip to Beijing with an intriguing report: the People's Republic of China was moving slowly but surely towards acceptance of a free-enterprise market, and inviting investment by foreign capitalists'.[28] But – like Thatcher – Reagan was understandably much more focused on the end of the Cold War than on the economic transformation of China.

There is a further possible explanation for why westerners were relatively slow to understand the significance of what Deng was up to. Some commentators argue that the importance of the reforms of 1978 have been exaggerated and mythologized in retrospect by a Chinese

Communist Party keen to build a new, heroic narrative that distracts attention from discomfiting political questions – in particular, the bloody suppression of China's democracy movement in 1989.[29] Those who want to demystify the Deng reforms of 1978 make several points. There had been a tentative emphasis on economic reform ever since Mao's death in 1976. The role of Zhao Ziyang, Deng's prime minister between 1980 and 1987, in promoting reforms has also been downplayed. Zhao was general-secretary of the Communist Party during the Tiananmen demonstrations of 1989, but was purged and put under house arrest for being too sympathetic to the democracy movement.

James Kynge, author of one of the best recent accounts of the rise of China, pours cold water on the idea that Deng had some sort of master-plan for economic reform in 1978. He points out that the immediate impetus for reform was a shortage of capital and a 'payments crisis'.[30] Kynge argues that many of the most important economic reforms of the eighties were initiated locally by peasant farmers or small businesses and encouraged by local government officials, who were actually ignoring directives from Beijing. He believes that 'Deng's contribution was not that he conceived of all the strategies that would lay the foundations for China's economic take-off, but that he was willing to ride with whatever homespun formulae seemed to yield the growth the country so desperately needed.'[31] Deng himself might even have privately agreed with that verdict. He famously described his method as 'crossing the river by feeling the stones'.

But this kind of easygoing practical attitude was, in fact, a massive contribution to the development of China. The history of China under communist rule had been, in large part, a tragic story of the triumph of ideology and zealotry over common sense and humanity. The results were the mass starvation of the Great Leap Forward and the terror and destruction of the Cultural Revolution.

Deng freed China from the tyranny of centrally imposed ideology. Almost all his most famous statements about politics and economics are expressions of pragmatism. Perhaps his most often-quoted remark was 'It doesn't matter if the cat is black or white, so long as it catches mice.' In 1978 he justified the abandonment of orthodox Marxism by telling the party, 'Engels never flew on an aeroplane. Stalin never wore Dacron.'[32] Deng saw no virtue in a hypocritical embrace of poverty. 'Poverty is not communism' was another of his much-quoted sayings.

Deng's pragmatism meant that he was more than willing to learn from the outside world. He rejected both the socialist purity of those party members who wanted to avoid being tainted by the capitalist world and the 'Middle Kingdom mentality' of Chinese nationalists. One of his first reformist moves was to press to allow more Chinese students to study overseas. As he noted, 'Not a single country in the world, no matter what its political system, has ever modernized with a closed-door policy.'[33]

Deng opened China to foreign education, trade, investment and technology. His decisions meant that the story of the modernization of the Chinese economy was inextricably bound up with the story of globalization.

Yet the Chinese route to globalization also posed a challenge to liberal theorists in the West. In 1989 it seemed as if the final piece of the puzzle – political liberalization – was about to be slotted into place. Eastern Europe was in ferment and Gorbachev's reforms had opened up the Soviet system. A visit by the Soviet leader to Beijing in May 1989 helped further to radicalize the democracy movement in China and to push the Chinese communist system towards crisis. The students in Tiananmen Square also looked to the West for inspiration – famously building a replica of the Statue of Liberty.

Yet while the communist regimes of Eastern Europe proved willing to cede power peacefully, Deng Xiaoping showed that there was also a violent and ruthless side to his pragmatism. On 4 June he sent the tanks into Tiananmen Square and crushed the student movement. Thousands are thought to have died in Beijing and around the country.

The West's reaction to Tiananmen was a strange mixture of horror and complacency: horror at the bloodshed, but also a complacent sense that China would ultimately have to embrace democracy. The Chinese government had won a battle against the democratic movement sweeping the world, but it could not win the war. Popular liberal theory held that, ultimately, economic freedom and political freedom went hand in hand. China could not buck the system for ever.

BRITAIN, 1979:

Thatcherism

Margaret Thatcher believed in wealth creation rather than wealth redistribution. She believed in the individual rather than the collective. She believed in the private sector rather than the public sector. She was the champion of the small entrepreneur and the shopkeeper, rather than the trades-union boss or the senior civil servant. She was determined to cut red tape, regulation and taxes. She believed in the market, not the state. One of her most famous and pithiest statements was 'You can't buck the market'[34] – a phrase that more than most sums up the global ideological drift from 1978 until the collapse of Lehman Brothers in 2008.

Thatcher was given her chance because by the late seventies Britain was in the grip of a powerful sense of national decline. It was a characteristic of the Age of Transformation that in country after country, free-market reforms were pushed through against a background of national economic crisis. From China to India to Brazil, running out of money was a salutary experience: a crisis in government finances provoked economic reform.

Britain had its own version of this searing experience. The spectacle of the United Kingdom having to go 'cap in hand' (the phrase that was always used) to borrow from the International Monetary Fund in 1976 crystallized a sense of national humiliation and decline. Throughout the seventies, British governments had struggled and failed to control trades-union militancy. It was increasingly common to argue that the country was being 'held to ransom' by the unions – which seemed able to cut off the electricity and leave the dead unburied, while they pursued their disputes.

As a child in London in the seventies, I found it rather exciting to grow up in a world of power cuts and urban riots. But adults of voting age found the atmosphere of perpetual national crisis much less accept-able. Thatcher's victory in the election of May 1979 was secured by the misery of the 'winter of discontent' of 1978–9 – a series of crippling strikes that fed Britain's feeling of national malaise.

In the run-up to the vote on 4 May 1979, both Thatcher and the prime minister she would replace, James Callaghan, sensed that epochal change was in the making. 'There are times, perhaps once every thirty years, when there is a sea change in politics,' Callaghan remarked. 'It then doesn't matter what you say or do.'[35] Callaghan's musings were remark-ably prescient. He anticipated not just his defeat by Margaret Thatcher but also the beginning of a new cycle in politics, and he accurately estimated how long it would last: thirty years. Thatcher herself later recalled, 'The British people had given up on socialism. The thirty-year experiment had clearly failed and they were ready to try something else.'[36]

Thatcher, elected at the age of fifty-three, was Britain's first ever woman prime minister. But she was extraordinary for reasons that went well beyond her gender. She was the leader of a Conservative Party that had come to prize clubby consensus in the highest reaches of govern-ment, social peace rather than confrontation, allied to upper-class notions of *noblesse oblige*. But Thatcher was a tough conviction politician who was determined to destroy ideological and political enemies, whether in the trades-union movement or within her own party.

The strengths of her views and her language were startling to many members of the British establishment. In 1978 she informed Sir Anthony Parsons, a prominent British diplomat, that she regarded fellow Conservatives who believed in consensus politics as 'Quislings, traitors'.[37] She castigated Jim Prior, a member of her first cabinet, as typical of the 'political calculators' who 'see the task of Conservatives as retreating gracefully before the Left's inevitable advance'.[38] When she clashed with striking miners in the mid-eighties, she described their leaders as the 'Fascist left'.[39]

Thatcher was determined not to accept the argument that the task for a leader of post-imperial Britain was 'the orderly management of decline'. Under her leadership, both the Conservative Party and Britain would go on the offensive.

Unlike her political ally, the easygoing Ronald Reagan, Thatcher was ferocious and often bullying in her cabinet. Yet some of her colleagues later came to accept that as a radical reformer with many reluctant colleagues, she was compelled to hector and harry. John Campbell, her biographer, suggests that 'her aggressive manner' might have been 'the only way that Mrs Thatcher, as a woman, could have asserted her authority in the circumstances of 1979–81'.[40] But while Thatcher could be fierce with fellow politicians, foreigners and senior civil servants, she was noted for her kindness and devotion to her staff.

Historians and political scientists still debate how much of the political programme that came to be known as 'Thatcherism' had really been planned and thought through when she took office in 1979. From the mid-seventies Thatcher and some of her closest colleagues, in particular her intellectual soulmate, the future education secretary, Sir Keith Joseph, were intrigued by the economic ideas of Milton Friedman, who was awarded the Nobel Prize for Economics in 1976 – the year after Thatcher became Tory leader. Thatcher and Joseph were convinced of the need to take on the trades unions and to beat inflation. But sceptics point out that some of her other trademark policies, in particular privatization, were little mentioned in the election manifesto of 1979.

Thatcher's philosophical preferences and powerful personality were, however, evident from the very beginning. All of her most important policies flowed from her fundamental belief in small government: tax-cutting, privatization, deregulation, an assault on inflation and on trades-union power. All were intended to weaken the state and boost private enterprise.

One of her very first acts as prime minister was to embrace the judgements and discipline of the market by lifting exchange controls, allowing the free movement of currency in and out of Britain. It was a very bold act that her first chancellor, Geoffrey Howe, likened to walking off a cliff just to see what happened.[41]

The Thatcher government's removal of exchange controls in 1979 was widely emulated around the world and so was crucial to the increase in international capital mobility that underpinned globalization. As the historian Harold James notes, this liberalization of capital flows meant that 'economic issues became globalized – in other words, it was ever harder for national authorities to control them'.[42]

By 1981 three of Thatcher's signature policies were in place: the abolition of exchange controls, cuts in direct taxation and moves to curb the power of trades unions. Britain was in the midst of a deep recession and manufacturing industry was suffering badly. But the foundations for a boom in the City of London had been laid.

In 1982 the evocatively named LIFFE futures trading exchange opened in the City. In 1986 the Thatcher government pushed through the 'Big Bang' of financial deregulation in the City, which Andrew Marr suggests 'has a claim to be the single most significant change of the whole Thatcher era'.[43] The brash City trader, along with the striking miner, became one of the emblematic figures of the Thatcher era.

Thatcher herself seemed ambivalent about the surge in conspicuous consumption in the City. She never quite shook off her Methodist origins and perhaps she also sensed that the electorate disapproved of the champagne-swilling, Porsche-driving City 'wide boys'. In 1985 she remarked cautiously, 'Top salaries in the City fair make one gasp, they are so large.'[44] Conservative commentators, as opposed to the lady herself, were less ambivalent. Simon Jenkins, a former editor of *The Times* and prominent columnist, wrote approvingly in 1987, 'The young men and women of the City have been the advance guard of Britain's overdue capitalist revolution.'[45]

But while the City traders were the most conspicuous beneficiaries of the Thatcher era, the benefits were spread more widely. Between 1979 and 1987 Britain experienced a 21 per cent rise in average real incomes. Thatcher encouraged home ownership by selling off public housing. Between 1985 and 1989 house prices doubled in Britain – before the inevitable bust came when interest rates shot up in the early nineties.

The boom in the City and in the middle-class suburbs of south-east England changed the intellectual atmosphere in Britain. As a student at Cambridge University in the early eighties, it seemed to me that all the intellectual energy and self-confidence was on the right. The student and academic left, which had been a powerful force in the sixties and seventies, was beaten and forlorn. A few left-wing students rattled tins to collect money for the striking miners. But the spirit of the times seemed to be more accurately captured by the increasingly extravagant May balls, in which students flounced around in evening dress, looking like extras from Evelyn Waugh's *Brideshead Revisited*. The 'Brideshead' style, with its celebration of aristocratic dissipation, enjoyed a new vogue after Waugh's book was turned into a television serial in 1981.

The southern boom was just one aspect of the Thatcher era, however. The deindustrialization of much of northern Britain was the other side of the coin, leading to big job losses in traditional industries such as mining, steel, shipping and manufacturing. The contrast between the boom in the South and the bust in the North became a theme of many of the most successful British films about the Thatcher era, from *Billy Elliot* to *The Full Monty*.

Thatcher's time in office began with a wrenching attack on inflation, which provoked a deep recession and soaring unemployment. By 1981 her government faced surging unemployment, the biggest collapse in industrial production since 1921, urban riots and denunciation of her budget by 364 of Britain's most prominent economists (including five former chief economic advisers to the government), who wrote to *The Times* arguing that her policies would 'deepen the depression, erode the industrial base of our economy and threaten its social and political stability'.[46] The previous Tory prime minister, Edward Heath, had softened his policies in response to industrial unrest. But Thatcher's determination to press on cemented her reputation as the 'Iron Lady' – a sobriquet initially bestowed on her by the Soviet Union in 1977.

The beginnings of an economic revival and massive disarray in the opposition Labour Party might have been enough to secure Thatcher re-election. But it was the 'Falklands factor' – victory in a war against Argentina in the South Atlantic, after Argentina had invaded the Falkland Islands in 1982 – that made Thatcher's re-election the following year inevitable. Thatcher herself drew a direct connection between victory in the Falklands and her economic programme at home. In July 1982 she proclaimed triumphantly, 'We have ceased to be a nation in retreat. We have instead a newfound confidence, born in the economic battles at home and found true 8,000 miles away.'[47]

Emboldened by re-election in 1983, Thatcher pressed on with policies that were to define her era. A year-long bitter dispute with the miners' unions helped to break the trades-union power that had crippled successive British governments in the seventies.

The privatization of state-owned companies like British Airways, British Telecom, British Gas, British Aerospace and Rolls-Royce widened shareholding, gave another boost to the City and was generally perceived as boosting the efficiency of the economy. It also gave the world a new approach to industrial policy and a new word – 'privatization'.

The Thatcher government had cut the top rate of tax from 83 per cent to 60 per cent soon after coming into office, and the basic rate from 33 per cent to 30 per cent. In 1988 Nigel Lawson, her reforming chancellor, cut the top rate again to 40 per cent – literally provoking howls of outrage from the opposition in the House of Commons.

By the end of the eighties, the success of Thatcherism in Britain was drawing widespread international interest and imitation. Two of Thatcher's advisers published a book with the exuberant title *Privatizing the World*. Thatcher's belief that 'the state should not be in business' was becoming global conventional wisdom by the end of the decade.

Thatcher herself became increasingly conscious and proud of her international reputation. She exulted that 'People are no longer worried about catching the British disease. They are queuing up to obtain the new British cure.'[48] In even more grandiloquent mode, she claimed as early as 1982 that Britain was 'teaching the nations of the world how to live'.[49] On a visit as prime minister to Mikhail Gorbachev's Russia in 1990, she noted wryly that the new mayor of Moscow appeared to be a disciple of her own economic guru, Milton Friedman.[50] In her memoirs she boasted proudly, 'Britain under my premiership was the first country to reverse the onward march of socialism.'[51]

By the end of her period in office Thatcher was increasingly worried that the European Union posed a threat to her free-market policies in Britain. She was, by contrast, an unabashed admirer of the United States in general and of Ronald Reagan in particular. Her speech-writer Ronnie Miller remarked, 'She loved America...and America loved her back.'[52] John Campbell, her biographer, believes that 'a part of her would really rather have been American'.[53]

As the Soviet bloc began to crumble, the partnership of Thatcher and Reagan took on a global significance. Thatcher was not exaggerating hugely when she wrote in her memoirs, 'The West's system of liberty, which Ronald Reagan and I personified in the eastern bloc, was increasingly in the ascendant; the Soviet system was showing its cracks.'[54]

While Thatcher and Reagan's support of democracy in Eastern

Europe fits a narrative in which the advance of economic and political freedom throughout the eighties were essentially inseparable, elsewhere things were more complicated. The exigencies of the Cold War and Thatcher's admiration for capitalism and aversion to socialism meant that she enjoyed cordial relations with some right-wing dictators and excoriated some genuine freedom-fighters. Thatcher notoriously referred to Nelson Mandela's African National Congress as a 'terrorist' organization, and there are warm references in her memoirs to dictators such as Suharto of Indonesia and Chile's General Augusto Pinochet.

Yet while Thatcher may have exaggerated the extent to which she and Ronald Reagan always represented 'freedom', there is no doubt about the potency and importance of their transatlantic partnership and their promotion of free markets. Together with Mikhail Gorbachev and Deng Xiaoping, Thatcher and Reagan were the dominant figures of the Age of Transformation.

3

THE UNITED STATES, 1980:

The Reagan Revolution

All new American presidents seek to capture the spirit of the age in their inaugural addresses. Ronald Reagan did it more completely than most when he stood, facing west behind the Capitol building, in January 1981 and proclaimed, 'In the present crisis, government is not the solution to our problems, government is the problem.'

As soon as he had finished speaking and before heading off to lunch with members of Congress, Reagan paused and performed his first official act as president. As he later wrote, 'I signed an executive order removing price controls on oil and gasoline; my first effort to liberate the economy from excess government regulation.'[55]

Ronald Reagan had been preaching small government conservatism for decades. But it was not until the presidential election of 1980, when he was almost seventy, that the United States finally seemed ready for his message. The country had turned to Reagan, as *Time* magazine saw it, because it was 'sick and tired of the vast, clogged federal machine; sick and tired of being broke; fed up with useless programs, crime, waste, guilt; not to mention shame in the eyes of the world'.[56]

Like Margaret Thatcher in Britain, Reagan came to power determined to reverse what he saw as an historic and debilitating trend towards ever more intrusive government. Thatcher was taking aim at what she regarded as a socialist consensus that had reigned in Britain since the end of the Second World War. Reagan, who had once been a supporter of Franklin Roosevelt's New Deal of the thirties, said that he believed that the rot had set in with Lyndon Johnson's Great Society social programmes of the sixties – although some critics reckoned that his real target was actually the New Deal itself.[57]

Both Reagan and Thatcher saw themselves as engaged in a moral as well as an economic crusade. And the reforms they pursued were strikingly similar. During Reagan's first term there were tax cuts. There was deregulation. There were cuts in the welfare state. There was an assault on trades-union power. There was a squeeze on inflation.

As a Hollywood star, Reagan had experienced top marginal tax rates of 94 per cent. As president he set about 'reducing federal income tax rates from top to bottom'.[58] Within six months of taking office he had pushed through new legislation, cutting the top rate of tax from 70 per cent to 50 per cent. The measure was hailed by his supporters as 'the biggest tax cut in American history'.[59] The Tax Reform Act of 1986 increased personal exemptions so ensuring that six million more poor Americans would pay no income tax at all. It also cut the marginal rate of tax for top-earners further from 50 per cent to 28 per cent – bringing it down to less than half the level when Reagan took office. Corporation tax was cut from 48 per cent to 34 per cent.

Liberals complained that the poor were being made to pay for these cuts and that a welfare state was being replaced with 'trickle-down economics'. Sean Wilentz, a historian of the period, laments that 'Important social programs for the needy and the underprivileged – public assistance, food stamps, school lunch and job training programs, Social Security disability payments – had been slashed.'[60] Conservatives, however, still remember this assault on the welfare state as a high point of the Reagan era. In 2009 Christopher DeMuth, head of the American Enterprise Institute, a leading conservative think-tank in Washington DC, identified the restraint of domestic spending as one of four key elements of Reaganism: the others were tax cuts, 'stable money' (low inflation) and deregulation.[61]

Indeed, Reagan's deregulation of price controls in the oil and gas industry on his first day in office was just the start. On the same day he imposed a hiring freeze on all federal agencies. The following day he abolished the Council on Wage and Price Stability.[62] The deregulatory impulse was also controversially extended to environmental legislation and to the financial sector.[63]

The new president also quickly took on the unions. In the summer of 1981, about seven months into his first term, Reagan clashed with air-traffic controllers in a dispute that hugely disrupted air travel across the country. (I remember it well, since I was stranded at JFK Airport as an eighteen-year-old student trying to get back to Britain for my first term at university.) Reagan ordered striking air-traffic controllers back to work. When they refused to fall into line, he ordered them to be sacked and replaced with reassigned military personnel. Eventually, union resistance and the union itself crumbled.[64]

The assault on inflation was masterminded by Paul Volcker at the Federal Reserve. Volcker had been appointed by Jimmy Carter in 1979. He was determined to eradicate double-digit inflation by squeezing the money supply. It worked. Inflation fell from over 13 per cent to a little over 6 per cent in 1982. But there was also a high price to pay. Unemployment soared to 9.7 per cent in 1982, the highest rate since the thirties.[65]

The narrative of the 'Reagan revolution' (as his supporters swiftly dubbed it) was very similar to the story of Thatcherism in Britain. There was a deep and alarming recession that did particular damage to manufacturing industry. But both leaders were conviction politicians, who pressed on when some of their fainter-hearted followers ('wets' as

Thatcher dismissively called them) wavered. Thatcher insisted that 'the lady's not for turning'. Reagan was determined to 'stay the course', although he noted laconically in his memoirs that 'the turnaround took a little longer than I expected'.[66]

When the turnaround did arrive in the United States, it was long and sustained, and aided by lower oil prices. When Reagan took office in 1981 inflation was averaging 12 per cent and interest rates had temporarily soared to over 20 per cent. By the time he left office, eight years later, inflation was at 4.4 per cent and interest rates were below 10 per cent. Unemployment had also dropped from 7.2 per cent to 5.5 per cent in 1988.[67] The Reagan years after 1982 were marked by the longest peacetime economic expansion in American history.[68] Some twenty million new jobs were created between 1983 and 1989 and economic growth averaged a very healthy 3.5 per cent a year.[69] But the Reagan years were also marked by a sharp increase in income inequality. The long trend towards a more equal America that had begun after the Roaring Twenties was put into reverse. As Robert Wade of the London School of Economics points out, in 1980, when Reagan took office, the richest 1 per cent of Americans received around 9 per cent of the country's GDP. By 2006 the richest 1 per cent gobbled up 23 per cent of national wealth.[70]

In the US and the UK, the success of the free-market reforms of the eighties was closely associated with a boom in the financial services industry, which was swiftly reflected in house prices and popular culture. In the US, the boom was captured in the film *Wall Street*, the catchphrase 'greed is good' and in Tom Wolfe's novel *The Bonfire of the Vanities*. The Dow Jones industrial average, which stood at 950 on the day Reagan took office, reached a peak of over 2,700 in August 1987 – before the stock market crash of October of that year.[71]

Some of Reagan's critics on the left never accepted that his economic policies had succeeded. They saw them as a cruel sleight of hand, fuelled by unsustainable tax cuts and deficit spending and hopelessly tilted towards the wealthy. Yet while Reagan never won the battle of the academy, he was vindicated in the way that matters most to politicians – with success at the ballot box. In 1984 he once again asked Americans the question he had posed during the presidential election of 1980 – 'Are you better off than you were four years ago?' They answered massively in the affirmative and gave him a sweeping re-election victory. In both the US and the UK, conservatives exulted that they had discovered a potent political formula for gaining blue-collar votes – a combination of lower taxes, social conservatism, popular capitalism and patriotism. In the US, these voters were called 'Reagan Democrats'; in the UK, they were labelled 'Essex man', after a working-class county just outside London.

Reagan and Thatcher also shared a common outlook on the world. Both were suspicious of détente, and both were determined to take a tougher line with the Soviet Union. The two leaders recognized each other as kindred spirits. Reagan first met Thatcher in the late seventies, when she was leader of the British opposition and he was between his first two runs for the presidency. He recalled in his autobiography, 'I'd planned on spending only a few minutes with Margaret Thatcher, but we ended up talking for almost two hours. It was evident from our first words that we were soulmates when it came to reducing government and expanding economic freedom.'[72]

For all their ideological similarities, the personalities of the two leaders were very different. Thatcher was a master of detail, driven, slept little, bullied her colleagues and thrived on confrontation. She was not a natural speaker and was ill-at-ease and mannered on television. Reagan was famously vague, relaxed, genial, fond of an afternoon nap and a brilliant performer on television.

The late Peter Jenkins, a British political commentator, argues plausibly that Thatcher 'wouldn't have tolerated him in her own Cabinet for a moment'.[73] She is alleged to have said of Reagan, to one of her senior officials, 'Poor dear, he has nothing between his ears.'[74]

Even some of Reagan's close aides and admirers in the US could be startled by his intellectual laziness and personal style. Pat Buchanan, a

White House aide who later ran for president himself, was surprised to see the president passing the time in a cabinet meeting by sorting out jelly beans into different colours. Alan Greenspan, who served as an adviser to Reagan during the 1980 campaign, later recalled a cross-country flight with the candidate, during which he was meant to brief him on economics. He later recalled, 'I think I heard more clever stories during that flight than in any other five-hour period in my life…but I couldn't get Reagan to open the briefing book.'[75] But although Greenspan was taken aback, he was not put off. He believed that the most important thing about Reagan was 'the clarity of his conservatism… Like Milton Friedman and the other early libertarians, he never gave the impression he was trying to be on both sides of the issue.'[76] Reagan was no intellectual but, in Greenspan's view, 'though his grasp of economics wasn't very deep or sophisticated, he understood the tendency of free markets to self correct and the fundamental wealth-creating power of capitalism'.[77]

Reagan's intuitions seemed to be vindicated by the economic boom of the mid-eighties. Economic success at home built him a political platform for re-election. But it was triumph in the Cold War that finally sanctified him as a hero of the conservative movement.

Once again, Reagan and Thatcher's instinctive responses to events in the Soviet Union were very similar. As a Cold Warrior and an 'Iron Lady' both leaders might have been expected to view Mikhail Gorbachev's reforms with some suspicion. In fact, they both realized their significance very quickly. Thatcher proclaimed that Gorbachev was 'a man I can do business with'. Reagan embraced the Soviet leader and pursued arms-control with an ardour that made some of his harder-line conservative supporters worry that he had gone soft in the head.[78]

By the end of the Age of Transformation Reagan and Thatcher were seen as a duo all over the world – by both the left and the right. In Latin America, economic reformers were often at pains to distinguish their modest market-based measures from the 'neo-liberalism' of Reagan and

Thatcher[79] – neither of whom were particularly popular figures south of the Rio Grande, after the Falklands war and Reagan's support of the Contra rebels in Nicaragua. By contrast, Reagan and Thatcher were popular heroes in much of Central and Eastern Europe – a fact that caused a certain amount of pain and confusion to their left-wing and liberal opponents back home.

The fall of the Berlin Wall and the collapse of the Soviet Union took place after Reagan left office. Yet these events cast a retrospective glow of vindication over his presidency. Reagan was able to argue with some justice in his memoirs, published in 1990, that the previous decade had witnessed a 'stunning renaissance of democracy and economic freedom'[80] around the world.

Reagan's attitude to democracy was, as with Thatcher, more equivocal than either leader would later care to acknowledge. The Cold War ensured that, at times, the Reagan administration got into bed with some brutal bedfellows – from Jonas Savimbi's Unita rebels in Angola to the Nicaraguan Contras. Yet the Reagan administration's attitude to democracy promotion did evolve and become a little less equivocal and two-faced. The decision in 1986 to turn America's back on Ferdinand Marcos, a pro-American autocrat in the Philippines, and to support Corazon Aquino's 'People's Power' movement was an important turning point – pushed from within the Reagan administration by Paul Wolfowitz, who later became an important neoconservative and an architect of the Iraq War of 2003.

By the early nineties it was not just conservatives who recognized that Reagan had accomplished something important. Indeed, Reagan and Thatcher truly presided over an Age of Transformation because in the end they forced the left to accept their key ideas. In Britain, Tony Blair realized that to make the Labour Party electable he had to accept the Thatcherite settlement – and promise not to raise income taxes or nationalize industries. (It took the financial crisis of 2008 to force the Labour Party back to these old policies.)

In the US, Teddy Kennedy, the hero of the liberal left, later reflected admiringly that Reagan had succeeded because 'above all else he stood for a set of ideas'.[81] When Bill Clinton declared in his State of the Union Address in 1996 that 'the era of big government is over', he was accepting the triumph of the ideas that Ronald Reagan had proclaimed in his very first inaugural address in 1981.

4

THE EUROPEAN UNION, 1986:

Embracing the Market

Viewed from a distance of twenty years, the success of Ronald Reagan and Margaret Thatcher might encourage the view that – to adapt a favourite phrase of the Iron Lady – 'there was no alternative'.

In fact, there was an alternative and it was pursued briefly, but with a great deal of vigour, in France from 1981 to 1983. The old rivalry between Britain and France was revived as Thatcher pushed her programme of free-market reforms, while France under President François Mitterrand pursued hard-left policies. Thatcher and Mitterrand held a certain fascination for each other. She got on well with him, but also slightly distrusted him because he was both French and a socialist. He remarked, with a characteristic interest in the female form, that she had 'the eyes of Caligula and the lips of Marilyn Monroe'.[82]

Towards the end of her time in office, Thatcher began to feel out-manoeuvred by the French and President Mitterrand over the issue of European political integration. But in the early eighties, it was Thatcher who was clearly the more successful leader. France's experiment with 'socialism in one country' failed, just as Thatcher's internationally oriented free-market reforms were beginning to pay dividends in Britain. That, in turn, gave a boost to the forces of the free market across the European Union and the world.

It is easy to view the European story as something of a sideshow in the great story of globalization. Certainly, over the long run, the rise of China and India are likely to dwarf the significance of the formation of a single market and even a single currency inside the European Union. For the last generation, the economy of the EU has grown much more slowly than that of the United States – let alone those of the rising Asian powers. But it would be a mistake to see the Europeans as bit-players in the creation of a globalized world. Taken as a whole the European Union single market that was put together in the mid-eighties is now the world's largest economy – bigger than the United States or China. And, for all its troubles, the euro, the European single currency, is so far the only plausible alternative to the US dollar as a global reserve currency.

At the beginning of the eighties, however, communism was still a force even in Western Europe. In April 1981, in my gap year between school and university, I travelled to Paris to watch a mass rally for Georges Marchais, the French Communist Party leader who was running in the presidential election that year. The rally was held, evocatively, in the Place de la Bastille, the birthplace of the French Revolution. A red flag was hoisted to the top of the square's monumental column, as Marchais addressed 70,000 chanting, flag-waving communists. Marchais ultimately finished fourth in the election with over 15 per cent of the vote.

The narrow victory of François Mitterrand in the presidential election of May 1981 led to the formation of France's first socialist government since 1956. This was a government of the broad left. Mitterrand appointed four communist ministers to his first cabinet. It was the first time since 1947 that the Communist Party had participated in government – and their presence was more than a mere sop or an effort at coalition-building. Many of the new government's most ardent supporters genuinely wanted to dismantle the capitalist system.[83] Mitterrand swiftly launched into an ambitious and radical agenda – what the historian Tony Judt calls 'a phantasmagoric programme of anti-capitalist legislation'.[84] The new French government pushed through higher wages and a shorter working week. It lowered the retirement age to sixty and increased the number of paid holidays. It nationalized thirty-six banks and five of France's largest industrial corporations. In contrast to Thatcher's liberalization of capital flows, opening the British economy to the rest of the world, the French government imposed new exchange controls, in an effort to wall France off from capital flight.

The French programme swiftly ran into trouble. France's effort to push ahead with socialism in one country threatened to violate the country's commitments to the other members of the European Economic Community (EEC) – later to become the European Union. By 1982, as Tony Judt notes, there was 'mounting panic in business circles and signs that currency, valuables and people were moving abroad with increasing urgency'.[85]

The U-turn began in June 1982. Faced with rampant inflation, a widening trade deficit and a run on the currency, the Mitterrand government imposed a prices-and-wages freeze, initiated a crackdown on inflation and pushed through cuts in public expenditure. By 1984 there were no more communist ministers in the French government – and the French communists had begun a long decline into political irrelevance, paving the way for the rise of the far-right. In 1986 the French shift to the right was completed when conservatives won the parliamentary elections. Although Mitterrand was still president, he was now 'co-habiting' with a right-wing prime minister, Jacques Chirac, who set about reversing the nationalizations of the early eighties.

By the end of the decade, France too had embraced the global vogue for privatization. The major banks were returned to the private sector. TF1, the main state television network, was privatized – a move that was bolder than anything Thatcher was able to attempt with the British

Broadcasting Corporation. The big French oil companies, Elf and Total, were also privatized. The whole process raised the number of shareholders in France from 1.5 million to 6.5 million.[86] By the mid-eighties Mitterrand was able to recognize and embrace the importance of the psychological shift that France had undertaken during his presidency, remarking, 'I will have been the president of France's entry into modern economic competition.'[87] Given the crucial importance of France and French officials to the construction of the European Union, this was a conversion that mattered to the entire continent.

The man who helped Mitterrand to unpick France's experiment with socialism was Jacques Delors, his finance minister. Softly spoken, bespectacled, religious and a genuine man-of-the-left, Delors was also a pragmatist who had been unhappy with the hardline socialism of the early Mitterrand years. Appointed as minister of finance in the first Mitterrand government, Delors watched unhappily while his colleagues stoked up inflation through higher public spending. As he later told his biographer, Charles Grant, 'As the left hadn't been in government for so long, we had to satisfy a part of its dream... The speculators were against us. One can't say I was against everything the government did, but I tried to limit the damage.'[88]

It was Delors who in June 1982 persuaded Mitterrand to change course and accept a devaluation of the franc and cuts in public expenditure. 'The time of austerity has arrived,' he told the press.[89] Delors's victory was not instantaneous. He still had to fight off a rival camp that was urging Mitterrand to try even harder-line socialism, involving import controls and massive borrowing – policies that Delors dubbed 'Albanian'.[90] But it was Delors who won the battle of Mitterrand's ear, persuading the president that protectionism always led to economic decline. The president later recalled, 'During this period I saw many people. In the end Delors had the best-crafted arguments. So the Delors plan won.'[91] A second austerity programme in March 1983 cemented the shift away from socialism.

It helped that the Delors plan delivered swift results. The trade balance improved. By 1984 French exports and industrial output were reviving strongly. The success of the Delors plan in France resonated around Europe. Britain's left began to moderate its opposition to Thatcherism and, as Grant puts it, 'abandoned policies of socialism in one country, partly because it had seen them fail in France'.[92]

In West Germany Chancellor Helmut Kohl, the leader of the Christian Democrats, had taken power in an internal party coup in 1982. In 1983 he won an election, defeating a left-wing opposition that had wanted to attack unemployment through much higher public spending and that was keen on Mitterrand-style wealth taxes and social legislation. By contrast, Kohl pushed his country towards a warmer attitude to the market. He was also favourably impressed by the French finance minister. He let President Mitterrand know that he approved of the idea of appointing Jacques Delors as head of the European Commission – the policy-making, law-enforcing heart of the EEC in Brussels.

Delors arrived in Brussels in January 1985. Within a year, he had formed an improbable and short-lived alliance with Margaret Thatcher that had important long-term consequences. Delors hit upon the idea that the next great project for Europe should be to create a genuine common market by ripping up the rules and regulations that still inhibited cross-border trade across Europe. He would focus on the 'four freedoms' – freedom of movement of people, capital, goods and services.

To achieve his goal, Delors needed the backing of the political leaders of the European nations. He could count on the backing of his sponsor, President Mitterrand, and Chancellor Kohl was already a supporter. It was Margaret Thatcher's decision to embrace the creation of a true European market that was critical to Delors's success in pushing through the Single European Act of 1986. Britain had always been the big state that was most wary of grand new European projects and Thatcher had started her period in office with a bruising battle with the other European leaders over the UK's financial contribution to the EEC.

But by the mid-eighties Thatcher's prestige was high at home and abroad. Her backing for the single-market project was vital.[93]

The motivations of the two leaders were very different. Delors was certainly a believer in the free market, at least by French standards. In 2000 he frankly told an audience of fellow French socialists, 'I've always thought, notably in France, that there was not enough market... The market will teach us better than any speech to think, act and produce according to the diverse needs of the world's consumers.'[94] But his main motivation in Brussels was, above all, to promote European political unity. For him the Single European Act was largely a means to those ends. As he told a French radio station, 'If this job was about making a single market I wouldn't have come here in 1985. We're not here just to make a single market – that doesn't interest me – but to make a political union.'[95]

Thatcher, by contrast, found the idea of a European political union abhorrent for both ideological and practical reasons. She was a patriot and a believer in national sovereignty and the Westminster system. She was also a liberal in the nineteenth-century British tradition, who once notoriously remarked 'there is no such thing as society'. Although that remark has been much wrenched out of context, it did reflect her individualism and her distrust of European-style corporatism. By contrast, Delors saw the European tradition as midway between that of the US and Japan – 'Society is more present than it is in the United States. The Europeans have always had a kind of balance between the individual and society.'[96]

But for Thatcher the promotion of the Single European Act was a chance to divert Europe into an avenue in which it could do some real practical good – by promoting economic liberalism. Since the British prime minister believed that free trade was the natural state of affairs, she was slow to recognize the political implications of the creation of a Single European Act. It would involve more than a simple bonfire of national regulations. It could also lead to new laws and regulations at a

European level to govern and enforce the market. That would involve handing new powers to the European Commission, run by Delors. It would also involve allowing the EEC to make more decisions by majority vote, allowing individual countries such as Britain and France to be outvoted. It might even involve the harmonization of indirect taxation at a European level. Delors was well aware of these political consequences. They were the main reasons he was in favour of the creation of a single market in the first place.

Towards the end of the creation of the Single European Act, Thatcher began to develop misgivings and to fight aspects of the new treaty, for example its mentions of the possibility of the creation of a single European currency. But the Thatcher–Delors partnership lasted long enough to bring the new act into existence.

By 1988, however, the two were squabbling bitterly over Delors's plans to match the liberalization of markets with a 'social charter', creating pan-European rights for workers. The deepest rift of all came over the next step in the process of European integration – the creation of a new European Union, with a single currency and an emerging 'common foreign and security policy'. The political implications of these steps were crystal clear to Thatcher and totally unacceptable. Her opposition was visceral and emotional. In the House of Commons, she denounced Delors's plans for deeper European integration with the cry, 'No, no, no.' The *Sun* newspaper gleefully summarized and endorsed her position with the headline 'Up Yours Delors.'[97]

Thatcher's increasingly imperious behaviour and her open contempt for many European politicians convinced some of her colleagues that she was going slightly mad. Eventually, this unhappiness triggered an internal party revolt. Thatcher was challenged for the leadership of the Conservative Party, lost the contest and resigned as prime minister in November 1990.

John Major, Thatcher's successor, eventually agreed the Maastricht Treaty of 1991 that laid the groundwork for the single currency. But he did so only after securing a number of 'opt-outs' for Britain. Even so, Thatcher became a bitter opponent of Maastricht.

In retrospect, the Thatcher–Delors disputes captured one of the central dilemmas of globalization. Does the increase in global trade and investment simply involve cutting back the powers of national governments to interfere in the workings of capitalism and the free market? Or does it require the creation of new structures of government – but at an international, rather than a national, level? It was an argument that was to explode into the open many years after both leaders had retired – with the international financial crisis of 2008.

THE SOVIET UNION, 1985–91:

Glasnost, Perestroika and Collapse

J ust after 3 a.m. on Monday 11 March 1985, Mikhail Gorbachev left an emergency meeting at the Kremlin and headed home. Eight hours earlier, Konstantin Chernenko, the leader of the Soviet Union, had died. At a rapidly convened meeting of the Soviet leadership in the Kremlin, it had become clear to Gorbachev that he was on the brink of achieving his ambition to take over the leadership of the Communist Party and the country. Arriving home, he found his wife Raisa waiting for him. The couple decided to leave their apartment – which was probably bugged – and to go for a walk in the cold and deserted Moscow streets to talk matters over. As Gorbachev later recalled, 'It was then that I said we cannot go on living like this, we must change.'[98]

The pace of the changes unleashed by Gorbachev was breathtaking. The Soviet Union had been in existence for sixty-eight years when he took power. Within six years it was swept away.

It is safe to say that this was not the change that Gorbachev had in mind when he went for his chilly late-night walk in March 1985. Like most of the great reformers of the Age of Transformation – from Deng

Xiaoping to Margaret Thatcher and Manmohan Singh – his starting point was the need to revive a national economy. Like the Chinese and Indian leaders, Gorbachev saw the world markets as the route to salvation. He told Alan Greenspan that he wanted to make his nation 'a major trading force in the world'.[99]

The two Russian words that the rest of the world swiftly learnt to parrot during the Gorbachev years were *glasnost* and *perestroika*, openness and reconstruction. It was economic reconstruction that was Gorbachev's first priority. *Glasnost* was employed to rally support for his reforms.

But Gorbachev's more tolerant attitude to discussion and dissent also reflected his personality and relative youth. He was fifty-four in 1985, and was clearly a new type of Soviet leader. After the stiff and doddery gerontocracy of the Brezhnev years, here was a new man – confident, vigorous, comfortable speaking without notes. When Gorbachev had visited Britain in 1984, shortly before Chernenko's death, Margaret Thatcher had swiftly noticed the difference between the old and new style of Soviet leaders.

Whatever his motives, Gorbachev's conservative critics within the Soviet Union were quicker then he was to spot, and fear, the profound political implications of the reforms the new Soviet leader embarked upon. The decision to ease the tight central controls over economics and politics swiftly triggered changes that led to the end of the Communist Party's monopoly on power and the dissolution of the USSR itself.

Conservative defenders of the Soviet order were, however, profoundly mistaken if they believed that nothing needed to change. It would be inappropriately Marxist to argue that Gorbachev's reforms were the inevitable product of the economic situation that he inherited. The new leader had a choice. But, equally, there is no doubt that Gorbachev had inherited a genuinely dire economic situation. The Soviet Union had benefited hugely from the spike in oil prices in the seventies. But by the mid-eighties the oil price had fallen sharply – helping the Western European and American economies to boom, but ending the fiscal windfall to the USSR. External debt was rising fast. The USSR owed the outside world $30.7 billion in 1986; three years later the figure had reached $54 billion.[100] To make matters worse, the country was involved in a draining war in Afghanistan, which the USSR had invaded in 1979. And the new arms race initiated by Ronald Reagan was also imposing a huge financial strain. On taking office, Gorbachev discovered that the USSR was spending 20–30 per cent of GDP a year on the military. By comparison, the US, even at the peak of the Reagan defence build-up, was spending less than 7 per cent a year.[101]

The Soviet Union's own official statistics told a worrying story of decline. Economic growth was said to have averaged 7.5 per cent a year in the late sixties and over 5 per cent annually in the early seventies, but was estimated at just 2.5 per cent a year by the early eighties.[102] Unofficial figures suggested that the Soviet economy was shrinking by the time Gorbachev took power. In the fifties and sixties it was still possible for western economists and intellectuals to laud the success of the centrally planned Soviet economy. By the eighties, however, the USSR's advanced scientific and military base could no longer disguise its broader economic failings. In a dismissive phrase that did the rounds at the time, the Soviet Union was 'Upper Volta with rockets'. As a young journalist visiting Moscow for the first time in 1987, I noticed that even the ceremonial part of the Soviet capital was decrepit and down-at-heel. It was nobody's idea of the future.

Gorbachev's reforms were watched with fascination by the rest of the world. But despite this – and despite the fact that the man himself has written and spoken volumes about his intentions – there are still plenty of open questions about what he was trying to do. When, if ever, did he come to believe in democracy? Did Gorbachev ever really believe in the free market?

Part of the problem is that Gorbachev said different things at different times. He seems to have become more radical in both his politics and his economics as events unfolded and as conservative opposition mounted. But the first high-profile economic reform of the Gorbachev era had little to do with the market. It was an anti-alcohol campaign, imposed on the direct orders of the Kremlin in mid-1985 and earning the new Soviet leader his first nickname – 'Lemonade Joe'.[103] Other early attempts at reform also steered clear of direct market incentives – they involved the encouragement of experiments in the management of state enterprises and support for high technology.

Yet Gorbachev was also clearly aware from an early stage of the demoralizing effects of the communist system. In a remarkable tele-vised public speech in May 1985 at the Smolny Institute in Leningrad, he told his audience, 'In a family you feel it when something is taken from your pocket, but if it's the state's pocket nobody feels it directly.'[104] Margaret Thatcher was making the same point in a different context, when she said, 'There's no such thing as society. There are individual men and women, and there are families.'

Like Zhao Ziyang in China, Gorbachev had cut his teeth as a pro-vincial party boss, trying to raise agricultural productivity in the countryside. He too noticed how much more peasants produced if they were given the incentive to farm their own land. By the mid-eighties, as the journalist Angus Roxburgh points out, it was estimated that 'Collec-tive farmers with private plots provided over a quarter of the country's food from only 3 per cent of its land.'[105] In 1978, while still working in Stavropol province, Gorbachev had sent a memo to Moscow suggesting ways of increasing incentives in farming.

Now, seven years later and in charge of the entire Soviet system, Gorbachev had the chance to increase incentives right across the econo-my. He was given political and intellectual support by a new group of reforming economists including Abel Aganbegyan, Leonid Abalkin and Grigory Yavlinsky – people who, as Francis Fukuyama, the politi-cal scientist, puts it, were the products of a 'remarkable intellectual revolution…within the Soviet economic establishment'. They were familiar with liberal economics and were 'convinced that the centralized Soviet administrative-command system was at the root of the USSR's economic decline'.[106]

Gorbachev had been consulting Aganbegyan since the early eighties and the economist was called in to advise on some of the new general-secretary's early speeches. Yet Gorbachev was clearly not completely convinced, or – if he was – he was still disguising his conversion. In June 1985 he proclaimed that 'Not the market, not the anarchic forces of competition, but above all the plan must determine the basic features of the economy.'[107]

It was in late 1986 that the Politburo took the radical decision to legalize small-scale private businesses. The new law had its limits. Only particular categories of workers were allowed to open new businesses, and the lines of work were also limited – they included private tutoring, translation and working as a handy-man. Another law allowing the formation of private co-operatives gave further limited scope for latent entrepreneurial instincts in the Soviet system. Moscow's first private restaurant was opened in 1987. It caused a sensation – and soon became a compulsory stop for foreign journalists and visiting dignitaries. By the end of 1987 there were 700 new co-ops in Moscow alone.[108] It sounded impressive.

But, in a broader perspective, the results were disappointing. As Judt points out, by 1989 'there were still just 300,000 businesspeople in the whole Soviet Union, in a population of 290 million'.[109] Private enterprise on that relatively small scale could not be expected to transform the moribund Soviet system. Worse, it would always struggle to flourish in a command economy that did not allocate resources by price. How were the new businesses to get their resources, if they could not buy them on the open market? But if the command economy was abandoned, what other powers would the Communist Party have to surrender? And if the market was given full rein, could the Soviet Union even describe itself as socialist any more?

By 1987 a conservative backlash was clearly taking place, both within the party and in sections of the press. Gorbachev and his allies fought back by increasing the pace of both economic and political reforms. Gorbachev had made the link between encouraging individual initiative in the economy and in the broader political and social life of the Soviet Union. In early 1987 he proposed reforms that encouraged not just shopfloor democracy (workers electing their managers), but also internal elections within the Communist Party. As the conservative backlash grew against his reforms, Gorbachev gave more encouragement to the liberal elements in the Soviet Union – dissidents like Andrei Sakharov were released, banned books were published, history was re-examined. By early 1988 he and his inner circle were considering the introduction of contested parliamentary elections.

Gorbachev's conservative critics who feared that he was sowing the seeds of destruction for the entire Soviet system had a point. Once Gorbachev had decided that the idea of 'choice' should be extended from economics to politics and then to international relations, the system could not survive. In late 1988 he gave a speech at the United Nations proclaiming that 'Freedom of choice is a universal principle. There should be no exceptions.'[110]

At the time few people realized that such a sentiment amounted to a death sentence for the Soviet empire. Did Gorbachev himself know? Whatever his intentions, within nine months, the countries of Central Europe had taken the Soviet leader at his word and broken free from the Soviet empire.

Gorbachev miscalculated badly if he thought that he could insulate the Soviet Union itself from the upheavals that had taken place in the old Soviet empire. Nationalist forces in the Baltic states and then in the other Soviet republics – whose existence and legitimacy Gorbachev barely acknowledged – took huge encouragement from the revolutions in Central Europe. Lithuania made a unilateral declaration of independence in 1990. Gorbachev briefly resorted to violent repression.

Soviet troops killed thirteen Lithuanian demonstrators in January 1991 – but the Baltic independence movements could not be stopped. The Soviet Union itself was beginning to break up.[111]

In August 1991 bewildered reactionaries within the crumbling Soviet system attempted to depose Gorbachev, staging a coup while he was on holiday in the Crimea. Gorbachev survived, but the end was near for both leader and nation. The failed coup attempt gave a further impetus to separatism within the Soviet Union. Throughout late August and September, the constituent republics of the Union of Soviet Socialist Republics broke loose and declared independence. On 8 December 1991 the leaders of the Russian, Ukrainian and Belarussian republics met near Minsk and effectively dissolved the country. Belatedly, Gorbachev accepted the situation and resigned. On Christmas Day 1991 the Soviet flag was lowered over the Kremlin for the last time and replaced by the Russian flag. Two days later, Boris Yeltsin, the president of Russia who had signed the Minsk agreement to dissolve the Soviet Union, moved into Gorbachev's old office in the Kremlin. The Gorbachev years were over and the Soviet Union was no more.[112]

Gorbachev had broken up the nation he ruled, but he had not revived its economy. He was hailed as a hero in the West, and soon took up a lucrative career giving speeches and advertising Louis Vuitton luggage. But he was widely reviled at home and in China, whose Communist Party had taken a different course.

The rival paths followed by China and the Soviet Union make a fascinating contrast. In China, the flowering of private enterprise wrought a dramatic economic transformation within a generation – and the Communist Party retained power. The opposite happened to the Soviet Union. The political system crumbled, but the economic transformation never really happened. What accounted for the difference?

One obvious distinction is that the Soviet system had no successful examples of reform upon which to draw. By contrast, many experts in Asia swiftly saw that China was emulating the successful path of manufacturing and export-led growth that had been pioneered first by Japan, and then by the other 'flying geese' of East and South-east Asia – Taiwan, South Korea, Hong Kong, Singapore, Malaysia and Thailand. Even if the bosses of the Chinese Communist Party were not, in late 1978, consciously emulating other Asian nations, the entrepreneurs whom they allowed to open factories in China's new Special Economic Zones knew the formula. In many cases, they were simply moving manufacturing operations wholesale from elsewhere in Asia to southern China.

But while there was an 'overseas Chinese' business community that could help private enterprise to take root in China, and then plug it into the international trading system, there was no equivalent 'overseas Russian' community. The Soviet Union was also starting from a different situation. It was a richer and more advanced country than China. (Indeed, even in 2010, per capita income in Russia is still considerably higher than in China.) There were more people with middle-class lifestyles who were threatened by a collapse in the old system – and many fewer poor peasants who could be used as a reserve army of cheap labour. The Soviet system – and its Russian successor – also suffered from the 'oil curse': the temptation to rely on natural resources as an easy route to wealth. The giant international firms that did eventually spring up in the Russia of the nineties were almost all in the oil and gas industries.

There was one other vital missing ingredient that China enjoyed and the Soviet system lacked – time for economic reforms to start to take effect. Six years into the Chinese economic reforms, foreigners were only beginning to notice the physical transformation of the country and the rise of private enterprise. Six years after Gorbachev had started his reforms, the whole Soviet system had collapsed.

For reasons of self-preservation, the Chinese Communist Party has made a close study of what went wrong with the Gorbachev reforms in the Soviet Union.[113] The core Chinese conclusion seems to be that Gorbachev put the cart before the horse. He should have concentrated on economic reforms first and only slowly and tentatively allowed free speech and challenges to the one-party state.

Why did Gorbachev take the opposite route? Some analysts argue that he simply blundered. Others believe that he was converted to democracy early in his tenure in the Kremlin. Whatever his true motivations, at a vital moment in 1989 he lacked the brutality and ruthlessness of a Deng Xiaoping. In June of that year, Deng sent the tanks into Tiananmen Square. Soviet leaders had done the same thing in Hungary in 1956 and Czechoslovakia in 1968. But when the countries of Eastern and Central Europe moved to break free again in 1989, Gorbachev kept the Soviet Union's troops and tanks in their barracks. The most dramatic chapter of the Age of Transformation was about to be written.

EUROPE, 1989:

The Year of Revolutions

The single most dramatic event of the Age of Transformation was the fall of the Berlin Wall on 9 November 1989. The wall had divided Europe. It had separated the communist world from the capitalist world, and the Soviet bloc from the democratic world. The sight of thousands of East Germans streaming through the wall and into West Berlin on that November night was the sign that the Cold War was over. A single global economic and political system was being formed – a 'new world order' as President George H. W. Bush called it.

The fall of the Berlin Wall was a victory for the western powers and for individual freedom. It was also a victory for western consumerism. The symbol of the failure of East Germany swiftly became the Trabant – the small, unglamorous, underpowered national car of East Germany, which looked so pathetic next to the powerful Mercedes and BMWs that flaunted the economic power of West Germany. Western journalists noted with a certain glee that the very first acts of East Berliners, newly arrived in the West, were often to stock up on consumer goods and such scarce luxuries as bananas. Communism had literally failed to deliver the goods. Capitalism, by contrast, promised prosperity as well as political liberty. Ronald Reagan, with his gift for simple slogans, had evidently got it right when he proclaimed that 'freedom works'.

Economic failure was one of the root causes of the collapse of the Soviet bloc. In that sense the Central European revolutions of 1989 had very similar roots to the profound changes that swept China, India and even Britain and the United States during the Age of Transformation. But there was also one major difference. The transformations elsewhere were almost always dictated by national governments that had decided on a radical change of direction. The transformations that came to countries like Poland, Czechoslovakia and East Germany in 1989 had deep local roots. But they were dependent on political change in Moscow. It was Mikhail Gorbachev's decision not to send Soviet tanks onto the roads of Central Europe that allowed the countries of the Soviet bloc to break free.

The change in Soviet thinking involved the abandonment of the 'Brezhnev doctrine' – the notion that the USSR claimed the right to impose 'socialism' right across the Soviet bloc. Leonid Brezhnev, the Soviet leader in 1968, had defined the doctrine shortly after Soviet tanks had overthrown the Czech government to stop the experiment with political liberalization known as the 'Prague Spring'. In the typically dead language of the high Soviet era, he had proclaimed that 'the sovereignty of each socialist country cannot be opposed to the interests of the world of socialism'.[114] It fell to Gennady Gerasimov, Gorbachev's sharp-tongued spokesman who liked to show off his quick wit and mastery of western culture, to confirm the change. Asked if Gorbachev's speeches meant that the Brezhnev doctrine was dead, he joked that it had been replaced by 'the Sinatra doctrine'. From now on, the countries of Central Europe could do it their way.[115]

Gorbachev had visited Beijing in May 1989 – an event that had helped to stir the hopes of the student demonstrators there. On 4 June 1989, just as the Chinese were sending the tanks into Tiananmen Square, Poland was voting in its first free elections since the imposition of communist rule. The Polish communists went down to a catastrophic defeat – and accepted it, partly thanks to the intervention of Gorbachev himself. When General Wojciech Jaruzelski, the leader of the communist government, considered reimposing martial law in the wake of the election defeat, he was warned off by the Kremlin.[116]

Later in the year, when the East German government contemplated using violence against the street demonstrations that were undermining the regime, Gorbachev's opposition was once again crucial. The Soviet leader had visited East Berlin on 7 October for the fortieth anniversary celebrations of the foundation of the East German state. As in Beijing a few months earlier, his presence acted as a spur to opponents of the regime. At a torchlight procession through Berlin, members of the communist youth group were heard chanting, 'Gorby, save us!' By the time Gorbachev left the following day, demonstrations had broken out all over the country. On the night of 9 October the East German leadership was on the brink of launching a 'European Tiananmen' against protesters in Leipzig. In the end, the leadership held back, partly because of the intervention of civic leaders in Leipzig itself. The other crucial factor was Gorbachev. There were 380,000 Soviet troops stationed in East Germany. But when the Soviet leader had left East Germany, he had left firm instructions that they were to stay in their barracks.[117]

The Sinatra doctrine allowed nations like Poland and Czechoslovakia to reclaim their political independence. But it would be a mistake to believe that the countries of the former Soviet bloc were simply passive recipients of a political gift handed to them from Moscow. The groundwork for the restoration of political and economic freedom in Central Europe had been laid by dissidents, trades unionists, intellectuals and ordinary people across the region over the previous decade and more.

The wellsprings of political dissent were a mixture of economic and political grievances. The simple demand for freedom of thought and expression had never disappeared. In 1977 a group of Czech dissidents had given eloquent expression to it through 'Charter 77' – a brave demand for civil and political rights whose signatories included Vaclav Havel, a Bohemian (in both the geographic and spiritual sense) and playwright who was to become president of post-communist Czechoslovakia.

But the economic, social and environmental failures of the Soviet bloc were also becoming increasingly obvious. The economies of Central Europe had very little going for them. They lacked the Soviet Union's reserves of oil and natural gas. They were incapable of responding to consumer demand in the manner of a Western European economy. They could not produce cheap manufactured goods with anything like the speed, efficiency and low costs of the emerging Asian economies. That left heavy, polluting, uncompetitive industries like steel and shipbuilding. Official corruption and the black market flourished. Shops were drab and shortages were rife. Increases in the price of food had provoked strikes in Poland in 1976, which were repressed with violence and arrests by the regime. In an effort to keep their economies afloat and to satisfy demand for consumer goods, the countries of the Soviet bloc borrowed more and more from overseas. The foreign debts of Eastern Europe stood at just $6.1 billion in 1971. By 1988 the figure had reached $95.6 billion.[118]

Trades-union protest returned to Poland in the early eighties. The rise of the Solidarity movement was the first sign of a broad-based challenge to communist rule. In August 1980 shipyard workers in the Polish port of Gdansk went on strike for higher pay and for the reinstatement of sacked workers, including their leader Lech Walesa. As part of the strike settlement, the government recognized the right to form independent trades unions. But the rise of independent social forces posed an obvious challenge to the communist system. The Soviet Union was still firmly wedded to the Brezhnev doctrine in the early eighties and staged showy military exercises on the Polish frontier in the winter of 1980–81 to make its point. In December 1981 General Jaruzelski imposed martial law.

The other great spur and encouragement to Polish dissidents was the emergence of an active, charismatic and anti-communist Polish pope – John Paul II. Indeed, some observers reckon that the real beginning of the unravelling of the Soviet bloc was not the foundation of Solidarity, but John Paul's first papal visit to his native land and the open-air masses he celebrated there in June 1979.[119] For the rest of the eighties, Poland's communist government struggled to keep the lid on dissent. The continuing crisis of the Polish economy and the government's inability to force through reforms without provoking strikes and unrest meant that by 1989 the Polish government was forced into political negotiations with Solidarity, known as 'round-table talks'. That, in turn, led to the Polish elections of June 1989. After its humiliation in those elections, the Communist Party had little option but to step aside. In September 1989 Tadeusz Mazowiecki became the first non-communist prime minister of post-war Poland. All of this happened months before the collapse of communist governments in the rest of the Soviet bloc.

There is a certain disgruntled feeling in modern Poland that their country's unique role in the downfall of communism has not received its proper recognition. The most memorable images of the revolutions of 1989 all seem to be drawn from elsewhere – the fall of the Berlin Wall, Czechoslovakia's 'Velvet Revolution' in telegenic Prague, the grisly murder of Nicolae Ceauşescu, the Romanian dictator, in December 1989.

It is true that none of these countries had the long history of anti-communist struggle that Poland had amassed throughout the eighties. It was also the Poles who gave Central Europe the model of 'round-table talks' that was widely emulated elsewhere.

Still, the writing of history is not a competition. Wherever the revolutionary virus was first incubated, it spread remarkably quickly in Central Europe in 1989.

In Hungary, younger elements within the Communist Party wanted to emulate Gorbachev's reforms in the USSR. Hungary started to open up in late 1988 and early 1989, passing laws that allowed for a transition to a multi-party system. In May 1989 the Hungarians removed the electric fencing that separated their country from Austria and so from Western Europe. In September the border was formally opened. This development put intolerable pressure on East Germany. As thousands of East Germans rushed across the newly opened Austro-Hungarian frontier, so the government in East Berlin was both humiliated and panicked, setting in train the events that led to the opening of the Berlin Wall in November.

The collapse of East German communism swiftly helped to spark the Czech Velvet Revolution of November 1989, which in turn encouraged the revolution in Romania the following month. The British author and academic Timothy Garton Ash captured the speed and the contagious nature of events when he joked to Vaclav Havel in November 1989, 'In Poland it took ten years, in Hungary ten months, in East Germany ten weeks, perhaps in Czechoslovakia it will take ten days.'[120]

The new leaders who came to the fore in Central Europe in 1989 were quite clear that, as well as rejecting a failed system, they were embracing a proven western political and economic model. Garton Ash, who observed many of the revolutions at first hand, later argued that one of the themes of 1989 was 'no more experiments, no more third ways'.[121]

While many on the western left still agonized about the failings of the free-market system and the weaknesses of western democracy, the Central European revolutionaries had few such doubts. Of course, they had their political differences. In Czechoslovakia, Vaclav Havel, who became the first post-communist president, was in the western social democratic tradition, while Vaclav Klaus, his finance minister, was a hardline Thatcherite.

But these shades of emphasis were insignificant compared to the broader intellectual trend. The countries of Central Europe formed an orderly queue to join the European Union – and to embrace the political and economic values that it stood for (as well as to get their share of generous EU subsidies). Those values were democracy, capitalism and an acceptance of globalization. These broad boundaries could accommodate both a radical free-marketeer like Thatcher and the soft socialism of a Delors. Nonetheless, 'European values' as embodied by the European Union were lucid enough to provide a clear alternative template for the nations turning away from communism. As the historian Tony Judt put it, Europe 'represented not an ideological alternative but simply the political norm... Europe stood – squarely and simply – for normalcy and the modern way of life.'[122]

The collapse of the Berlin Wall eventually more than doubled the size of the European Union. In 1989 there were just twelve members. Twenty years later, the Union had twenty-seven members. It was the world's largest economic bloc, stretching from Portugal to the Baltic states and from Bucharest to Belfast.

The political transformations of 1989 also had implications that stretched far beyond Europe. The existence of the Soviet bloc had provided moral, intellectual and financial support to leftist political movements all over the world. So the rejection of the Soviet system in its Central European heartlands – and the revelation of its moral and economic bankruptcy – had global ramifications.

In South Africa, the leadership of the African National Congress that was struggling against apartheid had traditionally been closely entwined with the Communist Party and so, indirectly, with the Soviet Union. But by the time apartheid was brought down in the mid-nineties and South Africa achieved its freedom, the Soviet Union no longer existed. The collapse of the Soviet Union freed white South Africa of its fear of the 'red menace' and made it easier to contemplate the end of apartheid. The government of the new South Africa did contain members of the Communist Party. But the ministers in Nelson Mandela's first government donned suits and ties, pursued orthodox economic policies and embraced globalization. The idea of 'round-table talks' that helped to bring a peaceful end to communism in Central Europe also served as a model for the negotiations that brought a peaceful end to apartheid and a transition to democracy in South Africa.

The collapse of the Soviet model also had profound implications for the left in India and Latin America. In Delhi, economic reformers were increasingly coming round to the opinion that 'there was no alternative' to an embrace of open markets and global capitalism. And in Latin America, communist Cuba now looked like a beleaguered outpost of a dying ideology, rather than the standard-bearer for an alternative to capitalism and the American way.

LATIN AMERICA, 1982–91:

The Triumph of Democracy and Markets

The collapse of communism in the Soviet bloc provided the most memorable visual images of the Age of Transformation. But the transformation of Latin America during the same period was almost as dramatic.

In 1978 there were only three democracies in the whole of Latin America. By the end of the decade, democracy had triumphed across most of the continent. The archetypal Latin military dictator, in his braided uniform, had been largely consigned to the past, replaced by civilian presidents in suits. Cuba, once held up as the harbinger of a revolutionary future for the continent, now looked like an anachronistic hold-out. Brazil and Argentina were civilian-run democracies. Mexico, although still a one-party state, was halfway through a democratic transition that would be completed by 2000. Even Chile – where free-market reforms had been pursued by a military dictatorship under General Augusto Pinochet – had turned back towards democracy with the election of a civilian government in 1989.

The democratic transformation of Latin America was accompanied by a free-market revolution. The Latin dictatorships had generally

pursued protectionist and state-led economic strategies. Their democratic successors were much more likely to follow orthodox economic
strategies: a crackdown on inflation; a welcome for foreign investment;
a more open trading regime; privatization.

Latin America's transformation illustrates how contagious political
and economic ideas can be – jumping across borders with all the energy
of a determined virus. The continent had been through periods of
synchronized political change before. There were nine military coups
across Latin America between 1962 and 1966.[123] In 1973 even Chile,
which had been a democracy since 1932, fell victim to a military coup.

The fear of communism instilled by the Cold War contributed to the
anti-democratic wave in Latin America in the sixties. The return of
democracy was also part of a global process. The fall of authoritarian
governments in Spain and Portugal in the seventies – and their replacement by democratic governments – inevitably had a profound influence
in the former Spanish and Portuguese colonies of Latin America.

The Carter presidency from 1976 to 1980, with its emphasis on placing human rights at the centre of US foreign policy, also put pressure on
Latin America's authoritarian regimes. During the Cold War, the United
States had worried about the 'domino theory' in which one country after
another would fall prey to communism. In Latin America in the Age of
Transformation, a reverse domino theory took hold, as one country after
another fell to democracy.

The first domino was the Dominican Republic, where a presidential
election in 1978 was won by the opposition. Military rule ended in
Ecuador in 1979, in Peru in 1980, in Honduras in 1981, in Bolivia
in 1982, in Argentina in 1983, in El Salvador and Uruguay in 1984, in
Brazil and Guatemala in 1985 and in Chile and Paraguay in 1989. The
last dominoes to fall were Haiti, Nicaragua and Panama – all of which
held free elections during 1990.[124] The way in which democracy came
to the continent established a pattern that was later to become familiar in Central Europe.[125] Authoritarian and military regimes were not

overthrown in violent revolutions. Instead, there were peaceful transi-
tions, as the generals sat down with civilian politicians to negotiate the
move to democracy.

Clearly, changing global politics profoundly influenced the course of
events in Latin America. But – as in much of the rest of the world – it
took an economic crisis to really clear the way for the policies that
defined the Age of Transformation. It was the debt crisis of 1982 that
sparked the change, discrediting both the Latin dictatorships and the
economic policies that they had pursued. As Michael Reid, a journalist
and author, puts it, 'When the 1982 debt crisis broke, the dictatorships
bucked under the opprobrium of economic failure.'[126] In Argentina,
defeat in the Falklands war of that year was also crucial in discrediting
the country's military junta.

In 1982 Mexico defaulted on its debts, provoking an international
financial crisis. The whole of Latin America had been piling up debt
during the seventies. But with the collapse of international confidence,
capital was pulled out and governments across the region were forced to
slash public spending. Some resorted to printing money to fill the gap
in their finances and this – combined with falling currencies – touched
off continent-wide inflation.

The economic crisis provided an opening for a new generation of
outward-looking Latin American economists, who took the export-led
success of the East Asian Tigers as a new model for their continent.
Many had trained in the United States and were determined to break
with the failed protectionist policies of Latin America's past.

The pace of change in the rest of the world helped to convince Latin
American leaders that the reformists were right. On a trip to Europe in
early 1990, just after the fall of the Berlin Wall, Mexico's President Carlos
Salinas de Gortari realized that his country needed to change fast, if it
was to compete for investment with the new markets that were opening
up in Eastern Europe. At the World Economic Forum in Davos, he
approached Carla Hills, the US trade representative, with the idea of

negotiating a free-trade agreement between Mexico and the United States – the germ of the North American Free Trade Area (Nafta) that was to come into being in 1994.[127]

Latin America did not simply passively receive lessons in free-market economics from the rest of the world. Prominent regional economists like the Peruvian Hernando de Soto became important contributors to the new liberal economics – with de Soto doing much to argue the case for the importance of property rights for the poor.[128]

Nonetheless, the new economics pursued across the continent came with the approval of the International Monetary Fund and the World Bank. Since both mighty institutions were based in Washington, the free-market prescription became known as the 'Washington Consensus'[129] – a phrase dreamed up by John Williamson, an economist at the Institute for International Economics. Across Latin America governments pursued the new consensus policies: cutting tariffs and taxes; making life easier for foreign investors; allowing markets to set interest rates and exchange rates; cutting regulation; privatizing.

The story told so far sounds like a liberal morality tale in which economic and political freedom advance hand-in-hand. In fact, things were a little more complicated than that – and the main complication to this uplifting narrative was Chile.

Chile embraced the economics of the Age of Transformation well ahead of the rest of Latin America – indeed, ahead of Britain, China and the US. The country became a laboratory for free-market reforms as early as 1975. The Harvard historian Niall Ferguson argues that 'Thatcher and Reagan came later. The backlash against welfare started in Chile.'[130] Awkwardly, for those who like to believe that political and economic freedom are indivisible, the Chilean reforms were launched after a military coup that overthrew the leftist government of Salvador Allende in 1973. Chile's policies of slashing tariffs and taxes, inflation-fighting, privatization and pension reform were regarded as a model by free-market reformers around the world. But they took place against a background of the imprisonment, torture and murder of dissidents.

General Pinochet's embrace of the market came in 1975, after a flying visit by Milton Friedman – the doyen of the Chicago school of economists, who was to receive the Nobel Prize for Economics the following year. The assault on inflation began a month after Friedman's visit. Under the Pinochet government, Friedman's 'Chicago boys' – many of them Chilean economists who had trained at the University of Chicago – were given a whole country as their canvas.[131]

Margaret Thatcher was a strong admirer of both Friedman and Pinochet. When the retired general visited Britain in 1999, the retired prime minister entertained him to tea. When, shortly afterwards, he was arrested in Britain on human-rights charges, she sprang to his defence, writing to *The Times* that Pinochet had been 'a good friend to this country' during the Falklands War.[132] Thatcherites admired the general's anti-communism, as well as his role as a pioneer of radical free-market reforms.

Ronald Reagan's relationship with the advance of freedom in Latin America also had its ambiguities. In 1979 Jeane Kirkpatrick, a professor at Georgetown University, had developed an influential theoretical justification for American support for authoritarian regimes in Latin America and elsewhere that so impressed Reagan that he appointed her as his first ambassador to the United Nations. Kirkpatrick argued that 'traditional authoritarian regimes', such as the military regimes then in power in Argentina, Chile and Brazil, were 'less repressive than revolutionary autocracies ... more susceptible to liberalization' than 'totalitarian' communist governments and 'more compatible with US interests'.[133] Hence, it was both morally respectable and strategically important to support them, while fiercely opposing communism.

Kirkpatrick's determination not to undermine pro-American governments in Latin America meant that she reacted with alarm when Margaret Thatcher's government decided to fight Argentina over the Falkland Islands in 1982. She accurately foresaw that military defeat would undermine the Argentine junta and lobbied for a negotiated settlement.[134] In the event, the Reagan administration threw its weight behind Britain. But the episode underlined the ideological ambiguities of the Cold War – some of which were later air-brushed away by the triumphalist neoconservative narrative about the onward global march of freedom during the Reagan years.

If Reagan and Thatcher sometimes displayed ambivalence to aspects of the transformation of Latin America, that ambivalence was heartily reciprocated by many of the region's reformers. Britain's war with Argentina did not make Thatcher particularly popular in Latin America. A long tradition of anti-Americanism – bolstered by dislike of the Reagan administration's policies in Central America – made it difficult for reformers to be too closely identified with the 'neo-liberalism' of Reagan.[135] Latin reformers preferred to argue that the market reforms they were recommending were simply mainstream economics, and had nothing to do with the ideology of radical, right-wing governments in Britain or the US.

The role of Latin America in the story of globalization can sometimes be overlooked. The story seems less earth-shaking than the collapse of the Soviet bloc – or the transformations of India and China. This is partly a matter of size. The population of the entire region is 550 million people – less than half the size of either China or India.

But the rise of Latin America is still an important part of the story of the 'new world order' that replaced the Cold War. By 2010 Brazil, with a population of close to 200 million and the tenth largest economy in the world, was widely recognized as a key emerging global power. Goldman Sachs, the investment bank, helped to confer this status by making Brazil one of the BRICs – the four emerging powers that Jim O'Neill, the bank's chief economist, argued would help define the next century. Unworthy suspicions that Goldman had included Brazil – alongside China, India and Russia – simply to make a catchier acronym were shelved as Brazil's growing international status became more apparent.

In June 2009 the BRICs held their first ever summit meeting in Russia – providing a rare example of an investment bank's research paper provoking a geopolitical change.[136]

Another plausible reason why Latin America's role in the story of globalization has been downplayed is that the economic record of free-market reforms there is much patchier – and so less interesting and alarming to North Americans and Europeans than the seemingly inexorable rise of China and India. There was a sharp continent-wide recovery in Latin America in the mid-eighties, but it was followed by a downturn. By the end of the decade most countries had conquered hyper-inflation and brought sanity to their government finances. The cutting of tariff barriers did spur trade. Countries like Brazil, Chile and Mexico experienced export booms.

Even as growth strengthened in the nineties, however, it was still punctuated by financial crises. The 'Tequila crisis' in Mexico in 1994 showed that the country was still prone to debt and currency disorders. It provoked a short but very deep recession and required emergency loans of billions of dollars from the US. The emerging-market panic of 1998, which started in Russia, sparked another bout of capital flight in Latin America – mirroring the debt crisis of 1982 that had provoked the free-market reforms in the first place. There were severe downturns and bank runs across Latin America.

When I visited Argentina for the first time in 2002, I encountered the tail-end of that country's crisis, leaving me with a vivid impression of what a financial system in crisis looks like. The banks resembled mini-fortresses, buttressed by corrugated iron – with one narrow door through which customers filed, in the hope of withdrawing money. The result of the crisis was four years of economic stagnation, which left the 'Washington Consensus' a 'damaged brand' – in the words of Moisés Naím, a journalist and former Venezuelan trade minister.[137]

Nonetheless, Latin American economies recovered and almost all of the region's democracies survived. In the George W. Bush years,

Venezuela became the focus for the America-bashing, anti-capitalism of Hugo Chavez, Bolivia also followed a populist path under Evo Morales and Castro's Cuba tottered onwards. But the biggest countries in Latin America, Brazil and Argentina, largely resisted the anti-American temptations of previous generations. They also avoided the other traps of the past, refusing to turn inwards economically or to look to the barracks for political salvation.

The effects of the Age of Transformation on Latin America proved durable – and that mattered across the world. For, as Michael Reid has argued, Latin America 'has become one of the world's most important and testing laboratories for the viability of democratic capitalism as a global project'.[138]

In 2002 Brazil elected Luiz Inácio Lula da Silva as its new president. Lula was the seventh child of a desperately poor family from the northeast of Brazil. His formative political experiences came leading metal workers' strikes in the years when Brazil was still a military dictatorship. For many years, his Workers Party espoused radical leftist policies. But in his victorious 2002 campaign, Lula espoused centrist and pragmatic economic policies. After his election, his first major foreign trip was to the World Economic Forum in Davos. Asked to explain his transformation, Lula frequently replied, 'I changed, Brazil changed.'[139] It was a pleasingly understated way of encapsulating the transformation of an entire continent.

8

INDIA, 1991

The Second Asian Giant Awakes

By the middle of 1991, India was on the edge of political and economic disaster.

In May of that year, Rajiv Gandhi, the prime minister, was assassinated by a suicide bomber while campaigning in the south of the country. Gandhi's death and the subsequent election brought a new prime minister to power. Narasimha Rao was seventy years old, quiet and uncharismatic. He looked ill-suited to the challenges ahead.

Shortly after the Rao government was sworn in, in mid-June, Manmohan Singh, the new finance minister, told a closed-door meeting of senior politicians that India was on the verge of bankruptcy. Its foreign reserves were down to the equivalent of two weeks' worth of imports. In order to secure an emergency $2.2 billion loan from the IMF, India had had to physically transport part of its gold reserves to London.[140]

But India's handling of the economic crisis proved the wisdom of the old observation that 'crisis' and 'opportunity' are often one and the same. The Rao government seized the chance to push through radical economic reforms that dealt not just with the immediate crisis, but with the root causes of more than forty years of relative economic failure. In doing so, it plugged India into the global economy and dramatically raised the country's growth rates. Thirteen years after the opening of China, India became the last major world power to join the globalization game. Although India was late to the party, its arrival may eventually prove every bit as consequential as the opening of China.

For a huge nation with an ancient history, India had to put up with a lot of condescension after achieving independence in 1947. While the East Asian economies roared ahead in the seventies and eighties, India seemed stuck with slow growth and tragic and humiliating levels of poverty. Some analysts spoke of a 'Hindu rate of growth' – implying that there was something timeless and spiritual about India that made the country poorly equipped for the cut-and-thrust of the global economy.[141] Others, like Singapore's founding father, Lee Kuan Yew, speculated that perhaps India's disputatious democracy was holding the country back.

The Indian economic crisis of 1991 had been a long time in the making. After achieving political independence in 1947, India had sought to achieve economic independence as well. The country committed to a policy of protectionism, state ownership and central planning.

With the benefit of hindsight this looks like a staggering error. But protectionism chimed naturally with the Indian nationalist desire for 'self-reliance' in the post-colonial era. As the historian Ramachandra Guha puts it, 'Gandhian protesters had burnt foreign cloth to encourage the growth of indigenous textiles; now Nehruvian technocrats would make their own steel and machine tools rather than buy them from the outside.'[142] Central planning was even in vogue in post-war Britain, where India's first prime minister, Jawaharlal Nehru, had been educated and where a young Manmohan Singh studied economics in the early fifties. As Singh later recalled, 'the predominant mood of the times at that time was that in poor countries you needed strong government intervention to move the economy onto a path of self-sustaining growth'.[143] Nehru was also a keen admirer of the Soviet Union. He had been much impressed when he first visited the country in the twenties, and now wanted India to pursue a 'socialistic pattern of society'.[144]

Under the Nehruvian system, Indian industry found itself suffocated by regulation, smothered by a monopolistic public sector and cut off from foreign technology and capital. While the East Asian Tigers opened their doors to foreign multinationals, India went in the opposite direction, expelling firms like IBM and Coca-Cola in the late seventies. Gurchuran Das, an economic journalist, writes that Indians 'having set out to create socialism found that [they] had instead created statism'.[145]

By the early nineties the country was on the brink of a major economic breakdown. The crisis of 1991 had its roots deep in the policies of Nehruvian socialism pursued since independence. But it also had more immediate causes. The government of Rajiv Gandhi had borrowed heavily overseas. But the Gulf crisis in 1991 caused a surge in the oil price and meant that India did not have enough money to buy oil. The familiar symptoms of a financial crisis – in particular, capital flight – began to kick in. The key figure in the economic team assembled by Prime Minister Rao to deal with the crisis was Manmohan Singh – a cerebral, former civil servant and central banker. As Singh explained later, 'There were no foreign lenders who were willing to finance our current-account deficit. Our foreign exchanges had literally disappeared, so we were on the verge of bankruptcy.'[146] Singh made no effort to conceal the starkness of the situation from Narasimha Rao – 'I said to him that we are on the verge of collapse…We must convert this crisis into an opportunity to build a new India.'[147]

Turning the crisis into an opportunity meant shrugging off years of accumulated Indian economic policy and thinking. As a student in the fifties, Singh had won Cambridge University's Adam Smith prize for economics. But the economics he had learnt at Cambridge and practised in India as a civil servant was not really in the tradition of Smith – it was more Keynesian and statist. However, Singh had been deeply impressed by the economic development of East Asia, and in particular by a visit to South Korea and Taiwan in 1987. In 1960 India and South Korea had been at roughly equal stages of development and income levels. But within two generations South Korean per capita income had risen to roughly twenty times the level of India. The South Korean economy was hardly free of government interference. But its emphasis on international trade and a dynamic private sector offered lessons that could be learnt by India.

Other key officials also saw the need and opportunity for reform in 1991 – including Palaniappan Chidambaram, who was commerce minister in the Rao government and who formed a reform alliance with Singh that was still going strong in 2008, when the two men were respectively prime minister and finance minister.

Although they shared many ideas, Singh and Chidambaram were very different characters, as I discovered when I met them both in 1996. Singh, who was as always wearing a Sikh turban in the light-blue colours of Cambridge University, has a diffident and scholarly manner. His other-worldly qualities were only emphasized by the fact our meeting took place in the quiet splendour of the finance ministry – part of Delhi's grandiose complex of government buildings, designed by the British architect Edwin Lutyens. Chidambaram is a much more emotional character. I met him in the relatively tawdry surroundings of the Indian trade ministry. A broken-down car on bricks sat in the ministry courtyard and Chidambaram seemed anxious and almost distressed when I met him. I asked the trade minister what was worrying him. He replied that he had just met the trade minister of Finland, and then asked rhetorically, 'Do you know how many people live in Finland? Five million.' He paused for dramatic effect. 'We have five million blind people in India.'[148] It was a graphic reminder of the almost overwhelming scale of the problems facing those attempting to govern a vast nation of over a billion people.

And yet, faced with the crisis of 1991, Rao, Singh and Chidambaram moved with speed and boldness. In early July Singh devalued the Indian rupee to give exports a boost. He and Chidambaram then used the

devaluation to abolish export subsidies and to set about radically liber-
alizing and deregulating India's trade regime. Next came the 'licence
Raj' – the system of government permits that regulated who could set up
a new business or offer a new product. A dramatic reduction in the
number of industrial sectors controlled by the state was announced on
the morning of 24 July 1991. That evening Manmohan Singh presented
his budget and quoted French novelist Victor Hugo, proclaiming that
'No power on earth can stop an idea whose time has come.' The idea
that Singh was referring to was 'the emergence of India as a major
global power, an economic power... freedom from poverty, ignorance
and disease. You get that with India becoming a major player in the
world economy.'[149]

Over the next two years, the Rao government pushed through a
collection of market-based reforms to gladden the heart of any economic
liberal. Industrial licensing was virtually abolished. Businesses such as
telecoms, airlines and banking were opened up to the private sector.
Laws on foreign investment were liberalized – and capital began to pour
into the country. The stock market was also opened up for foreign investment. Tariffs were cut dramatically. So were taxes. The exchange rate
and interest rates on government securities were henceforth to be set by
the market.[150]

The recovery in the economy was swift. As Singh later recalled, 'The
economy turned around much sooner, much quicker, and much more
deeply than I anticipated.'[151] This had the vital effect of ensuring that
the political backing for a more open Indian economy was maintained,
even after the immediate crisis passed. When Singh's Congress Party
lost power in 1996, the next Indian government, led by the Hindu-
nationalist BJP, embraced the economics of reform and opening.

Over the following decade, the pace of subsequent Indian reforms
often frustrated the more ardent liberal reformers, who looked back with
nostalgia to the early days of the Singh reforms. Singh himself came in
for criticism for pursuing reform too timidly.[152] But the changes put in

place between 1991 and 1993 had created a momentum of economic growth that continued to gather pace – even as the speed of reforms slowed. The choke-holds that had suffocated Indian entrepreneurialism had been loosened enough to allow new businesses to spring up. In the eighties average economic growth in India had hovered around 5 per cent a year. In the nineties, this rose to 5–7 per cent a year. By 2006 and 2007 India was growing at more than 9 per cent and looking, in the words of Bill Emmott, a former editor of *The Economist*, 'more "East Asian" all the time'.[153]

The Indian reforms of 1991 were the last part of a transformation that had created a truly global capitalist economy in the space of just thirteen years. India changed because the world had changed. The most direct influence on Manmohan Singh was the dynamic growth of the capitalist economies of East Asia. But the collapse of the Soviet system was also crucial. For many years India had looked to the Soviet bloc for inspiration – and so the collapse of the Soviet system had a profound impact. As Singh later explained, 'This was a telling proof that a command-type of economy was not as secure as we had thought … We thought (we) … could look at the Soviet Union as a new civilization. And here was an economy and its society and its politics which could not defend itself against all its internal contradictions. Therefore the collapse of the Soviet Union – the end of the Cold War – was also a major factor influencing thinking on economic reforms in our country.'[154] Singh also admitted to a 'great admiration' for Margaret Thatcher, although he downplays her influence on Indian economic thinking.

The rapid rise of the Indian economy in the nineties – allied to the country's size – meant that it swiftly became not just another big player in the global economy but a potent symbol of the very process of globalization. Thomas Friedman's *The World is Flat*, which was published in 2005 and rapidly became the single most popular book ever written on globalization, began its narrative in Bangalore, the capital of the Indian IT industry.

The rise of Bangalore is indeed a breathtaking story and it is one that was directly attributable to the Indian economic reforms. The IT industry could simply not have emerged under the old licence Raj – where entrepreneurs would have had to refer to the government in Delhi to authorize every change in corporate strategy.

In 1996 foreigners were just beginning to notice the emergence of India's high-tech industries. When I visited Infosys in that year, it was a relatively modest Bangalore firm, with about three thousand employees, mainly doing low-level contract work for the big names of the IT industry on the west coast of America. When I returned thirteen years later, Infosys was the icon of the Indian economic renaissance – and a major global player in its own right, competing on equal terms with the most prestigious firms of the US and Europe. It occupied a vast Californian-style campus on the outskirts of Bangalore, employed 97,000 people and had a market capitalization of over $20 billion.[155]

India's embrace of market economics in 1991 and its emergence as a major global power gave a vital boost to globalization. But it also had important political and ideological implications. During the eighties India's relative failure compared to China had boosted those, particularly in Asia, who argue that democracy could actually undermine the stability and prosperity of emerging economies. But, just as victory in the Cold War was giving a boost to western self-confidence, so the newly confident Indians also weighed in on the side of democratic and liberal ideas. Manmohan Singh argued that 'Liberal democracy is the natural order of political organization in today's world.'[156] It was a perfect encapsulation of the confident liberal ideology that underpinned the new Age of Optimism that was dawning in 1991.

But, in that year, very few people in Washington would have had much time to pay attention to the progress of economic reform in India. They were preoccupied by the collapse of the Soviet Union. And – as so often – by turmoil in the Middle East.

THE GULF WAR, 1991:

The Unipolar Moment

President George H. W. Bush famously reproached himself for lacking 'the vision thing'. Unlike Ronald Reagan he was not a passionate advocate of the free market. Unlike Bill Clinton he was not particularly enthralled by globalization or modern technology (he was once baffled by a supermarket scanner). But the first President Bush did come up with a phrase that helped to define the Age of Optimism – 'new world order'.

President Bush's talk of a 'new world order' was not a reaction to the end of the Cold War. He used the phrase for the first time in a speech to Congress in September 1990, when Mikhail Gorbachev was still in the Kremlin and the Soviet Union was still in one piece. The president's rare flight of rhetorical fancy was, instead, provoked by Iraq's invasion of Kuwait – and the vision of a new world in which all the major powers could come together to defeat acts of international aggression.

Bush elaborated on his vision in a State of the Union Address shortly after the start of the first Gulf War against Saddam Hussein's Iraq. He told Congress, 'What is at stake is more than one small country; it is big ideas, a new world order, where diverse nations are drawn together in common cause to achieve the universal aspirations of mankind – peace and security, freedom, and the rule of law.'[157]

The president's phrase was latched on to by critics of both left and right. Some American right-wingers feared that Mr Bush had been captured by advocates of a 'one world government'; some left-wingers reckoned that he was talking about a newly rampant global capitalism. In fact, characteristically, his vision was rather more limited than that. As the historian Lawrence Freedman writes, 'Bush's concept for this new order essentially involved the old, post-World War II order, working as it should because now the United States and the Soviet Union could work together.'[158] Like many telling phrases, however, the 'new world order' eventually took on meanings that were never envisaged by its author. In the aftermath of America's victory in the Gulf War of 1991 and the collapse of the Soviet Union, it began to be associated with a new age dominated by US political power and a globalized economy.

The notion that America would naturally dominate a 'new world order' seemed obvious in the aftermath of the Cold War. But just three years earlier, even as the Reagan era closed, many American intellectuals and politicians were still transfixed by the rise of Japan. Yale professor Paul Kennedy's bestselling book *The Rise and Fall of the Great Powers*, which was published in 1988, captured and encouraged the fear that the United States might be in decline. Kennedy's concluding chapter was gloomy about America's economic prospects and very bullish about Japan. 'Just how powerful, economically, will Japan be in the early twenty-first century?' he asked rhetorically, before replying, 'the consensus answer seems to be much more powerful.'[159] But, as so often, the 'consensus answer' was the wrong answer. Japan's stock market peaked at the end of 1989 and began a long crash that gradually revealed the weaknesses of the country's 'bubble economy'. By the end of 1991 the sense that Japan's rise was inexorable and threatening was already beginning to dissipate – just as America regained confidence in its own power, after the first Gulf War.

The Gulf crisis began on 2 August 1990 with Saddam Hussein's invasion of Kuwait. Within days President Bush had announced that Iraq's forceful acquisition of Kuwait 'will not stand'.[160] Within weeks it had become apparent that military force would almost certainly be required to get Iraq out of Kuwait. Margaret Thatcher, nearing the end of her twelve years in power, made a memorable appearance on the scene urging President Bush not to 'go wobbly'.[161]

After the painstaking process of assembling diplomatic support at the United Nations and assembling a huge military coalition in the Gulf, hostilities began with air strikes on 16 January. The ground invasion followed on 24 February and lasted just three days. The expulsion of Iraq from Kuwait was achieved easily. Allied casualties had been relatively low, with the coalition forces suffering fewer than four hundred deaths. The final phase of the war had been, in the morally discomfiting phrase of the time, a 'turkey shoot' of fleeing Iraqi troops.

It was only in retrospect, however, that an easy victory in the Gulf War looked inevitable. I was working as a journalist in Washington DC in the months before the conflict broke out and can well remember the intense anxiety about committing US troops to a war in the Middle East. Memories of Vietnam were still fresh and were frequently evoked. Some serious analysts estimated that the US could lose up to fifteen thousand troops trying to force Iraq out of Kuwait.[162]

President Bush exulted that easy victory in the Gulf War had 'kicked the Vietnam syndrome once and for all'.[163] It certainly transformed American attitudes to the use of force. The US had beaten a large, battle-hardened army on the other side of the world and assured the security of the world's oil supplies in a matter of weeks. American politicians began once again to believe in the possibility of swift military victories.

America's revived willingness to contemplate war was a defining feature of the new Age of Optimism that dawned in 1991. It can be seen in the contrast between the Congressional votes authorizing the first and second Gulf wars. In 1991 the case for war was clearly much

stronger, since Saddam Hussein had actually invaded a foreign country. In 2003 President George W. Bush was essentially asking America
to wage a pre-emptive 'war of choice', based on assumptions about what
Saddam might do in the future. Nonetheless, Congressional support for
the second war with Saddam was much stronger than for the first. The
Senate voted to authorize the use of force by just 52–47 in 1990. Twelve
years later, the vote to go to war was 77–23. Richard Haass, who worked
for both the first and the second President Bushes, thinks that the
disparity in the votes reflected the traumatic effect of the terrorist attacks
on New York and Washington DC in 2001: 'Many of those voting this
time around simply did not want to be on record in the wake of 9/11
opposing a war that was then popular.'[164]

The national trauma suffered by America on 9/11 undoubtedly had
a lot to do with the country's willingness to go to war in 2003. But the
renewed faith in the possibility of swift military victory that was a legacy
of the first Gulf War of 1991 was also critical.

By the end of 1991 the phrase 'new world order' had come to signify
far more than a better-functioning United Nations. Although in Europe
in particular, 1989 is often seen as the most transformational year in
the Age of Transformation, for the world as a whole 1991 was at least as
significant. The opening of India had put in place the last big piece of
the globalization puzzle. The collapse of the Soviet Union had definitively ended the ideological and geopolitical struggle that had defined
world politics since 1945. And the easy victory of the US-led coalition in
the Gulf War gave American politicians an intoxicating glimpse of a new
world defined by an unanswerable combination of American technological, military, economic, ideological and political power. The unipolar
moment had dawned.

PART TWO

The Age of Optimism
1991–2008

INTRODUCTION

The Age of Optimism was a period of unparalleled American power. Economic power with the US as the core of the global economy. Financial power with Wall Street directing the flows of money around the world. Military power with the US outspending the whole of the rest of the world combined. Technological power with America at the heart of the computer and internet revolutions. This led to intellectual power – the power to create a new narrative for the world.

With the collapse of the Soviet Union in 1991, an enticing vision of a 'new world order' beckoned. It was of a more peaceful world in which all the major powers embraced similar political and economic visions of democracy and free markets. This idea was captured in a new buzz word – 'globalization' – which became the dominant political and economic theme of the Age of Optimism that ran from 1991 until 2008.

The first four chapters of this section look at the ideas that under-pinned the Age of Optimism, and at the people most associated with them. The remaining chapters look at how far America's confidence in democracy, markets, the 'democratic peace' and the power of technology was shared in Asia and Europe. It explains why all the world's major powers bought into globalization and how a long period of economic growth created a win-win world that diminished the chances of international conflict.

The first American writer to capture the spirit of the new age was Francis Fukuyama, whose famous essay on the 'end of history' was published in the summer of 1989, just as the revolutionary transformation of the Soviet bloc was gathering pace. Fukuyama's argument was that the end of the Cold War might signal 'the end point of mankind's ideological evolution', heralding the eventual triumph of western-style liberal democracy across the world. Although Fukuyama's ideas were widely attacked as hubristic (and equally widely misunderstood), a version of his thesis underpinned US foreign policy during the Age of Optimism. The administrations of Bill Clinton and George W. Bush both placed the promotion of democracy at the centre of their foreign policies – and both believed that they were putting themselves on the right side of the end of history by doing so.

When Fukuyama proclaimed the 'end of history', he was thinking above all about politics and the triumph of liberal democracy. But when Americans asked themselves what it was that had led to victory in the Cold War, democracy was only one part of the answer. The other key element, it was generally agreed, was free markets. In the Age of Optimism many people also began to believe in something like the 'end of economic history'.[165] The big economic debates seemed to have been settled. Across the world, this was the era of smaller government, lower taxes, privatization, deregulation, market opening and globalization.

Alan Greenspan, who had been appointed the chairman of the Federal Reserve in 1987 and who was to serve until 2007, epitomized the economic ideas of the Age of Optimism. Greenspan was a libertarian, with an instinctive distrust of government meddling. He believed that 'You can't tell when a market is over-valued and you can't fight market forces.' The long boom of the Age of Optimism ensured that

Greenspan became a revered figure, not just in the United States, but around the world. For the US was not just the core of the world economy, it was also the intellectual centre of the economics profession. It was no accident that the free-market ideas that were promoted all over the world during the Age of Optimism came to be known as the 'Washington Consensus'.[166]

One reason why the United States itself retained its faith in globalization during the period from 1991 to 2008 was that the American economy was growing fast. By the nineties it was clear that the US was at the forefront of a technological revolution. The rise of high-tech companies like Microsoft, Apple and Google on the west coast of America seemed to more than make up for the loss of industrial jobs in the Rust Belt. America's ability to spawn exciting new products and companies made US business culture, in the words of Alan Greenspan, 'the envy of the world'.

The technological revolution also deeply influenced the political thinking of the era, strengthening America's belief that countries that blocked democracy and the free flow of information would fail. As Bill Clinton explained to an audience in the Pentagon in 1998, 'Bit by bit the information age is chipping away at the barriers economic, political and social that once kept people locked in and freedom and prosperity locked out.'[167]

The rising powers of Asia and the European Union had their own reasons to embrace globalization in a spirit of optimism. The economies of China, India and most of South-east Asia were growing at unprecedented rates. New opportunities also beckoned for the countries of Central Europe, which were at last free to embrace democracy and free markets. The European Union doubled in size, as a result, and became the world's largest economy.

Yet not every major power was satisfied with its place in the 'new world order'. The big exception was Russia. The country's chaotic transition to a market economy in the nineties had left many ordinary people worse off than under communism. In the process, both political and economic liberalism were discredited. By the end of the decade, Russia's leadership was also in an angry mood – convinced that western leaders had betrayed a promise not to expand the Nato military alliance up to Russia's borders. Nonetheless, many members of the Russian elite had a direct personal stake in the new globalized order – in the form of Swiss bank accounts and houses in London.

In the wake of the Asian and Russian economic crises of the late nineties, the anti-globalization movement found its voice. The anti-globalizers pointed out that large parts of the world – in particular, in Africa and the Middle East – had failed to benefit from the economic growth unleashed by globalization. Some argued that most of the wealth created by globalization had been captured by international elites: western bankers, Russian oligarchs, Asian manufacturers – the Davos crowd, in short.

The most violent and shocking assault on globalization and the US-led 'new world order' was launched on 9/11. The al-Qaeda attacks on New York and Washington were a symbolic assault on the two main underpinnings of the Age of Optimism – globalization and American power – with the hijacked planes crashing into the World Trade Center and the Pentagon.

The United States responded to this assault with a reassertion of American military power and free-market ideology that is examined in the final chapter of this section. For the neoconservatives, who pushed for the invasions of Iraq and Afghanistan, the war on terror provided an opportunity for the United States to remake the world – crushing its enemies and exporting the virtues of democracy and free markets.

The Iraq and Afghan wars, however, made the limits of American power painfully clear. The wars of the Bush era ate away at American optimism. But the Age of Optimism was definitively brought to a close by the Wall Street crash of 2008. The US was plunged into its deepest recession since the thirties, with double-digit unemployment and a spiralling national debt. The economic crisis was also a huge blow to America's self-esteem and international prestige. The Age of Optimism had seen an American effort to remake the world in its own image. But the model formed in America had failed in America.

DEMOCRACY:

Francis Fukuyama and the End of History

I n early 1989 Francis Fukuyama returned to Chicago University, his alma mater, to give a lecture. His talk was part of a series on the decline of the West, organized by his old professor, Allan Bloom, author of the celebrated and gloomy conservative tract *The Closing of the American Mind*.[168] There was only one problem. In early 1989 Fukuyama was in anything but a gloomy mood. As he later recalled, 'I said I'll give a talk, but it's not going to be the decline of the West, it's going to be the victory of the West. And they said, okay, fine, whatever. So I gave the talk in February of 1989.'[169]

The thesis that Fukuyama outlined in Chicago became famous as 'the end of history'. A softly spoken Asian-American, with an academic manner and conservative views, Fukuyama was aged thirty-six in 1989. He had done his doctorate on Soviet foreign policy. After a period working in the State Department during the Reagan administration, he returned to the study of Soviet politics at the Rand Corporation, a think-tank just outside Los Angeles. As he followed the course of Gorbachev's reforms in 1988, Fukuyama realized that Soviet communism had collapsed as an ideological system. The West had won.

So when Professor Bloom contacted him, he pushed back against his mentor's instinctive pessimism. In Chicago Fukuyama argued that 'What we may be witnessing is not just the end of the Cold War, or the passing of a particular period of post-war history, but the end of history as such: that is, the end point of mankind's ideological evolution and the universalization of Western liberal democracy as the final form of human government.'[170] By June 1989, when a revised version of Fukuyama's talk was published as an article in the *National Interest*, a highbrow Washington magazine, the world was ready for his message. The Soviet empire in Eastern Europe was tottering. The first free Polish elections had just taken place, the Iron Curtain was beginning to crack with the dismantling of the border between Hungary and East Germany. In China that same month, the tanks had rolled into Tiananmen Square and crushed the student movement, but the Chinese government seemed to be faltering. Talk of the collapse of communism and the final triumph of democracy did not seem fanciful.

The buzz generated by the 'end of history' thesis was intensified by the fact that, by the time his article appeared, Fukuyama was back in government, working as deputy director of the State Department's policy planning staff in the administration of the first President Bush. It was all too tempting to read the Fukuyama thesis as the expression of the secret views of the US government. The fact that policy planning was the department from which George Kennan had spelled out the doctrine of 'containment' – defining US foreign policy during the Cold War – added to the mystique.

In fact, Fukuyama's article was a curious piece of work – whimsical and full of long digressions on obscure Hegelian philosophers, it reads like the scribblings of a very clever, but ill-disciplined graduate student. Eager journalists and foreign diplomats, keen to divine the secret thinking of the Bush administration, found themselves poring over sentences such as: 'I want to avoid the materialist determinism that says that liberal economics inevitably produces liberal politics, because I believe that both economics and politics presuppose an autonomous prior state of consciousness that makes them possible.'[171]

But the obscure language and Hegelian philosophizing didn't matter. Fukuyama's central insight was powerful and brilliant. The end of the Cold War had ended ideological competition. Liberal democracy would reign supreme.

In subsequent years, it has become almost compulsory for political commentators to take a sideswipe at Fukuyama and to dismiss the 'end of history' thesis as hubristic nonsense.[172] Part of the problem is often a misunderstanding of what Fukuyama was actually saying. He was not predicting the end of events. His argument was rather that the battle of ideas had ended. Communists had stopped believing in their own system, and there was no new ideological challenger to liberal democracy on the horizon. This did not mean that all countries would become liberal democracies immediately, or that conflict would disappear from the world. Instead, Fukuyama predicted a 'steadily expanding post-historical world'[173] of liberal democracies that would clash intermittently with a 'historical' world of countries that had not yet made the transition to liberal democracy.

Fukuyama's more grandiloquent statements were clearly meant to provoke and were open to challenge. But, equally clearly, he was on to something. As he pointed out in the book that grew out of his original essay, the spread of liberal democracy since the establishment of the United States in the late eighteenth century has been truly remarkable. In 1790, he argued, there were just three parliamentary democracies in the world – the US, Britain and Switzerland. (Some might dispute even this, given slavery in the US and the fact that Britain only moved to a universal franchise in the twentieth century.) By 1848 there were five democracies, by 1900 there were thirteen, by 1960 there were thirty-six and by 1990 there were sixty-one. There had been rises and falls in the number of democratic states, with the rise of fascism and communism, but the overall trend was inexorably upwards.[174]

In 1989, moreover, the new long wave of global democratization that had begun in Western Europe in the mid-seventies was about to gain renewed impetus. Freedom House, a New York-based think-tank that tracks the progress of democracy around the world, records that in 1989 there were sixty-nine electoral democracies in the world, accounting for around 41 per cent of nation-states. Twenty years later, in 2009, there were 119 electoral democracies, accounting for 62 per cent of countries.[175] Questions of definition mean that Freedom House's numbers are slightly different from those offered by Fukuyama in 1991. But the overall trend is unmistakeable.

The collapse of the Soviet system and the global advance of democracy seemed to vindicate the Fukuyama thesis and a simplified version of his ideas deeply influenced US foreign policy during the Age of Optimism. Like Fukuyama, US officials decisively turned their back on the 'declinism' that had become fashionable in the late eighties, when the US was still worrying about the rise of Japan. Instead, a new and optimistic American foreign policy was based on a belief in the triumph of the western system and the unstoppable rise of democracy and free markets.

Al Gore, Bill Clinton's vice-president, eloquently summed up the new thinking in a brainstorming session in the White House in 1994: 'Ours is becoming a global civilization,' he told the president and his advisers. 'There is a universal sense that democracy is humankind's chosen form of political organization and that the free market is humankind's chosen form of economic organization.'[176]

This 'universal sense' was not confined to the United States. In the nineties, securing democracy in the former Soviet empire became a defining mission for the European Union. Manmohan Singh, the architect of the Indian economic reforms, sounded like an Asian echo of Fukuyama when he asserted, 'Liberal democracy is the natural order of political organization in today's world. All alternative systems ... are in varying degrees an aberration.'[177]

For the United States, however, the 'end of history' thesis answered one question but posed another. Was history going to end of its own accord, or might it need a helping hand? Put in less abstract terms – should the US simply wait for democracy to triumph around the globe? Or should it pursue a policy aimed at actively promoting democracy?

One interpretation of the 'end of history' thesis was that Americans should take a well-earned rest after the Cold War, and enjoy their 'peace dividend'. Newt Gingrich, the architect of the Republican resurgence in Congress in the mid-nineties, favoured a more expansive foreign policy. But he was aware that the optimistic spirit in the US was actually fostering introspection. He later described the mid-nineties as 'a little bit like *The Great Gatsby*: a feel-good period with relatively modest threats in which the most powerful nation in the world had near hegemonic supremacy.'[178]

There were others, however, who wanted America to take a much more active role in promoting democracy. Anthony Lake, President Clinton's first national security adviser, wanted to make 'democratic enlargement' the centrepiece of the new administration's foreign policy. President Clinton himself took up the call in a speech to the United Nations in 1993: 'In a new era of peril and opportunity,' he proclaimed, 'our overriding purpose must be to expand and strengthen the world's community of market-based democracies.'[179]

The group of Republican foreign-policy activists who later became famous as 'the neocons' under President George W. Bush were pushing for similar policies. During the Clinton years, the debate was important – but not urgent. After the terrorist attacks on 9/11, however, the question of how far America should go to promote democracy overseas became much more critical and controversial.

President Bush's 'freedom agenda' and his constant emphasis on the imperative to spread liberal democracy around the world owed a great deal to the intellectual positions staked out by Fukuyama in 1989. But the position of Fukuyama himself was ambiguous. His early political career placed him firmly in the neoconservative camp. His first govern-ment jobs in the Reagan administration involved working for neocon Paul Wolfowitz, another protégé of Allan Bloom.[180] When the neocons organized a lobby group and think-tank called the Project for the New American Century (PNAC) in 1997, Fukuyama was one of the twenty-five co-signatories of their founding manifesto, alongside such luminaries as Wolfowitz, Dick Cheney and Donald Rumsfeld – all of whom later served in very senior positions in the administration of George W. Bush. PNAC demanded a more assertive US foreign policy based around democracy promotion, economic freedom and a renewed commitment to national security. Fairly quickly, PNAC also became closely associated with the campaign for 'regime change' in Saddam Hussein's Iraq.

Yet even before 9/11 and the subsequent drive for war with Iraq, Fukuyama was clearly beginning to feel uncomfortable with the company he was keeping. In an essay in *Commentary* magazine in 2000, he chided his fellow neoconservatives for their complete silence on international economics and globalization.[181]

In the aftermath of the Iraq War, Fukuyama broke decisively with his old friends. In a book published in 2006, he acknowledged that he had 'long regarded myself as a neoconservative'. But he went on, 'I have concluded that neoconservatism . . . has evolved into something that I can no longer support.' Specifically, neocon ideas 'were used to justify an American foreign policy that overemphasized the use of force and led logically to the Iraq War'. But, in the year preceding the invasion, Fukuyama had come to believe that the war 'didn't make sense'.[182]

Many of Fukuyama's old colleagues felt betrayed by his repudiation of neoconservatism. And Fukuyama himself acknowledges that his 'end of history' thesis could indeed have been read as providing the basis for the neocon view of the world. Some neoconservatives, he noted, 'compared me to Lucy holding the football for Charlie Brown, and then pulling it away at the last minute . . . I had teed up this football saying that there's this global move to democracy that's unstoppable, and I pulled it away just before they invaded Iraq.'[183] Fukuyama, however, insists that nothing he said in Chicago in February 1989, or in his subsequent article and book on the 'end of history', could be read as a justification for the invasion of Iraq. Yes, he believed in a worldwide trend towards democracy. But 'the idea that American power can be used to dramatically speed up this process in a country that's got a lot of cultural restraints is something I never believed in'.[184]

Democracy advanced around the world during the Age of Optimism. But Fukuyama's 'end of history' thesis seemed to become more, not less, controversial. By the end of the Bush administration, many foreigners regarded American talk of the globalization of democracy and the president's freedom agenda as a mask for US aggression. The idea of 'democracy promotion' even divided Americans.

But while faith in the universality of democracy was never, in fact, universal during the Age of Optimism, there were other parts of the liberal internationalist creed that really did seem to have conquered the world in the years between the collapse of the Soviet Union and the financial crisis of 2008. The most important idea of all was faith in market economics.

PROSPERITY:

Alan Greenspan and the End of Economic History

When Bill Clinton gave his first speech to a joint session of Congress in February 1993, his staff choreographed the occasion with great care. Hillary Clinton was sitting in the front row of the Senate gallery. Alan Greenspan, the chairman of the Federal Reserve, was placed right next to her. It was a deliberate message of reassurance to the markets and to ordinary Americans. It said, in effect, 'Don't worry. Greenspan is here.'

No man better embodied the economics of the Age of Optimism than Alan Greenspan. Appointed as chairman of the Fed for the first time in 1987 under Ronald Reagan and then reappointed by three successive presidents, Greenspan had his hands on the controls of the most powerful economy in the world throughout the period – leaving office only in 2006, just two years before the global financial crisis. His success in piloting the economy through the storms of the stock market crash of 1987, the Asian and Russian financial crises of 1997 and 1998, and the bursting of the dot.com bubble of 2001, turned him into a mixture of a guru and a lucky charm.

Greenspan's press was adulatory. In 2001 Bob Woodward – perhaps the most famous American journalist of the time – published a biography of the Fed chairman entitled simply *Maestro*.[185] Bill Clinton was by no means the only US politician to recognize Greenspan's talismanic qualities. George W. Bush was careful to reappoint him when he became president in 2001. John McCain, the Republican candidate in 2008, once joked that if Greenspan were to die, the only thing to do would be to put dark glasses on him and prop him up behind his desk. In an area of technological, political and economic transformation, Alan Greenspan seemed like a fixed point of quiet, adult good sense.

The humming American economy was at the core of a prolonged world boom, so the Greenspan cult became global. In 2002 he was awarded an honorary knighthood (becoming Sir Alan Greenspan) by Britain's Queen Elizabeth.

Greenspan himself was mild-mannered and courteous. As a young BBC producer in the mid-eighties I once wrote him a note to apologize for a foul-up that had left him hanging around a studio, wasting time. I was surprised to get a handwritten letter by return of post, telling me not to worry. Even as Fed chairman, he remained engagingly unassuming for a man at the receiving end of so much adulation.

Born into a New York Jewish family of modest means, he was educated at the same Manhattan high school as Henry Kissinger – although the two men did not meet at school. As well as being a gifted mathematician and economist, Greenspan was a talented musician. As a young man, he briefly played in the same jazz band as the legendary Stan Getz. But Greenspan's nerdy side was always well to the fore. He helped out the other members of his jazz band by doing their tax returns for them. Many years later, when he was wooing Andrea Mitchell, who became his second wife, he ended a dinner date by inviting her back to his apartment, 'where I showed her this essay I'd written on anti-trust for Ayn Rand'.[186]

The reference to Rand is perhaps as revealing as Greenspan's unusual mode of courtship. For Greenspan was not a mere technician or a number-cruncher. He was a man of powerful libertarian and free-market convictions, who both captured and moulded the spirit of his age.

As a young man, Greenspan had been captivated by the personality and ideas of Ayn Rand, a Russian exile, philosopher and bestselling novelist who, as Greenspan puts it, 'championed laissez-faire capitalism as the ideal form of social organization'.[187] Debating with her, Greenspan later remembered, was 'like starting a game of chess thinking I was good, and later finding myself in checkmate'.[188] Rand was short, force-ful, charismatic and dominated many of her youthful disciples. One of them, Nathaniel Branden, became involved in an affair with her, despite being twenty-five years her junior. (Rand convinced her own husband and Branden's wife to accept this arrangement.) Greenspan's devotion to Rand was entirely cerebral, but he became, in his own words, a 'young acolyte' who wrote 'spirited commentary for her newsletter'.[189] When he was appointed to his first senior government job as chairman of Presi-dent Ford's Council of Economic Advisers, in his late forties, Rand stood next to him at the swearing-in ceremony in the White House. And when Rand died in 1982, Greenspan attended her funeral, where one of the wreaths was a six-foot-high floral dollar bill.

Greenspan's reverence for Ayn Rand has sometimes been used to portray him as slightly kooky – almost the member of a cult. But by the time he assumed the chairmanship of the Fed at the age of sixty-two, Greenspan was perfectly capable of rejecting some of the more extreme ideas of his mentor. Rand's 'Objectivism', for example, held that all taxation was immoral because it involved the government's theft of private property. As a senior economic official in the US government, Greenspan was prepared to take a more pragmatic position.

Nonetheless, the Fed chairman carried with him Rand's belief in the joys and virtues of unfettered market competition. When his govern-ment career began, in the mid-seventies, he was out of tune with the ideological spirit of the time. At meetings of the Organization of Economic Co-operation and Development (OECD) – which brought together economists from twenty-four nations – Greenspan found himself almost isolated: 'only Hans Tietmeyer of West Germany and I were pressing for market-based policymaking.'[190] But by the time he assumed the chairmanship of the Fed in 1987, free-market ideas were once again in the ascendancy.

As chairman, Greenspan's instinct was always to defer to the judgement and wisdom of the markets. On one famous occasion – in the midst of a long bull market in stocks in 1996 – he did muse openly about the idea that the markets might be in the grip of 'irrational exuberance'. But the cautionary effect on investors was short-lived. After a while the stock market resumed its upward climb and Greenspan felt he had relearned a valuable lesson – something that Rand would certainly have told him: 'You can't tell when a market is over-valued and you can't fight market forces.'[191] As the journalist Justin Fox observes, 'This was Greenspan's ideology… Financial markets knew best… They regulated global economic affairs with a swiftness and decisiveness that governments couldn't match.'[192]

The fact that the chairman of the Federal Reserve held these views was critical to the development of the Age of Optimism, for this was a period of remarkable growth in financial markets, not just in the US, but around the world. As a foreign correspondent in Asia in the nineties, I observed the burgeoning of stock exchanges in countries that were still nominally communist, such as China and Vietnam. The first mutual funds aimed at foreigners were launched in India and soon showed rapid growth. On any trip to an Asian capital, one of my first visits would be to the offices of the big western investment banks – the likes of Goldman Sachs and Morgan Stanley – which were directing the flow of money and investment around the world.

For western leaders, struggling to convince voters (and themselves) of the virtues of globalization, the growth and power of the western investment banks was a crucial part of the argument. Let the Asians specialize in low-cost manufacturing, so the argument went, the West could corner the market in much more profitable areas like high-tech and high finance. Greenspan himself referred approvingly to hedge funds as 'a vibrant trillion-dollar industry dominated by US firms'.[193]

But for the financial industry to deliver, it needed to be let off the leash. Greenspan became a crucial voice arguing for deregulation. In 1999 he pushed for the changes that finally abolished the last vestiges of the Glass–Steagall Act – a law passed during the Great Depression that erected walls between commercial and investment banking. Glass–Steagall was intended to limit the risks that banks could take, but its opponents feared that it stifled innovation and opportunity, and drove financial business out of the US to less regulated markets like London. Both Greenspan and the major investment banks agreed that Glass–Steagall was a relic. The Fed chairman allowed himself a rare moment of open vanity in praising his role in pushing through the Financial Services Modernization Act of 1999 that finally scrapped the Act. It was, he later wrote, 'a milestone of business legislation, and I'll always remember it as an unsung moment of policymaking for which there ought to be a little song'.[194]

As well as pushing through deregulation, Greenspan supported those who wanted to fight off efforts to bring in new rules to regulate new areas of high finance – in particular, the growth in exotic financial derivatives. The surge in this market during the period of Greenspan's tenure at the Fed was mind-boggling. The value of derivatives traded 'over-the-counter', rather than through an exchange, rose from $866 billion to $454 trillion in the twenty years between 1987 and 2007.[195]

The extraordinary nature of these numbers did, naturally enough, cause a certain amount of alarm. The legendary financier Felix Rohatyn warned that derivatives could turn out to be 'financial hydrogen bombs'.[196] Congress began to move to regulate this new and largely unregulated market. But the industry was determined to resist regulation and Alan Greenspan agreed with them. Everything seemed to be going so well, and the financial industry was generating such massive profits, tax revenues and bonuses that it seemed like folly to intervene. As Greenspan mused in his memoirs published just a year before the crash of 2008, 'Why inhibit the pollinating bees of Wall Street?'[197]

The amount of money generated by the giant investment banks was undoubtedly a huge source of influence – and even of corruption and conflict of interest.[198] The alumni of Goldman Sachs, the most prestigious and profitable of all the banks, seemed to pop up everywhere. Robert Rubin, who became a powerful secretary of the Treasury under Bill Clinton, was a former co-chairman of Goldman Sachs. When the financial crisis finally broke in the twilight years of the Bush presidency, the US Treasury was once again being run by a former chairman of Goldman Sachs, Hank Paulson. The traffic between government and Wall Street worked in both directions. Jerry Corrigan, who had once cast a sceptical eye on the derivatives business as a regulator at the New York Fed, was later hired as a managing director by Goldman Sachs. The same process operated in Europe. Peter Sutherland, who as competition commissioner for the European Union in Brussels was partly responsible for the regulation of investment banking, later resurfaced as co-chairman of Goldman Sachs International in London. Mario Draghi, who headed the Financial Stability Forum that the G20 placed in charge of reforming global finance in the wake of the crash, was another Goldman alumnus.

But while the drive to fight off regulation of banks in general and derivatives in particular was led by a desire to maximize profits, it was also about principle and ideas. The lobbyists who led the banks' fight to keep the derivatives market largely unregulated were libertarians who believed passionately in what they were doing. Mark Brickell, the leader of the industry lobbying organization, was a follower of Hayek and a believer in the all-seeing wisdom of markets.[199]

Fortunately for Brickell and the derivatives traders, their views chimed with those of Alan Greenspan. The chairman believed that market participants – whose own financial interests were directly at stake – were far more likely to ensure that risks were adequately assessed than regulators, who would inevitably be many steps behind the market. It was a lesson that he traced all the way back to the 'simple, time-tested principle promulgated by Adam Smith in 1776: individuals trading freely with one another following their own self-interest leads to a growing, stable economy'.[200]

Towards the end of the Age of Optimism, and just before the crash, it became clear that the global financial market was so huge and so complex that no single individual or institution could fully comprehend its scope – and no regulator could control it. Yet this realization did not perturb Greenspan, who believed firmly in the market's ability to self-regulate: 'As I saw it…the largely unregulated global financial markets, with some notable exceptions, appeared to be moving from one state of equilibrium to another. Adam Smith's invisible hand was at work on a global scale.'[201]

By 2008 the world was facing the mother of all 'notable exceptions'. The global financial system was on the point of collapse and the world economy was entering its deepest recession since the thirties. Far from guarding their own interests and exemplifying the virtues of private profit-seeking, the giants of Wall Street had either collapsed like Lehman Brothers or had to be bailed out by the taxpayer to the tune of billions of dollars.

A chastened and agonized Alan Greenspan testified before Congress. His words seemed as hopeless and uncomprehending as the NASA operative who was heard to say, 'Obviously a major malfunction', just after the Space Shuttle Challenger blew up in 1986. When Congressman Henry Waxman put it to the former Fed chairman, now aged eighty-two, that 'you found that your view of the world, your ideology, was not right. It was not working,' Greenspan was honest and shell-shocked enough to agree. 'Precisely,' he replied. 'That's precisely the reason I was shocked because I had been going for forty years or more with very considerable evidence that it was working exceptionally well.'[202]

The question of what precisely had gone wrong swiftly became the subject of fierce debates that will keep economists busy for decades to come. But the most plausible explanations all pointed to weaknesses in Greenspan's belief in the self-righting, self-regulating magic of the global marketplace. In retrospect, it seemed clear that a credit bubble had built up in the United States – promoted by Greenspan's policy of very low interest rates and by the 'global economic imbalances' that had allowed huge trade surpluses to build up in Asia and then to be recycled in the US. Greenspan's faith in deregulation and in the self-interest of the major investment banks as the best guarantee of the health of the financial system also looked complacent and mistaken.

But it was too easy, in the aftermath of the crash, to blame it all on the misjudgements of the ageing 'Maestro' and his indulgence of Wall Street financiers. It was not Greenspan's fault that he had become the object of irrational veneration. And in embracing the free market, the financial industry and globalization, he was simply part of a much broader ideological trend that swept the world in the Age of Optimism.

In the western world, the triumph of free-market ideology was signalled by the acceptance by the American and British centre-left of the Reagan and Thatcher revolutions. In his State of the Union Address in 1996, Bill Clinton proclaimed that 'the era of big government is over' and then launched into an ambitious reform that cut back welfare benefits in order to improve incentives to work – an idea that would have appealed only to hardline conservatives just a decade before.[203] In 1994, three years before they took power in Britain, Gordon Brown and Tony Blair – the duo who defined New Labour – visited Alan Greenspan in his office in the Fed in Washington. As Greenspan noted, 'Brown in particular espoused globalization and free markets.'[204] The Fed chairman was impressed.

In the spring of 1997, shortly before his election as the first Labour prime minister in eighteen years, Tony Blair gave a speech at the Corn Exchange in the heart of the City of London in which he announced,

'We accept, and indeed embrace, the role of free enterprise in the economy. There will be no retreat from any of that.'[205] In particular, Labour announced that there would be no retreat from the 40 per cent top tax rate introduced under Margaret Thatcher – a point of crucial importance to the City audience. Blair also took it upon himself to become an evangelist for free markets with the more sceptical left-wing parties of France and Germany. In 1999 he staged a joint summit with Gerhard Schroeder, the recently elected Social Democratic chancellor of Germany. The two men issued a joint statement proclaiming their faith in the importance of markets.

The free-market wave was even stronger in the developing world. After the shock of the Tiananmen uprising, Deng Xiaoping and the Chinese Communist Party doubled their bets on economic growth as the crucial stabilizing force in China. Free enterprise, foreign investment and export-driven growth were to be given their heads. In India, the new strategy for solving the old problem of persistent poverty was to encourage private enterprise. As leading reformer Palaniappan Chidambaram put it, 'Growth is the best antidote to poverty.'[206]

The point Chidambaram was making was vital. Free markets were being given their head in country after country across the world, not because they had triumphed in some rarefied debating contest but because they were delivering results – reducing poverty in some of the poorest countries in the world, and underpinning a long boom in the US and Europe. The reforms initiated by Deng Xiaoping are widely reckoned to have pulled as many as 200 million Chinese out of absolute poverty. The proportion of Indians living in absolute poverty has fallen from 60 per cent to 42 per cent since reforms began.[207]

In the United States too, the long economic expansion of the Age of Optimism seemed little short of miraculous. Bill Clinton had capitalized on economic anxiety in winning the presidency. His campaign team had adopted the celebrated slogan 'It's the economy, stupid.' But, at the end of his presidency, Clinton was able proudly to point out that the

United States was enjoying 'its lowest unemployment rate in three decades, the smallest welfare rolls in thirty-two years, the lowest crime rate in twenty-seven years, the highest home ownership in American history, and three consecutive years of budget surpluses'.[208] The George W. Bush years saw some economic turbulence, with the end of the dot.com bubble. But tax cuts, a housing boom and the Fed's policy of low interest rates under Greenspan succeeded in reinflating the economy and extending the long American expansion.

A prolonged period of global prosperity had one unlikely outcome. It turned economists and central bankers, normally the least charismatic of figures, into the heroes of the age. The veneration of Alan Greenspan in the United States was only the most extreme example of this phenomenon. In China Zhu Rongji, a former Central Bank governor and friend of Greenspan's, became prime minister between 1998 and 2003. In Europe, the managers of the European Central Bank were hailed for their skill in overseeing the successful introduction of the euro, the new pan-European currency introduced in 2002 that symbolized the growing ambition of the European Union. In India, Manmohan Singh, a distinguished academic economist, played a key part in the economic reforms, first as finance minister and then as prime minister. In Mexico, the North American free-trade agreement was negotiated in 1993 by Carlos Salinas, a president with a doctorate in economics from Harvard.

The self-confidence of economics as a profession was also rising. In 2004 Ben Bernanke, who was to succeed Greenspan as chairman of the Fed in 2006, gave a speech on a phenomenon he called 'the Great Moderation'. He drew attention to the 'substantial decline in macroeconomic volatility' over the past twenty years; or in non-economist speak, the emergence of a long, smooth economic boom whose peaks and troughs were much less pronounced than those experienced in more turbulent economic times. Bernanke considered three possible explanations for this happy outcome – luck, structural factors and better economic policy. He suggested that all three had played a part. But the great bulk of his speech was devoted to the contributions of better economic policy.[209] Perhaps, as Gordon Brown, Britain's finance minister, was fond of saying, there would be 'no more boom and bust'. The economics profession had cracked it.

The rising prestige of economics as a discipline was probably reflected in the steady rise of the circulation of *The Economist* during this period. When I joined the magazine (or newspaper, as it insists on calling itself) in 1991, global circulation was still below 300,000. By the time I left in 2006, weekly sales had broken a million worldwide.[210] This was significant because *The Economist* was not just a news weekly, it was also an energetic promoter of many of the economic ideas that underpinned the Age of Optimism – in particular, free trade and globalization. As Michael Mandelbaum, an American scholar, put it, *The Economist* was 'globalization's weekly chronicle'.[211]

In the United States, the growing prestige of economists and the technical complexity of their discipline and of the financial markets meant that economic advisers assumed the status of a particularly revered priesthood within policymaking circles. Derek Chollet and James Goldgeier, officials in the Clinton administration, noticed that 'Throughout the Cold War, the diplomats at the State Department and the military planners at the Pentagon dominated. Now, on many of the most important global issues, these traditional shapers of American foreign policy were left to defer to the people with experience in global markets. When [Robert] Rubin or [Larry] Summers argued for a particular course of action . . . the national security experts lacked the economic expertise to challenge them effectively.'[212]

The economists seemed to be, as the phrase went, 'the smartest guys in the room'. The press picked up on the new mood. When Greenspan, Rubin and Summers seemed to have staved off economic disaster in the wake of the Asian and Russian financial crises in 1999, *Time* magazine ran a breathless cover story on the three men, under the memorable headline 'The Committee to Save the World'. Years later, the cover still adorned Rubin's office wall in Manhattan. It was left to a few academic critics to argue that rescuing Wall Street investment banks from the consequences of their bad investment decisions was creating a very bad precedent, and storing up trouble for the future.[213]

But, as was to become even more evident in 2008, abstract considerations of 'moral hazard' in investment banking counted little, compared to the apparent threat of a meltdown of the global financial system.

More important, global finance was a vital part of globalization – easing the passage of capital around the world. And in the Age of Optimism, the promoters of globalization felt that the moral arguments were overwhelmingly on their side. It was the integration of global markets that was bringing about unprecedented reductions in global poverty and underpinning the long boom in the developed world.

Free markets and free men – economic freedom and political freedom – were also inextricably linked. It was no accident that the two economic gurus of Thatcher and Reagan – Hayek and Milton Friedman – were deeply concerned with human liberty. Hayek's most famous work was an attack on the power of the state called *The Road to Serfdom*. A collection of Friedman's most important lectures was given the title *Capitalism and Freedom*.

Even for the likes of Clinton and Blair, neither of whom were followers of Hayek or Friedman, globalization served moral ends. For Bill Clinton, in particular, it was a force for greater global peace and prosperity. In any case, it was pointless to try and block the progress of globalization. Clinton believed that a new world was being created by the inexorable and unstoppable power of new technologies.

Progress:

Bill Gates and the Triumph of Technology

The Age of Optimism was defined and shaped by a technological revolution. The rise of the personal computer and the internet created new industries, destroyed old ones, raised economic productivity, transformed social life and turbo-charged globalization.

America's technology boom was crucial to banishing a fear of national decline that had hovered stubbornly over the eighties, even as Ronald Reagan proclaimed 'morning in America' and the US triumphed in the Cold War. Japanese brands seemed to dominate everything from cars to consumer electronics. As Alan Greenspan later noted, 'even the TVs we depended on for news bore Sony, Panasonic and Hitachi brands. Not since Sputnik had America felt itself to be at such a scary disadvantage.' But then, said Greenspan, 'the technology boom came along and changed everything. It made America's freewheeling, entrepreneurial, so-what-if you-fail business culture the envy of the world.'[214]

While the power of high finance was celebrated on the east coast of the United States, the west coast was the capital of the technological revolution. The technology boom of the nineties gave the US a whole new set of world-beating companies to admire and inspire: Microsoft,

Apple, Oracle, Netscape, eBay, Amazon, Intel, Yahoo!, Google. It made businessmen and entrepreneurs heroes once again. By 1991 *Time* magazine had not selected a businessman as 'man of the year' for more than three decades. But in the nineties, it chose three businessmen from the technology and media industries – Ted Turner of CNN in 1991, Andy Grove of Intel in 1997 and Jeff Bezos of Amazon in 1999.

Bill Gates had to wait until 2005 until he got that particular honour, when he shared it for his charitable work, with his wife Melinda and with Bono, the rock musician. But the founder of Microsoft was – amid a great deal of competition – the dominant businessman of his era. Gates founded Microsoft in 1975 and launched the first version of his Windows operating system in 1985. The breakthrough version – Windows 3.0 – came out in 1990.[215] It made IBM computers a lot easier to use and secured Windows' position as the industry standard.

For many of the keenest technophiles, Gates was something of a villain since they regarded Microsoft products as inferior to those produced by Steve Jobs at Apple. Throughout the nineties, Gates and Microsoft were also dogged by accusations of anti-competitive practices and the company became the object of high-profile anti-trust cases in both the US and Europe, resulting in fines that ran into billions of dollars.

Nonetheless, Gates himself attracted remarkably little opprobrium for such a high-profile figure. After the dot.com bubble burst in 2000, corporate America became engulfed in a series of scandals from Enron to WorldCom. The pay of top executives was increasingly the subject of scandal and controversy. But few begrudged Gates his money. He had become the world's richest man through his own brilliance and drive. He was living refutation of the cynical old maxim that 'behind every great fortune lies a great crime'. In the best traditions of American philanthropy, Gates was determined to use his money to improve the world. The Gates Foundation, founded in 1994, committed billions of dollars to development, health and education.

As a journalist, I have always tried to make it a rule not to be overawed by anybody I meet. But Gates was an exception. I first met him in January 2008 (at Davos, inevitably). There *was* something genuinely awe-inspiring about seeing all that energy, determination and brilliance applied to the problems that he wanted his foundation to solve. Gates's mannerisms are slightly unusual. He has a habit of rocking backwards and forwards when talking about a subject that particularly engages him. When he is especially keen to make a point, he sometimes leaps to his feet and marches around the room, cursing and gesticulating. But there is no mistaking the force of Gates's intellect. On every topic that we discussed, from malaria prevention to clean water and AIDS, he seemed to have devoured the academic research and to be pressing for new advances.

But what was most striking about the founder of Microsoft was not his wealth or his mind. It was his optimism. Gates was convinced that the world's toughest problems could be cracked – if you could just find the right people and enough money, and then apply the power of technology. He was the epitome of the American 'can-do' spirit – a man with an almost nineteenth-century faith in progress that seemed to have been largely lost in Europe. And why not? Gates and the tech-pioneers of the west coast had already transformed the world once.

The technological optimism personified by Bill Gates coloured the entire era between the end of the Cold War and the financial crash of 2008. Faith, even euphoria, about the new possibilities unleashed by high technology underpinned American optimism about the economy, about globalization, about high finance, about politics, peace and democracy, about American military power and about the world's ability to combine rapid economic growth with protection of the environment.

Throughout much of the eighties, economists had wondered why the computerization of America was not leading to higher productivity – and the increased wealth that higher productivity generates. But in the nineties, the productivity gains started to emerge. Computerization really did seem to have given a big boost to the capacity of the American and indeed the world economy. Once again, Greenspan both epitomized and moulded the emerging consensus. In 1995, as the tech boom surged, he suggested to his colleagues at the Fed that the IT revolution meant that the world had 'entered what would prove to be a protracted period of lower inflation, lower interest rates, increased productivity and full employment'. It was, he suggested, the kind of technological revolution that only happened once or twice a century.[216]

The rise of the information technology industry in the US made it much easier to make the case for globalization. If traditional manufacturing industry was still at the core of the American economy, then competition with low-cost workers in Mexico or China would look much more frightening. But with America leading the world in the new, cleaner and more lucrative technologies of the personal computer and the internet, a new and attractive global division of labour beckoned. Why not outsource the dirty old factories to somewhere else in the world – and do the clever, lucrative, higher-value-added stuff in the US?

The rise of outsourcing in India after 2000 suggested that this rosy picture might be a little oversimplified. What if the Indians could do the clever white-collar stuff as well? Thomas Friedman's bestselling book on high-tech and globalization, *The World is Flat*, which was published in 2005, spent some time wrestling with the implications of internet-driven outsourcing. But, in the end, Friedman came down decisively on the side of the optimists, arguing that America would prosper in a flat world by investing more in education and technology.[217]

New technology was clearly at the very core of the new industries of the west coast of America. But it was also revolutionizing another iconic industry of the age – high finance. Wall Street banks became increasingly reliant on computing power to model risk and design fancy new products. The credit derivatives that blew up with such deadly effect in 2008 were a product of this new era of high-tech confidence. Bankers at J. P. Morgan who helped design the new products were bewitched by the new possibilities. As Gillian Tett of the *Financial Times* later wrote,

'Computing power and high-order mathematics were taking the business far from its traditional bounds, and this small group of brilliant minds was charting the outer reaches of cyberfinance.'[218] Bill Winter of J. P. Morgan recalled that 'There was this sense that we had found this fantastic technology which we really believed in and we wanted to take to every part of the market.'[219]

The technological revolution bred optimism not just about the American economy, but about politics and international relations. Bill Clinton believed profoundly that technology was transforming the world in ways that favoured the United States and the democratic world. In his first inaugural address, he tipped his cap to the technological revolution. 'Communications and commerce are global,' he declared. 'Investment is mobile. Technology is almost magical.' Clinton was well aware of the destructive power of new technologies and his security team worried about weapons of mass destruction. But, ultimately, he was on the side of the optimists. At times Clinton's faith in technology verged on the mystical. He told his economic advisers, 'With the internet, with technology, I can feel the change. I can see growth everywhere.'[220]

Given time, the technological revolution would solve the perplexing problem of an anti-democratic China. Clinton explained his thinking on a visit to China in 1998: 'In this global information age, when economic success is built on ideas, personal freedom is...essential to the greatness of any modern nation.'[221]

If information technology was indeed the key to the new economic age, then regimes that relied on controlling and suppressing information were surely doomed in the long-run. The argument was put eloquently in a book that deeply impressed Clinton, Robert Wright's *Nonzero*, which argued that technological advance was leading inexorably to greater co-operation between nations. Wright believed that autocracies were incompatible with the information age. He wrote that 'Even China, an authoritarian (and once-totalitarian) nation, had seen by the late nineties that it needed the Internet... The nation was more porous to outside information than at any point since the communist revolution. Conceivably, the regime could reverse this trend – but the price would be a dismal economic future.'[222]

Wright's theory was that the spread of technology throughout the ages had led mankind to ever deeper forms of co-operation; or, as he put it, 'non-zero-sumness'. Tech-driven globalization was taking this well-established process to new levels. As Wright put it, using his favoured jargon, 'The current age, in which relations among nations grew more non-zero-sum year by year, is the natural outgrowth of several billion years of unfolding non-zero-sum logic.'[223] Wright argued passionately that the world should no longer be thought of in 'zero-sum' terms, in which one country's gain was another country's loss. Instead, globalization had created a win-win world.[224] Despite Wright's taste for impenetrable jargon, Clinton was deeply impressed. In the president's opinion, *Nonzero* was 'a work of genius'.[225]

Many conservatives – of both the neo and traditional variety – found Wright's theories a little New Age for their taste. Even Clinton's infatuation with globalization seemed a little mushy and suspect. The team around George W. Bush were known to deride the very term 'globalization' as a 'Clinton word'.

But American conservatives fell prey to their own form of technological euphoria during the Age of Optimism. They became firm believers that the technology-driven 'revolution in military affairs' had created a new era of unanswerable American dominance.

The vision of swift, relatively bloodless military victory first entranced America in the first Gulf War of 1991, when television audiences were introduced to computer-guided cruise missiles, zeroing in relentlessly on their targets in Baghdad. Air power seemed to prove its credentials once more in the Balkan wars of the mid-nineties. In the run-up to the invasion of Iraq in 2003, Donald Rumsfeld, the defence secretary, seemed determined to use the impending war to prove his own belief in the new era of high-tech warfare that would require far fewer troops than some of his own generals were calling for. In the aftermath of the swift fall of Baghdad, Rumsfeld seemed to have been vindicated. President Bush exulted that 'We've applied the new powers of technology... to strike an enemy force with speed and incredible precision...We are redefining war on our terms.'[226]

Even the threat of environmental catastrophe was somehow softened and vitiated by the technological euphoria of the period. The threat of global warming hung over the Age of Optimism. It was a central topic at the Earth Summit convened by the United Nations in Rio de Janeiro in 1992. Al Gore, Bill Clinton's vice-president, was famously passionate about the subject – although he was a much more whole-hearted campaigner once he had left mainstream politics. But Clinton himself was not overly concerned. In his autobiography of over a thousand pages, global warming gets just four mentions.

If even a liberal globalist like Clinton was relatively relaxed about global warming, conservatives were openly sceptical. It was not that they necessarily doubted the scientific evidence – although some did – it was that many believed that technology would solve the problem. *The Economist* epitomized this mood in an article on environmental scares, published in December 1997. 'Forecasters of scarcity and doom,' the magazine announced, are 'invariably wrong'. It traced the history of environmental scares all the way from Thomas Malthus's predictions of impending famine in the eighteenth century up to contemporary predictions that the world was running out of oil or food. As the article illustrated, forecasters of scarcity and doom had consistently failed to anticipate how new technologies would solve the problems that worried them. So, for example, the Green Revolution in agriculture had confounded the neo-Malthusians of the twentieth century. The magazine continued, 'Today the mother of all scares is global warming. Here the jury is still out.' But it was pretty clear what *The Economist* expected the eventual verdict to be. 'Every other environmental scare has been either wrong or badly exaggerated,' it argued.[227]

If even a centre-right magazine, published in Europe, took this position, American conservatives could be expected to be even more sceptical about global warming – and bullish about the prospects for new technology cracking the problem. President George W. Bush embodied both trends. In his first term in office he was notably reluctant to make a fuss about global warming. In 2001 the president formally withdrew American support for the Kyoto Protocol, arguing that it was 'fatally flawed'. As Strobe Talbott, president of the Brookings Institution, notes, 'When the Environmental Protection Agency, in May 2002, endorsed the view... that the problem was of humankind's making, Bush... said only, "I've read the report put out by the bureaucracy."'[228] A year later, the federal funding and warm words that Bush awarded to an initiative to build a hydrogen-powered car reflected his eagerness to find a high-tech solution to global warming.

By the end of the Age of Optimism, *The Economist* had joined the ranks of those who regarded global warming as both real and threatening. So had President Bush, a little reluctantly – and so, with rather more fervour, had John McCain, the Republican presidential candidate in 2008.

But the slowness to take global warming seriously demonstrates an important truth about the Age of Optimism. This was a period when a technological revolution seemed to promise a solution, not just to environmental problems, but to some of the oldest and most vexing political and economic dilemmas – from how to combine high growth with low inflation to how to persuade the nations of the world to make peace. Bill Clinton, in particular, came to believe that technology-driven globalization was the key to international peace. The old rules of international relations – in which countries competed for resources and power – were being replaced by a new co-operative world, in which all countries grew richer together. The zero-sum world was giving way to a win-win world.

PEACE:

Bill Clinton and the Win-Win World

I n 1996 Thomas Friedman, a *New York Times* columnist and evangelist for globalization, argued that 'no two countries that both have
a McDonald's have ever fought a war against each other... People
in McDonald's countries don't like to fight wars; they like to wait in line
for burgers.'[229] The ebullient Friedman was only half-joking. His line of
argument captured one of the most important strands of thinking of the
Age of Optimism – the theory of the 'democratic peace'.

The 'democratic peace' was where the 'end of history', the 'end of
economic history' and faith in technology and in globalization all came
together. The idea was that capitalism, democracy and technology would
advance simultaneously – and global peace would be the end-product.

Friedman's 'golden arches theory of conflict prevention' sounded
crude. But for the generation that grew up during the Cold War, the
connections between the advance of capitalism, democracy and peace
seemed absolutely evident. When the Soviet bloc collapsed, the move
towards market economics was swiftly followed by democratic revolutions. Europe was now united by a common democratic, capitalist
and consumerist culture. That, in turn, had dramatically reduced the

threat of another world war breaking out on the old continent.

The technological euphoria of the Age of Optimism added an extra layer to the theory. The divided world of the Cold War had given way to a unified global economy, tied together by high-technology. The new technologies empowered individuals and broke down national boundaries. In a 'borderless world', the idea of nation-states going to war seemed positively antediluvian. In his second book on globalization, *The World is Flat*, Friedman came up with another version of 'democratic peace' theory to illustrate the argument. The 'Dell theory of conflict prevention' argued that war between China and Taiwan was made much less likely (impossible, said Friedman) by the fact that they were part of the same high-tech supply chain that manufactured Dell computers.[230]

Friedman was skilfully popularizing ideas that had been part of liberal theory for many years. The great British campaigners for free trade in the nineteenth century, Richard Cobden and John Bright, had always believed that international peace and international trade went hand-in-hand. In a world of free trade, countries could abandon the imperialist logic that argued that you needed physical control over territory to secure its wealth. You could simply buy the oil or the diamonds – or whatever it was you were after – on the open global market.

Once countries embraced economic liberalism, so the theory went, they were much more likely to embrace political liberalism as well. People who had got used to making their own decisions as consumers, workers and employers would eventually demand political rights too. The spread of democracy would then further strengthen the move towards international peace because democracies were highly unlikely to go to war with each other.[231] Once again, there was a body of theory to suggest why democracies were unlikely to fight. Political systems that stressed individual rights and a free press were less likely to tolerate the misery of war. Countries that shared the same political values were unlikely to feel threatened by each other. Democracies that gained their legitimacy through the ballot box would not need international conflict to rally people behind their governments. And citizens who gained fulfilment and dignity as consumers and voters would be less susceptible to the demagogic temptations of nationalism.

The idea of the 'democratic peace' didn't just work in theory. It also seemed to work in practice. There was plenty of academic research that showed that democracies were indeed much less likely to fight each other.[232]

The theory of the 'democratic peace' could have been tailor-made to appeal to Bill Clinton. As a southern Democrat and a centrist, he had spent his whole political career trying to find common ground between old adversaries – blacks and whites, conservatives and liberals. In 1991, shortly before he declared his candidacy for the presidency, he had given a well-received speech to the Democratic Leadership Council that summed up his inclusive approach. Democrats, he said, recognized that Americans 'are a community. We are all in this together, and we are going up or down together.'[233]

As president, Clinton took this philosophy and applied it to the world. James Steinberg, who was a senior official in Clinton's National Security Council, later recalled that Clinton 'didn't see that there had to be inherent competition among nations. The success of some was not threatening to others. It was their failure that was threatening.'[234]

This was a radical departure from the traditional 'realist' view of international relations that held that rivalry between nations was the way of the world. Clinton believed that globalization had changed all that. The great powers – America, China, Russia, India, Japan and the European Union – would get richer together. Indeed, in a global market, the economic success of each major power was increasingly dependent on the success of the others.

For the win-win world to be a reality, however, globalization needed to create more than economic growth – it needed to produce political convergence. If China got much richer, but remained a one-party dictatorship, that could threaten American interests. But if globalization turned China into a freer and more democratic country, then the chances of conflict with the US would surely diminish. That was the great attraction of 'democratic peace' theory.

As a candidate, Clinton had bashed the first President Bush for coddling the 'butchers of Beijing' in the aftermath of the Tiananmen Square massacre.[235] But, as president, he pursued a conciliatory policy based on trade, investment and globalization. This was not simply because Clinton was keen to avoid confrontation. It was also because he believed that the more China opened up economically, the more likely it was to change politically. Clinton made the point clear in a speech welcoming Chinese membership of the World Trade Organization in 2000: 'By joining the WTO, China is not simply agreeing to import more of our products. It is agreeing to import one of democracy's most cherished values, economic freedom. The more China liberalizes its economy, the more fully it will liberate the potential of its people... And when individuals have the power, not just to dream, but to realize their dreams, they will demand a greater say.'[236] As the scholar Michael Mandelbaum put it, Clinton's support for economic liberalization in China was 'a Trojan Horse to be wheeled inside the walls the Chinese Communists had erected against political liberalism'.[237] Similar policies were adopted towards Russia, where US support for economic liberalization was regarded as vital to bolstering the fragile democracy being established under Boris Yeltsin.

There was only one snag with 'democratic peace' theory in the Clinton years. The nineties were indeed a great decade for the advance of democracy. But they did not *seem* very peaceful. The break-up of Yugoslavia provoked the most serious war in Europe since 1945 with some three hundred thousand people dying in the fighting in Bosnia alone. The Rwandan genocide of 1994 led to the murder of some eight hundred thousand people – the worst example of genocide since the Holocaust.

How was one to account for this divergence between the beguiling

theory of the democratic peace and the horrifying facts? One answer
was that appearances were deceptive. Gareth Evans, a former Australian
foreign minister, was so appalled by the events in Bosnia and Rwanda
that he led the way in developing a new doctrine in international relations called the 'responsibility to protect' – justifying international
intervention to prevent 'mass atrocity crimes'. But even Evans points
out that, in the aftermath of the Cold War, 'contrary to conventional
wisdom, and perhaps all our intuitions, there has been a very significant trend decline…in the number of wars taking place'. This decline
applies to all forms of political violence: civil wars, wars between states,
cases of genocide and other mass atrocities.[238] Citing research by the
Human Security Report project in Canada, Evans claims 'an extraordinary 80 per cent decline since the early nineties' in deaths caused by
serious conflicts and political mass murders. In the first years of the
twenty-first century, some twenty thousand soldiers a year were dying in
wars around the world. This compares to an average of one hundred
thousand battle deaths a year between 1945 and 1990.[239]

The trends lying behind Clinton's vision of a win-win world – the
spread of democracy, markets and technology – were only part of the
explanation for the decline in political violence. Evans also points to
the 'end of the era of colonialism' and the 'huge upsurge in activity in
conflict prevention' and peacekeeping activity during the nineties.[240] The
end of the Cold War also ended the proxy war between the Soviet Union
and the US, in which both sides backed militias and rival governments
around the world to deadly effect. Some three million people died in the
wars in Indochina in the seventies. Another million people died in
the Angolan civil war – another arms-length conflict between the US
and the USSR. This deadly superpower competition ended with the
Cold War.[241]

Nonetheless, even if the overall picture was improving, the Balkan
wars and the Rwandan genocide horrified both Clinton and Kofi Annan,
the then UN secretary-general. Together with Tony Blair, Bernard

Kouchner (founder of the charity Doctors without Borders, and later France's foreign minister), Gareth Evans and others, they began to develop new ideas on 'liberal interventionism'. The central idea was that in the globalized world, the world's major powers could no longer accept 'mass atrocity crimes' – even if they took place within the borders of a state such as Rwanda, or as part of a civil war as in the former Yugoslavia. The logic was partly humanitarian. But there was also a national security justification. Clinton believed that the biggest security threats to the West were now likely to come from failed states like Somalia, Afghanistan, Rwanda and Yugoslavia.

America's increasing willingness to contemplate military intervention overseas during the Clinton years was not just a reflection of the president's humanitarian concerns or his theories about globalization. It also reflected increased American confidence in the country's ability to use military force overseas successfully. This confidence was a legacy of the first Gulf War in 1991.

The line from the Gulf War of 1991 through to the Nato campaigns in Bosnia and Kosovo during the Clinton years and finally to the invasion of Iraq in 2003 is clear, in retrospect. But it was not a straight line. Clinton's initial experiences with military intervention were humiliating and discouraging. The US retreated from Somalia after eighteen American soldiers were killed in Mogadishu in 1993. Shortly afterwards, the US navy, on a mission to deliver civilian engineers and trainers to help a UN mission in Haiti, was forced to turn back when faced with an angry mob on the dock. These experiences were so off-putting that Richard Holbrooke, a senior US diplomat under Clinton, referred to the 'Vietmalia' syndrome – linking the scarring experiences of Vietnam and Somalia.[242] But the Clinton administration regained its faith in liberal interventionism in the Balkans. It was the US that pressed for the Nato bombing campaign that turned the Bosnian War around. And in 1999 Nato defeated Serbia in the Kosovo War through the use of air power alone – and without the loss of a single American soldier.

But how did Clinton square his belief in the peaceful power of glob-alization with his increasing willingness to use military force around the world? The president attempted to explain in a ceremony at the White House in the midst of the Kosovo War: 'Most of us have this vision of a twenty-first century world with the triumph of peace and prosperity and personal freedom… within a framework of shared values, shared power, shared plenty… This vision, ironically, is threatened by the oldest demon of human society – our vulnerability to the hatred of the other. In the face of that, we cannot be indifferent, at home or abroad. That is why we are in Kosovo.'[243]

It was a good, emotive summary of the attitudes to war and peace that characterized America during the Age of Optimism. The United States believed that economic globalization and free markets were a force for prosperity and peace around the world. But where markets failed to bring peace, prosperity and stability, the US was prepared to intervene with military might.

Bill Clinton, a restless conceptualizer, was the man who best expressed the idea of a win-win world (although he never used that precise phrase.) But George W. Bush, his successor, embraced the same philosophy.

The notion that Clinton and Bush shared the same approach to the world would probably have upset both men – and would certainly have horrified their most diehard supporters. The styles of the two presidents were certainly very different. Where Clinton instinctively reached for common points between nations, Bush was famously inclined to Manichean distinctions between freedom-loving countries and an 'axis of evil'.

And yet, behind the rhetoric, the continuities were striking. Clinton's justifications for the use of American military might during the Kosovo War foreshadowed many of the ideas used by Bush after 9/11 – in particular, the way he highlighted terrorism and weapons of mass destruction as threats to freedom and prosperity. And Bush's attitude to new, emerging powers was strikingly similar to Clinton's. Like Clinton, as a presidential candidate Bush had flirted with a more confrontational approach to China. Once he was in the White House, he pursued a policy based on co-operation and economic openness. Bush explained his approach in 1999: 'Economic freedom creates habits of liberty. And habits of liberty create expectations of democracy... Trade freely with China, and time is on our side.'[244]

The underlying American assumptions about globalization and 'democratic peace' remained unchanged throughout the Age of Optimism.

But what did the rising powers of Asia think?

The Optimistic East:

Kishore Mahbubani and the Asian Century

O n the night of 30 June 1997, the Foreign Correspondents Club in Hong Kong was packed. The crowd had gathered to watch television coverage of the ceremonies marking the end of British colonial rule over Hong Kong and its return to China. The people at the bar were journalists, they were westerners and they were drunk – so the mood was raucous and irreverent. The official ceremonies, with their anthems, flags and sombre-looking officials, were greeted with jeers and laughter. Suddenly, from behind the bar, there was a shout – 'Shut up, all of you!' It was a Chinese woman, one of the bar staff. She was watching the raising of the Chinese flag over Government House with rapt attention, and tears streaming down her face.

The return of Hong Kong to China was a landmark in the rising power of China. The forced ceding of the territory to Britain after the Opium Wars was one of the more humiliating moments of China's 'century of humiliation'. Margaret Thatcher, who handled the negotiations with the Chinese during the eighties, found it hard to believe that it was really necessary to hand over Hong Kong, which she regarded as a temple of free-market capitalism and a tribute to the wisdom of British colonial rule. Again and again, British officials had to explain to Thatcher that, in a phrase that she herself made famous in another context, 'there is no alternative'. International law, power politics and time were all on China's side.

The Chinese played their hand with skill, patience and determination. The Hong Kong handover was accomplished without force. It was just made clear that Hong Kong could not hope to survive beyond the expiration of the British lease in 1997 without Chinese approval. A rising China could not be denied its destiny.

The whole process epitomized an approach to the world in the Age of Optimism that China called 'peaceful rise'. The phrase was invented by a Chinese academic named Zheng Bijian – but it encapsulated the philosophy laid out by Deng Xiaoping. China should concentrate on building up its economic strength over the long-term. To do this, it needed a stable and permissive international environment. So China should avoid alarming the world's dominant power – the United States. Or as Deng put it: 'Observe developments soberly, maintain our position, meet challenges calmly, hide our capacities and bide our time, remain free of ambition, never claim leadership.'[245]

The only time during this period when China flamboyantly violated the principles of 'peaceful rise' was when it staged threatening missile tests near Taiwan in 1995 and 1996. China believes that Taiwan, like Hong Kong, is an inalienable part of Chinese territory. Taiwan was run by the heirs to the nationalist government that the communists had driven off the Chinese mainland in 1949 – and the idea that the island might declare formal independence was regarded as intolerable. China's missile tests were intended to demonstrate that, in the last resort, China would invade rather than concede independence. But they backfired because they provoked the US into sending aircraft carriers to the Taiwan Straits in 1996, in an overt display of military might intended to support Taiwan and deter China. Shortly afterwards, the Chinese missile tests stopped.

China had backed down. But it had also learned a valuable lesson. Overt confrontation with the US was counter-productive. In the years after the Taiwan Straits crisis, China concentrated on pursuing high economic growth and ever-deeper involvement with the international market and the American economy. A major goal of national policy was achieved when China successfully joined the World Trade Organization in 2001, thereby gaining the protections and market access that WTO membership conferred. Behind the scenes, China was also increasing its military spending at double-digit rates every year – perhaps to ensure that it was better placed when the next Taiwan crisis arose.

But the public face of Chinese power was almost always careful and restrained. Indeed, by the time I met Zheng Bijian at a banquet in Beijing in 2007, even the phrase 'peaceful rise' had been modified, lest it sound too provocative. The new formulation was 'peaceful development with harmonious characteristics'. It was only when it came to Taiwan that there was even a hint of steel. Here Zheng's formula was 'Taiwan is a core national interest for China. We have no flexibility on this issue.'[246]

With Chinese officials following Deng's advice to 'hide our capacities and bide our time', it was left to others to spell out the implications of the rise of China and the rest of Asia. Of course, in many ways it is absurd to look for spokesmen for a continent as vast and varied as Asia. And it was particularly odd when that role was assumed by the leaders of Singapore, a micro-dot of a city-state with a population of just five million.

But while the Singaporeans' efforts to speak for Asia were presumptuous, they were also worth listening to. The city-state self-consciously and successfully positioned itself as a hub for Asian trade and as a bridge between East and West. By the mid-nineties Singapore was the world's busiest port and was the second richest nation in Asia (on a per capita basis), after Japan. Lee Kuan Yew, the country's founding father, had increasingly assumed the role of an international elder statesman and spokesman for Asia. Lee had taken a brilliant degree in law in Cambridge in his youth – but he rejected the idea that Asian nations would necessarily converge on the western model. Instead, Lee positioned himself as a spokesman for 'Asian values' – which he defined as more communitarian and respectful of authority than the disorderly, individualistic West.

'Americans,' pronounced Mr Lee, 'believe that out of contention, out of the clash of different ideas and ideals, you get good government. That view is not shared in Asia.'[247] It suited Mr Lee to argue the case for authoritarianism, given Singapore's own distinctly equivocal relationship with democracy.[248] But Lee was also providing a thoughtful and closely argued rebuttal for the democratic evangelism of the United States during the Age of Optimism. In effect, he was laying out the intellectual justification for China's suppression of the pro-democracy movement in 1989. As far as Lee was concerned, premature democracy could be ruinous: 'Take the Philippines. They had democracy from the word go in 1945. They never got going. It was too chaotic.'[249]

Lee's distrust of democracy made him sceptical about the economic prospects of India. His Chinese heritage and authoritarian leanings may also have made him much more sympathetic to the Confucian cultures of East Asia. By the end of the nineties, however, it had become clear that India too was now part of the great Asian economic miracle. The leading spokesman for this new form of pan-Asian optimism was another Singaporean, Kishore Mahbubani, a diplomat and academic who had headed the country's foreign service.

Mahbubani's personal heritage made him as well placed as anyone to assume the all-but-impossible role of spokesman for 'Asia'. Born into a Hindu family in Pakistan, he was brought up in the majority-Chinese society of Singapore, alongside a substantial Malay community. For Mahbubani, the rise of Asia from poverty to riches was an intensely felt personal story, as much as an abstract historical process. As he recalled in his book *The New Asian Hemisphere*:

My childhood circumstances were modest (some would say poor).
Until the age of ten, I lived with four other family members in a
one-bedroom home. We had no refrigerator, no telephone, no
television. But the real inconvenience we suffered was that we had
no flush toilet... And if I were asked to name the date when my
life entered the modern world, I would date it to the arrival of the
flush toilet. On that day I felt that there had been a magical
transformation of my life. Suddenly I felt that I could lead a life
of greater dignity.[250]

By the middle of his career, Mahbubani was a member of the Davos
crowd in good standing – a former Singaporean ambassador to the
United Nations and dean of the Lee Kuan Yew School of Public Policy.
Small, dapper and invariably well turned-out, Mahbubani had not
forgotten his origins. They infused his outlook on the world with a
strange mixture of optimism, gratitude, pride, Asian chauvinism and
an impatience for the assumptions made by pampered westerners. They
had never known deprivation or hardship – and yet they presumed to
lecture Asians? At a seminar in Singapore in 2007, I saw him reproach
some visitors from the Brookings Institution in Washington for a failure of imagination and sympathy when it came to Asia. 'You've never
known what it feels like to be made to feel inferior to another culture,'
he complained.[251] That was why, Mahbubani argued, western assumptions that other Asians were terrified by the rise of China were
misplaced. On the contrary, he insisted, most Asians felt admiration and
fellow-feeling for China's rise from poverty and 'thought they were going
to make it'.[252] The Asian story, he insisted, could not be told just in
abstract figures. It was about 'the empowerment of hundreds of millions
of individuals who previously had felt a total sense of powerlessness in
their lives'.[253]

The transformation in the fortunes of millions of individual Asians
was, Mahbubani believed, going to be reflected in the transformation of

the fortunes of the continent as a whole. For the seer of Singapore, the great story of our age was the rise of Asia and 'the irresistible shift of global power to the east'. As he wrote, 'Asia's growth and success in the past few decades have exceeded Asians' wildest dreams... Asians today do not have to be convinced to be optimistic.'[254] Opinion poll evidence bears out Mahbubani's assertion of Asian optimism. An international poll taken in November 2005 found that 76 per cent of Chinese and 75 per cent of Indians counted themselves personally optimistic about the future – much higher figures than those recorded in the US or Europe.[255]

Mahbubani was well aware that rising optimism in Asia could cause pessimism in the West. But he embraced a version of Bill Clinton's view of a win-win world, in which globalization and rising prosperity potentially laid the conditions for a new era of peace and international harmony. As he wrote, 'Competition in the nineteenth century for political influence and territorial control was a zero-sum game. Competition in the second half of the twentieth century could become a positive-sum game. Growing economies could benefit, not harm, each other.'[256]

Unlike many thinkers in the West, Mahbubani was not a believer in 'democratic peace' theory. As far as he was concerned, democracy did not have much to do with it. The real underpinning of international peace was rising prosperity. 'At the root of the reason why North Americans and Europeans do not wage war among themselves is a powerful middle class that has little desire to sacrifice its comfortable life.'[257] The rise of an Asian middle class was therefore a massive force for global peace and meant that 'world peace is not a pipe dream'.[258] And, as Lee Kuan Yew liked to argue, if it took a period of authoritarianism to secure the stability necessary to create a Chinese middle class, that was surely a price worth paying? As a result, an early transition to democracy in China might not be as conducive to global peace as western theorists liked to believe.

Mahbubani's advance on the philosophy of his mentor, Lee Kuan Yew, was that he firmly positioned India as part of the great Asian success story. The transformation in the morale of the Indian middle classes and the rise of Indian companies during this period was certainly remarkable and palpable to a repeat visitor.

The India of beggars and holy cows and dusty, rutted roads still existed in Bangalore in 2008. But the campuses of big IT firms like Infosys felt as up-to-date as anything you could find in California. That was quite deliberate. It was an effort to ward off any lingering feeling of cultural inferiority of the sort that Mahbubani referred to. As one Infosys executive explained to me, setting up a Californian-style high-tech campus – complete with juice bars, shops and fitness centres – was meant to send a message to both employees and customers. Both groups are meant to take away a very clear message – that the Bangalore IT companies and facilities are not quaint Indian overshoots, competing on cost alone. They are as good as their competitors anywhere in the world. I was visiting Infosys the week after Lehman Brothers had collapsed in the US. Afterwards, I wrote that it was 'bracing to be in Bangalore last Friday, as Wall Street bounced around drunkenly. This is one place where a financial meltdown in the US looks like a temporary inconvenience.'[259]

There are, however, two important qualifications to the idea that 1991–2008 was an Age of Optimism in Asia. The first was the fate of Japan. After the bursting of the bubble economy at the end of the eighties, the Japanese economy entered a long period of stagnation that became known as the 'lost decade'. By 2009, with the economy still in the doldrums, it was beginning to look like a lost generation. And yet, for all that, Japan was still a nation that was comfortable with the prevailing international system. The years of rapid growth had gone, but Japan remained a wealthy and orderly country; the second largest economy in the world throughout the period, a title that was only ceded to China in 2010. As America's closest Asian ally, Japan was comfortable with the 'unipolar moment'. And, as a major exporting power, Japan had little reason to question the merits of globalization.

The Asian financial crisis of 1997–8 gave some of Japan's neighbours much more reason to ask fundamental questions about how the international capitalist system was working. In a sequence of frightening events that prefigured the global financial crisis of 2008, a series of Asian economies were hit by capital flight, collapsing currencies, defaulting loans, folding businesses and, finally, catastrophic-sounding collapses in economic output. The GDP of South Korea dropped by around 30 per cent between 1997 and 1998; Thailand suffered a 40 per cent fall.[260]

The economic crisis does not, however, change the overall narrative about the rise of Asia over the last generation. By 1999 even the most badly affected economies had begun to recover. A decade later, it was clear that countries like South Korea had been badly shaken – but had not permanently lost the economic gains they had made so painstakingly over the previous generations. They were still middle-income countries that had resumed their upward trajectory.

The crisis did, however, have three lasting effects. First, it ingrained a deep scepticism in many Asian minds about the competence and impartiality of the International Monetary Fund. The IMF was accused of advocating sadistic policies, which involved raising interest rates, cutting government spending and allowing failing banks to collapse. Some argued that these policies were more in the interests of western creditors and banks than of the Asian nations themselves. When the US and Europe were hit by their own financial crises in 2008, it was certainly noted in Asia that the policies pursued seemed to be the exact opposite of those urged on Asia a decade earlier – interest rates were slashed, banks were bailed out, governments indulged in massive deficit-spending.

A second major consequence of the Asian financial crisis was that it encouraged countries in the region to build up vast foreign reserves to give themselves defences and a cushion against future waves of speculation. By 2008, when the global financial crisis hit, China's reserves alone were almost $2 trillion. Cash piles of that sort gave Asian policy-makers a huge boost in confidence when dealing with their western counterparts.

Finally, the Asian financial crisis hastened a transfer of power within the Asian continent itself. The countries that were worst affected were Thailand, Indonesia and South Korea. The backwash was also felt badly in other South-east Asian Tigers such as Singapore and Malaysia. But the rising giants of Asia – China and India – were relatively little affected. Their economies slowed, but they did not tip into recession. The first part of the Asian story had been about the rise of Japan in the post-war era. Then came the first Asian Tigers – South Korea, Taiwan and Singapore. By the time I moved to Bangkok in 1992, the action had shifted to South-east Asia. Thailand, for a time, was the fastest growing economy in the world. Growth did return to Thailand and South-east Asia after the Asian financial crisis. But the world's attention had moved on. By 1999 it was clear that the really world-shaking developments were taking place in China and India.

As the citizen of a South-east Asian nation, Kishore Mahbubani could have regarded this as a worrying development. Instead, he chose to rejoice in the rise of Asia as a continent. For Mahbubani, the biggest worries concerned the West. Would the United States have the wisdom to welcome China's 'peaceful rise'? And would the European Union shake off its gloomy introspection?

The Singaporean was particularly scornful of Europe. He argued that Europe was simultaneously in thrall to a dangerous and distasteful form of cultural arrogance, and to defeatism. 'As most Europeans look ahead to the future,' he declared, 'they are becoming increasingly pessimistic.'

But while Mahbubani was right about Asian optimism, he was wrong about Europe. In the European Union, the twenty years after the fall of the Berlin Wall were also an Age of Optimism – an optimism that under-pinned some of the most remarkable and ambitious political and economic projects of the era.

EUROPE:

Günter Verheugen and the European Dream

I n early 2001 a small team from the European Commission in Brussels flew into north-western Bulgaria. A crowd of several hundred people watched their helicopters land on a muddy football field, turning their faces away at the last moment to shield themselves from the mud and dust hurled up by the helicopters' blades. The EU delegation, led by Günter Verheugen, scrambled out of the choppers and was swept off into town in a motorcade. In the city hall, the mayor of Vidin, a town with a population of around seventy thousand near the Serbian and Romanian borders, recounted a sad tale of decline. Local factories had closed since the collapse of communism. The war in Serbia and the blockage of the River Danube had dealt further blows to the economy. Unemployment was at 25 per cent. 'You represent hope for us,' he concluded, simply and plaintively.

This was the Europe bequeathed by the end of the Cold War. The fall of the Berlin Wall was a moment of huge hope and opportunity for Central Europe; but also a profound shock and a dislocation. Industries collapsed as the communist economies imploded. For several years, unemployment soared and living standards fell. Vidin was just an hour's flight from the modernity and prosperity of Milan. But it had been on the wrong side of the Iron Curtain and it was suffering badly.

Across Central Europe, a new class of capitalists became very rich, while the living standards of many ordinary people fell. Faced with similar conditions, democracy in Russia staggered and went backwards to the controlled autocracy of Vladimir Putin. The Central Europeans were very aware of the poor example and the lingering threat of Russia. As Radek Sikorski, a future foreign minister of Poland, put it to me in 2001: 'Imagine there is a big river dividing Europe. On the one side is Russia. On the other side is the European Union. We know which side of the river we need to be on.'[261] Günter Verheugen was the European Union's commissioner for enlargement. It was his job to hold out a hand from Brussels and to haul the Central Europeans safely across to the other side of the river.[262]

During the Age of Optimism, many Asian intellectuals and American conservatives treated the European Union with open contempt. The United States dominated the present; the future looked Asian. Europe was the past. The economy of the European Union was growing slower than that of the US, let alone China. European fertility rates were low, so the continent's population was shrinking. Europe was incapable of dealing with a war in its own backyard, so that the conflicts in the Balkans in the nineties had to be settled by American military and diplomatic might. Despite its pretensions to unity, the European Union split down the middle over the Iraq War in 2003. In the aftermath of that conflict, Max Boot, an American neoconservative, wrote: 'By the traditional measures of power, Europe is in decline: economic growth is anaemic, military budgets are in free fall, the fertility rate is declining.'[263] In the aftermath of 9/11, some American conservatives pointed to the rising Muslim population in Europe as a particular threat to the stability of Europe.[264]

Yet, for a continent in supposed decline, Europe seemed to 'represent hope' for millions of people around the world. Even in its imperial heyday, when European nations dominated the affairs of the planet, Europe had been a continent that people fled from. Poles, Italians and Irish moved in great numbers to the United States in search of a better life. The Spanish and Portuguese headed for Latin America; the British for Australia and Canada. But, by the end of the twentieth century, the European Union – along with the United States – was one of the two biggest beacons of peace and prosperity in the world. Immigrants, legal and illegal, were flooding into Europe – from Asia, Africa, Latin America, the Caribbean and the Arab world.

Alongside the uncontrolled and uncomfortable experience that Europe was having with immigration from poor countries – and, in particular, the Muslim world – the European Union was undergoing a much more controlled expansion and enlargement towards the east. This too demonstrated that, despite the derision it sometimes attracted, the Union exercised an almost magnetic attraction for its poorer neighbours. In 1990, just after the fall of the Berlin Wall, the EU was an organization of just twelve nations. By 2007 the Union had expanded to include twenty-seven countries and launched its own pan-European currency, the euro. It was a behemoth of almost five hundred million people, with an economy larger than that of the United States or China.

Günter Verheugen, the man who masterminded the biggest ever enlargement of the European Union, was an unlikely hero. Uncharismatic, with wispy grey hair and rimless spectacles, he had washed up in Brussels after his political career in Germany had run out of steam.

Like many modern Germans, Verheugen had an innate suspicion of anything that looked like nationalism, approaching the topic warily, like an unexploded bomb. In Bulgaria in 2001 I found myself talking to him outside an official banquet, as he pondered how to reply to a simple-sounding question from a German tabloid newspaper – 'Are you proud of being German?' For a politician in most normal countries, the answer to a question like that would be obvious. But Verheugen was troubled. He asked me whether I was proud of being British. I said I was. He turned to his French spokesman. He too was proud of being French. But Verheugen wouldn't go there. 'I can't say I am proud of being German,' he said. 'I am proud of what I have achieved. But I was born German. That is not an achievement.' The commissioner's subtle mind was a diplomatic asset. Over dinner, the Bulgarian foreign minister, Nadezhda Mihailova, told us that she reckoned that Monica Lewinsky had been directly placed in President Clinton's way by conspirators who were plotting to destroy him. It was a tricky dilemma for Verheugen. If he agreed, he was assenting to a conspiracy theory. If he disagreed, he risked insulting the minister. So he simply replied, 'Yes, that's what my wife thinks.'

But for all his modesty and good manners, Verheugen was also capable of inspiring. A couple of years later, I saw the commissioner receive an emotional standing ovation from students at Budapest's University of Technology, which had been at the centre of the failed Hungarian uprising of 1956. His speech had ranged widely – it had evoked the tragedies of the Second World War and of communism in Eastern Europe. It had appealed to a sense of European brotherhood. And it had held out the prospect of better times ahead. With Hungary on the brink of finally achieving EU membership, shepherded through the gate by Günter Verheugen, both the message and the man were received with huge enthusiasm.

Verheugen's Budapest speech was given in the very month that American troops entered Baghdad. Like President Bush and the US, the European Union and Verheugen were pursuing a 'freedom agenda' – based on a deep belief in spreading democracy, capitalism and liberal values. But the two crusades were conducted in completely different ways. The European way relied on bureaucrats rather than tanks. It was much more patient and long-term. It involved not so much 'nation-building' as 'nation-reconstruction'. Any country that aspired to join the EU had to align its laws with those of the Union, pushing through 80,000 new pages of laws and regulations. But the countries involved undertook this tortuous process willingly because they knew which side of the river they needed to be on.

The whole process was infuriatingly slow. In Washington, in the early 2000s, American policymakers often shook their heads in disbelief at the European Union's torpor. How could it be, they wondered, that more than a decade after the fall of the Berlin Wall, the EU had still not admitted countries like Poland and the Czech Republic? The answer was that joining the European Union was a complicated process that involved a deep form of mutual adaptation on both sides. The applicant countries had to remould their societies and governments. The existing members of the European Union also took on serious obligations. They would all eventually open their borders for potentially unlimited immigration from the much poorer new members. They would offer billions of euros in aid. They would invite much poorer countries to join them in a political union, and give them a vote on laws that would apply across twenty-seven nations.

Enlargement certainly took a long time. But, in the end, it worked. After the deep, post-communist recessions, growth – rapid growth – returned to Central Europe. According to the World Bank, between 1998 and 2003, more than forty million Central Europeans moved out of poverty.[265] In the immediate years after the 'big bang enlargement' of May 2004 – which saw ten new countries admitted to the Union – every one of the new Central European members was growing faster than the older EU states in Western Europe. As manufacturing industry migrated to the new, lower-cost centres in the EU, enthusiastic investors began to call Central Europe 'the China next door'. And as investors moved east, workers moved west – taking advantage of the higher wages and new opportunities to travel, afforded by European Union membership. Around half a million, mainly young, Poles moved to Britain in the years after enlargement. They were driven partly by the fact that unemployment was still high in Poland. But they were also taking advantage of the new opportunities offered by a freshly united

Europe. Enlargement was not just about reunifying Europe. It was also a key part of the story of globalization – the removal of barriers to the free flow of people, capital and goods.

Almost doubling the size of the European Union was a hugely ambitious undertaking. But it was not the only visionary step taken by Europe in the generation that followed the fall of the Berlin Wall. As well as setting themselves the target of widening Europe through enlargement, the leaders of the European Union agreed to 'deepen' Europe through further economic and political integration. In the Treaty of Maastricht, agreed in 1992, the Europeans agreed to create a common foreign policy and a common currency.

For the less instinctively integrationist countries, in particular Britain, this was all too far and too fast. The British responded with hostility and scepticism to the new moves. In 1993 John Major, the British prime minister who succeeded Margaret Thatcher, derided the plan for a single currency as having 'all the quaintness of a rain dance, and about the same potency'.[266] Yet, in due course, it happened. On New Year's Day 2002, euro notes began to be dispensed from cash machines in twelve countries across the European Union. (Britain, Sweden and Denmark were the three EU members who chose to stand aside from the euro experiment.)

Many economists wondered whether it could last. Their anxieties began to seem prescient after the financial crisis of 2008, when surging fiscal deficits across the euro area raised questions about the solvency of some of its members – in particular, Greece – and about the durability of the currency union itself. The optimism of a few years earlier, when the EU launched the euro, suddenly looked almost reckless.

But even at the height of the Age of Optimism, Europe's leaders worried about the continent's relative lack of economic dynamism. Anguished seminars about Europe's relatively slow growth, low productivity, lack of entrepreneurial drive and high unemployment were a staple of grey Brussels afternoons. And yet, almost without realizing it,

Europe had created the world's largest single market. By the turn of the millennium, the EU was the largest recipient of American foreign investment (far larger than China), and the biggest single market for Chinese exports. Germany alone was the largest exporter in the world – a title it only ceded to China in 2009. The size of the European market meant that decisions taken in Brussels had to be obeyed around the world. In 2001, when the EU authorities decided that a proposed merger between General Electric and Honeywell was anti-competitive, the two huge firms – both proudly American – had to abandon their plans. They simply could not afford to ignore the giant European market.

It was Europe's dream to replicate its economic power in the political arena. When the Europeans set about trying to write a constitution in 2002, Valéry Giscard d'Estaing, a former French president and the chairman of the constitutional convention, held out the hope that the European Union would one day be a global superpower, 'which will talk on equal terms to the greatest powers on our planet'.[267] Yet European pretensions to superpower status were consistently scuppered by popular scepticism – Mr Giscard d'Estaing's constitution was rejected in popular referendums in France and the Netherlands in 2005. The Union's internal divisions and lack of military might also undermined its ambitions. European failure in the Balkans in the mid-nineties was one bitter lesson. Then, in the midst of the constitutional convention, Europe split again – this time over Iraq. 'European unity is a joke,' complained Javier Solana, the hapless Spanish diplomat who was meant to represent the European Union to the world.[268]

And yet beneath the painful splits over Iraq between European governments, some thinkers discerned a deeper unity – the stirrings of a pan-European public consciousness. When millions of Europeans took to the streets in February 2003 to demonstrate against the move to war in Iraq – with massive demonstrations in London and Madrid, where the governments were committed to war, as well as in anti-war Paris and Berlin – Dominique Strauss-Kahn, a prominent French politician (later to become head of the IMF), exulted that 'On Saturday February 15th, a new nation was born on the street. The new nation is the European nation.'[269]

Even sceptical Americans could discern a distinctive European approach to the world. As the old 'West' split over the Iraq War, Robert Kagan, a high-profile American neoconservative, published an acute analysis of the divisions between European and American approaches to the world, entitled *Of Paradise and Power*. The United States represented power; Europe represented a post-political, pacifistic 'paradise'.[270] It was clear that Kagan was exasperated by what he regarded as moralistic free-riding by the Europeans on a US security guarantee. But the American was not being entirely ironic when he referred to Europe as a 'paradise'. In the twenty years after the fall of the Berlin Wall, an increasingly prosperous and unified Europe had plenty of reasons to feel optimistic.

Many in Brussels believed that, for all Europe's economic difficulties and foreign-policy divisions, the European Union was charting a way forward for the world. A globalized world, they argued, demanded new forms of global governance. While the United States and China were still fiercely nationalist and locked into a nineteenth-century view of the state, it was the Europeans who were showing the way forward for the twenty-first century. Robert Cooper, a prominent European Union diplomat, argued that the EU as an organization had transcended balance-of-power politics. In a new world, defined by 'the end of empire and the transformation of the state through globalization', 'the most hopeful feature is the emergence of the postmodern system of security in Europe'.[271] As Cooper saw it, a 'postmodern system' no longer relied on the balance of power between neighbouring states, but instead on deep economic and political integration.

This view that Europe represented the future was neatly encapsulated in a book published in 2005 by Mark Leonard, who was later to become the first head of the new European Council on Foreign Relations. Leonard's book, boldly titled *Why Europe Will Run the 21st*

Century, argued that 'Europe represents a synthesis of the energy and freedom that comes from liberalism with the stability and welfare that comes from social democracy. As the world becomes richer and moves beyond satisfying basic needs such as hunger and health, the European way of life will become irresistible.'[272]

And yet, while intellectuals in Brussels believed that the European Union represented a kinder, gentler approach to capitalism, globalization and international affairs, not all Europeans saw it like that. Many on the left came to believe that the European Union had betrayed its original mission by becoming an agent of unfettered globalization. As the Age of Optimism advanced, the European Union found itself a target of the international backlash against globalization.

16

THE ANTI-GLOBALIZERS:

From the Asian Crisis to 9/11

S eattle looked like the perfect place to celebrate world trade and globalization: a booming city on the Pacific rim; the home of Microsoft, Boeing and Starbucks, three of America's most internationally renowned companies. Where better to launch a new round of market opening under the auspices of the World Trade Organization?

And yet it was in Seattle in late November 1999 that it became clear that a broad-based movement against globalization had developed. The politicians, businessmen, economists and journalists who attended the summit – most of whom took the virtues of globalization for granted – initially had difficulty taking the Seattle protesters seriously. Philippe Legrain, who was there to report on the meeting for *The Economist* and who later joined the WTO, noted sardonically that the streets of Seattle were 'full of American college kids sporting Japanese cameras and Nike shoes railing against the iniquities of global trade'.[273] Yet by the second day of the demonstrations, it became clear that the Seattle protests were no joke. Thousands of people marched through the streets, demonstrating against everything from third-world debt to the threat posed by international trade to sea turtles. The protests turned nasty and the windows of Bank of America, Niketown and a variety of other stores were smashed. The streets filled with tear gas, broken glass and riot police. The delegates at the WTO meeting were under siege.

Larry Summers, the then US Treasury secretary and a distinguished academic economist, could not hide his contempt for those protesting against globalization in the name of international justice. 'There are children who are working in textile businesses in Asia who would be prostitutes on the streets if they did not have these jobs,' he remarked acidly.[274] The professional politicians were careful to be more respectful. Bill Clinton, as convinced an advocate of globalization as could be found in the upper reaches of western politics, nonetheless said that the environmentalists and trades unionists who had shown up on the streets of Seattle had valid points to which politicians needed to listen.[275]

For a couple of years after Seattle, demonstrators were a presence at almost any international meeting that could be said to have something to do with globalization. At the G8 meeting in Genoa in 2001, the Italian police actually killed a protester. In Gothenburg in Sweden in the summer of 2001, I was present at one of the last European Union meetings to be seriously hampered by anti-globalization protests. Mysterious, masked anarchists known as the 'black blocs' had turned the city into a war zone; the police had blocked off the streets with giant steel containers, hauled in from the docks.

And then suddenly it all stopped, and international summits once again took place in relative peace. What had changed? The answer was 9/11. Al-Qaeda's attacks on America seemed to take the wind out of the sails of the western anti-globalization movement. Partly, it was because in the wake of 9/11, security was intensified to the point where it became almost impossible for demonstrators to get close to a summit. The WTO took the precaution of having its next major meeting in Doha, in inaccessible Qatar. But the young westerners who made up the bulk of the anti-globalization protesters may also have lost some of their appetite for violent protest after 9/11. For, in its own way, al-Qaeda was also attacking an American-dominated, capitalist global order. The original anti-globalizers had been outflanked by a much more violent, ruthless and radical rejectionist movement.

The critics of globalization were so diverse that it is impossible to pick a single figure to epitomize the movement. They ranged all the way from a Nobel Prize-winning economist like Joseph Stiglitz, to fulminating journalists like Naomi Klein and – at the very extreme end – terrorist movements like al-Qaeda. The anti-globalization crowd included far-left radicals who despised global capitalism, and far-right radicals who believed that globalization was an excuse for the creation of a single world government. Some argued that globalization was destroying the livelihoods of western workers by subjecting them to merciless competition from Asians labouring for less than a dollar a day. Others argued that globalization involved the ruthless exploitation of the world's poor by western multinationals. Some critics, like Naomi Klein, made both arguments simultaneously. She believed that the dominance of the world economy by western multinationals was undermining democracy and increasing inequality across the world.[276]

In the immediate post-Cold War period, the first critics of globalization in the West focused on the threat to the jobs of workers at home. In the United States, the conclusion of the North America Free Trade Area (Nafta) with Canada and Mexico, led Ross Perot – a third-party presidential candidate in 1992 – to predict a 'giant sucking sound' of American jobs heading south across the border. On the Republican right, Pat Buchanan took on the internationalism of President George H. W. Bush with a raw nationalism that made a great play of the threat to American jobs. As Buchanan complained, 'Having declared free trade and open borders to be America's policy, why are we surprised that corporate executives padlocked their plants in the Rust Belt and moved overseas...firing twenty-dollar an hour Americans and hiring fifty-cent an hour Asians?'[277]

Both Buchanan and Perot made a major impact on American politics. But neither achieved a decisive breakthrough. Bill Clinton's victory in the 1992 presidential election ensured that, for the next eight years, the White House was occupied by a firm believer in the virtues of globalization. Moreover, the long economic boom of the nineties made it easier to manage protectionist sentiment. But the arguments never really disappeared. As it became clear that American real wages were stagnating, so the economic critique of globalization was refined. The new argument was that removing barriers to international trade and investment was an elite project that benefited only the rich and the highly skilled. It was certainly true that a firm belief in the tenets of globalization prevailed only among elite groups. A Pew poll in 2005 found that 84 per cent of Americans believed that 'protecting the jobs of American workers' should be the government's top priority; but only 24 per cent of a group of 'opinion-formers' agreed.[278]

It was a similar story in Europe. With unemployment stubbornly high, protectionist slogans could move voters. In 2005 France's referendum on the proposed European Union constitution was won by a 'No' campaign that based its arguments on fear of the 'Polish plumber' – shorthand for the low-wage competition that French workers had been exposed to after the enlargement of the European Union in 2004. Almost all French politicians paid lip-service to the need to protect the European social model from 'unfair competition'. But the big story was that mainstream European politicians remained committed to an open economy and to globalization. The enlargement of the European Union went ahead. And despite rejection in referendums in France and the Netherlands, the EU constitution was repackaged as the Lisbon Treaty and pushed through by parliamentary vote.

It was not until the late nineties that the argument that globalization was also bad for the developing world began to be made with real force. The trigger for this was the Asian economic crisis of 1997. Economic crises in Russia in 1998 and in Latin America in 2002 further strengthened the argument.

It was doubts about the impact of globalization on the world's poor that motivated Joseph Stiglitz to break with the elite consensus. Stiglitz was adored by the anti-globalization movement because he had emerged from within the citadel of the World Bank, waving his heretical texts. As a Nobel Prize-winner, he commanded instant credibility – making it much harder to brush off his arguments as self-indulgent or ill-informed. And as a former chief economist at the World Bank, his critique was a thrilling piece of apostasy.

Stiglitz's work, however, is far from a blanket condemnation of globalization. In a couple of early pages of his book *Globalization and Its Discontents*, he swiftly acknowledges that 'because of globalization many people in the world now live longer than before and their standard of living is far better'.[279] His anger and condemnation was focused on specific aspects of the process – in particular, his belief that policies advocated by the International Monetary Fund in response to the crises in Asia and Russia were wrong-headed, biased towards the interests of western banks and caused unnecessary misery. Stiglitz's work was an attack on what he regarded as 'market fundamentalism', leading to premature liberalization of trade and foreign-exchange regimes.

Yet while the globalization consensus wobbled after the Asian, Russian and Latin American crises, it fundamentally stayed in place. Open economies in a globalized world were clearly vulnerable to sudden financial crises – but turning your back on the world was not an attractive or practical remedy. South Korea and Thailand were two of the biggest victims of the Asian economic crisis. But the South Koreans only had to look across the border to North Korea to be reminded that economic isolation offered far worse and more devastating prospects. The Thais could perform the same exercise by looking across their western border into isolated, dictatorial, impoverished Burma, where a military junta had violently repressed the country's democracy movement in 1990.

What Joseph Stiglitz and Naomi Klein put their fingers on was a feeling that globalization was a project that benefited elites more than ordinary people. It was certainly true that the 'globalization consensus' seemed at its firmest in places where the international political and business elite gathered, like the World Economic Forum in Davos. It was also true that there were some common themes to the complaints made about globalization in countries as different as the United States, China, India and Russia. The link was a complaint that the faster growth associated with globalization had been bought at the expense of rising inequality – that it was Russian oligarchs, Chinese factory-owners and bankers on Wall Street who had creamed off most of the benefits and used some of the proceeds to buy consent from political elites.

For many of the left-wing critics of globalization, the answer was obvious – open up the process and make it more democratic. Stiglitz complained that the creation of a globalized economy had not been matched by the emergence of globalized politics: 'We have a process of globalization analogous to the earlier processes in which national governments were formed. Unfortunately, we have no world government accountable to the people of every country.'[280]

But while Stiglitz lamented the lack of a 'world government', a different wing of the anti-globalization movement was terrified by precisely this prospect. For Stiglitz, it was the economics of globalization that were open to criticism. But for conservatives in Britain and the United States, it was the politics of globalization that were most alarming. They believed that power was being drained away from nation-states by undemocratic supranational institutions, acting in the name of economic rationality or world peace.

In Britain, Eurosceptics focused on the ever-increasing power of the European Union. Some were gut nationalists. Others were traditional conservatives with detailed and logical critiques of the 'European project' and legitimate worries about its democratic credentials.

In the United States, it was the United Nations that was the focus of conservative suspicion and paranoia. The *Left Behind* series of sixteen bestselling novels – the first of which was published in 1995 – told the story of the 'End of Times', in which a Romanian politician named Nicolae Jetty Carpathia rose to become secretary-general of the UN, promising to restore peace and stability to the world. But Carpathia was, in fact, the Antichrist. Pat Robertson, a preacher and one-time contender for the Republican Party nomination, gave voice to these fears in his book *The New World Order*, which claimed to expose a vast conspiracy to create a 'one world government'.

It was easy for urban, secular elites to laugh off phenomena like the *Left Behind* series or the works of Pat Robertson. But right-wing paranoia about 'world government' and the United Nations also had the potential to spill over into violence – as became tragically apparent in the attack on the Alfred P. Murrah Federal Building in Oklahoma City in 1994, which killed 168 people. Timothy McVeigh, the man who drove the truck bomb into the building, nurtured a fanatical hatred of the federal government. He was also a man who was fascinated by the idea of a 'conspiracy between the United Nations and the United States to limit individual freedom and, ultimately, take over the world'.[281]

Until the attacks on New York and Washington on 9/11, the Oklahoma bombing was the worst ever terrorist atrocity on American soil. The 9/11 bombers, in a strange way, represented the mirror image of the fears of the Oklahoma terrorist. While Timothy McVeigh was angered by the notion that a world government might be imposed on the United States, al-Qaeda saw an all-powerful United States imposing its will on the rest of the world.

The al-Qaeda movement was motivated by many strands of thought, emotion and political analysis. And yet the symbolism of an attack on the economic capital of the United States and on the World Trade Center was hard to miss. As Martin Wolf of the *Financial Times* wrote, 'We can view this event as an episode in the resistance of the Islamic World to westernization, as witness to the abiding force of human evil, as the end of liberal optimism and as an assault on liberal globalization. All are valid, not excluding the last. The attack on the US was also an assault on globalization.'[282]

In the heyday of liberal optimism, during the Clinton years, it was easy to point to the most attractive forces driving forward globalization: new technologies, the spread of political freedom, the power of market economics, the creation of common interests between nations, even the wisdom of far-sighted politicians. But in the post-9/11 world, the Bush administration decided to reassert and demonstrate the most funda-mental force underpinning the international system – American power.

POWER:

Charles Krauthammer and the Neoconservatives

In February 2004, less than a year after American troops had swept into Baghdad, Charles Krauthammer gave a triumphal speech to the annual dinner of the American Enterprise Institute. The importance of the occasion and of the speaker was underlined by the fact that Krauthammer was introduced by America's vice-president, Dick Cheney.

Krauthammer was a syndicated newspaper columnist, who had overcome terrible personal setbacks to achieve his revered status in conservative Washington. Disabled in a diving accident as a young man and confined to a wheelchair, he had used his intellect and his forceful writing to become the most articulate popularizer of a foreign policy based on the unapologetic deployment of American power. Along with Francis Fukuyama, who was in the audience at the dinner, Krauthammer was one of the first analysts to spell out the implications of US victory in the Cold War to a wider audience. His article on 'The Unipolar Moment' had appeared in *Foreign Affairs* at the end of 1990 and stressed the awesome nature of American power after the collapse of the Soviet empire. The United States, he asserted, was the 'unchallenged superpower' and the 'centre of world power'[283] – and would be so for generations to come.

Perhaps unsurprisingly, given the personal odds he had overcome, Krauthammer was a believer in the power of will. In early 2001, well before the attacks on the World Trade Center and the Pentagon, he had called upon President George W. Bush to use American power without apology. 'America is no mere international citizen,' he had written. 'It is the dominant power in the world, more dominant than any since Rome. Accordingly, America is in a position to reshape norms, alter expectations and create new realities. How? Through unapologetic and implacable demonstrations of will.'[284]

Now, in the aftermath of the toppling of Saddam Hussein – flushed with a sense of righteousness and victory – Krauthammer returned to the theme of unanswerable American power. He told the assembled Washington grandees that 'On December 26th 1991, the Soviet Union died and something new was born, something utterly new – a unipolar world dominated by a single superpower unchecked by any rival and with decisive reach in every corner of the globe.'[285]

By tracing the roots of America's seeming triumph in Iraq in 2003 back to victory in the Cold War, Krauthammer was making an important point. The attacks on the World Trade Center and the Pentagon on 9/11 had not changed everything. On the contrary, they had led America to underscore something that the world already knew – there was only one superpower.[286] If America wanted to, it could overthrow governments on the other side of the world – in weeks.

And yet for most people in the United States and the rest of the world, the days and months after the 9/11 attacks did feel like a new epoch. George Will, a conservative columnist (but not a neoconservative), summed up the idea that an era had ended when he said that America had enjoyed a 'holiday from history' in the years between the fall of the Berlin Wall and 9/11.

The sense that a *Gatsby*-esque Age of Optimism had come to a close was compounded by a sour turn in the economy and the bursting of the tech bubble in the second half of 2000. Some $5 trillion in the market value of tech companies disappeared between 2000 and 2002.[287]

President Bush's rhetoric in the days after 9/11 also stressed the idea that America was facing a new world and would have to respond in new ways, with 'a lengthy campaign, unlike any other we have ever seen'[288] – a campaign that swiftly became known as the 'war on terror'.

As it became clear that the war on terror would involve invading not just Afghanistan, but also Iraq, so international attitudes to the US changed. European governments split over the Iraq War, with Britain, Spain, Portugal and Poland joining President Bush's 'coalition of the willing' – and France, Germany and Russia leading the opposition. European public opinion, however, was fairly united in its hostility to the invasion of Iraq. The popularity of the United States in international opinion polls plummeted in the run-up to the invasion, and did not recover for the rest of the Bush presidency.

Both Europeans and Americans had concluded that the Bush administration and the United States as a whole had charged off in an entirely new direction after 9/11. But that was misleading. Some things had indeed changed. Above all, neoconservatives like Krauthammer were much more suspicious of international institutions (and indeed foreign countries) than the Clintonians – and much more inclined to recommend that the US act unilaterally. This determination to go it alone chimed with the mood of many Americans after 9/11 and with the instincts of President Bush. The president's absolutist rhetoric about an 'axis of evil' also contrasted strongly with the more emollient and intellectual style of President Clinton and his belief that, in a globalized world, 'we're all in this together'.

But look at the fundamentals of the Bush foreign policy and it is clear that they remained deeply rooted in the assumptions of the Age of Optimism that had begun in 1991. President Bush, like President Clinton before him, believed firmly in spreading free markets and democracy around the world. Clinton's national security adviser, Tony Lake, had called it 'democratic enlargement'. Bush called it the 'freedom agenda'. But the idea was the same.

The Democrats recognized and responded to Bush's emphasis on freedom. The neoconservatives' use of the language of liberty made it easier to build a consensus for the Iraq War. The main justification for the war was the alleged threat from Iraqi weapons of mass destruction. But by locating the campaign against Saddam in a long American tradition of taking on tyrannies, the supporters of the war helped attract liberals to the cause. More Democratic senators voted for the Iraq War than voted against. Those in favour included the standard-bearer of the Clinton legacy, Senator Hillary Clinton.

Underlying Bush's policies was a strong sense of the morality and power of the United States. This too was shared by leading Democrats. It was Bill Clinton and his secretary of state, Madeleine Albright, who frequently referred to the US as the 'indispensable nation'. Clinton placed the promotion of democracy at the centre of his vision of the world, delighting in his second inaugural address in 1997 that 'for the very first time in all of history, more people in this planet live under democracy than dictatorship'. Albright herself recognized the continuities with Bush's freedom agenda. As she later put it, 'They picked up on a lot of the things we were doing and pushed them to their exponential degree.'[289]

Clinton too had worried about the possible conjunction of terrorism and weapons of mass destruction, which provided President Bush with a rationale for invading Iraq. In 1998 President Clinton had even signed the Iraq Liberation Act, which committed the United States to the goal of regime change in Iraq.

Above all, the willingness to use American military might was bipartisan. It had its origins in the easy victory of the first Gulf War of 1991. After a hesitant start, President Clinton had become increasingly confident in his ability to make effective use of the American military.

The Kosovo War in 1999 had been won without a single American casualty. After 9/11, the easy success in toppling the Taliban in Afghanistan in November, 2001 further strengthened the confidence of America in military power. Kenneth Adelman, a prominent neoconservative, summed up the prevailing mood in his circle when he predicted that the invasion of Iraq would be a 'cakewalk'. In the weeks before the invasion, I had lunch with a leading neocon and told him, half-seriously, 'I'll back this war, if you guarantee it will all be over in three days.' My lunch companion looked at me pityingly and replied, 'Of course it will be over in three days.'[290]

The confidence of the neoconservatives had many sources. At the end of the Cold War, the US seemed to enjoy full spectrum dominance – it was the world's largest economy, its technological leader, with the world's leading universities and its most powerful popular culture. American moral authority was also at a peak. The US had faced down the 'evil empire' and the peoples of Eastern Europe seemed suitably grateful.

But the unipolar moment was based above all on military might. At the beginning of the twenty-first century America was spending almost as much on its military as the rest of the world combined. The technological lead of the US military was also widening steadily, reflecting America's position at the cutting edge of the IT revolution. In the aftermath of swift victories in Afghanistan and Iraq, many neoconservatives were euphoric about US power. Max Boot, at the Council on Foreign Relations, enthused that America's military supremacy 'far surpasses the capabilities of such previous would-be hegemons as Rome, Britain and Napoleonic France'.[291]

This overwhelming confidence was reflected in Krauthammer's speech to the American Enterprise Institute almost a year after the fall of Saddam. Seated in the audience, Francis Fukuyama found it odd that Krauthammer and the applauding crowd seemed to regard the war as a 'virtually unqualified success...given that the United States had found no weapons of mass destruction in Iraq, was bogged down in a vicious insurgency, and had almost totally isolated itself from the rest of the world'.[292]

But Fukuyama's misgivings were unusual at that stage. In neocon circles most assumed that – in the soon-to-be-notorious words of President Bush – it was 'mission accomplished'. As confidence in American military might grew, so more neoconservatives began to flirt with the idea of imperialism. In what became one of the defining quotes of the era, an unnamed senior administration official told Ron Suskind of the *New York Times*, 'we are an empire now...and when we act, we create our own reality'. The notion of 'American imperialism' – once used solely as a term of abuse by anti-Americans and the left – began to be written of in more approving terms by conservative academics such as Max Boot and Niall Ferguson.

If the Bush administration really had adopted an imperial ideal, that would indeed have marked a decisive break with US foreign policy since the end of the Cold War. But as far as President Bush was concerned, the 'evil' that he was determined to battle against resided in caves, in failed states and in medium-sized powers such as Iran and North Korea.

When President Bush dealt with the world's major powers he followed the principles that governed American policy throughout the Age of Optimism. The US was placing its bets on globalization and international economic integration to smooth away international conflict and to provoke democratic change in potential adversaries such as Russia and China.

While some neoconservatives worried about a sinister and anti-democratic turn in Russian domestic politics under President Putin, Bush famously said that he had looked into the Russian president's eyes and 'got a sense of his soul'. Evidently, he liked what he saw. Worries about the outsourcing of white-collar jobs to India mounted during the Bush years. But the president himself actively sought a close strategic and economic alliance with a country that he regarded as an emerging superpower and a democratic ally. The Indian elite regarded the president as a firm friend of their country and a strong supporter of globalization. The Chinese worried, legitimately, that President Bush's overtures to India reflected a tacit desire to balance rising Chinese power. But overall, the government in Beijing regarded the Bush administration as a good thing.

In dealing with China President Bush adopted the ideas – although not the vocabulary – of President Clinton and his win-win world. James Miles of *The Economist* observed in March 2006: 'The Bush administration is trying to cajole China away from seeing the global balance of power in zero-sum terms and persuade it instead that a rising China and a strong America could not only coexist but thrive together.'[293] Robert Zoellick, one of the leading internationalists in the Bush administration, took the lead in urging China to be a 'responsible stakeholder' in the world community.[294]

There was an unconscious condescension in language like 'responsible stakeholder'. Throughout the Age of Optimism, America simply assumed that it was the world's standard-setter. The arc of world history was bending towards free markets and democracy. Countries that failed to accept economic and political liberalism would ultimately fail. Countries that embraced economic and political liberalism would become more like the United States. It was a win-win situation for America and the world.

Lying behind this belief was confidence in the continuing military and economic dominance of the United States. The whole neoconservative philosophy – exemplified by Krauthammer's speech in 2004 – was based on an unexamined assumption òf continued American economic supremacy.

By the end of the Bush presidency, however, the United States was becoming much more conscious of the limits of its own power. Both the Iraq and Afghanistan wars had turned into long, bloody and unpopular slogs. Then, in September 2008, the collapse of Lehman Brothers precipitated the biggest financial and economic crash in the United States since the Great Depression. The economic crisis was also a turning point in the presidential election. In the aftermath of the fall of Lehmans, Barack Obama established a lead over John McCain in the opinion polls that saw him win a decisive victory in November 2008.

The new president had called his second book *The Audacity of Hope*. But it had taken a disastrous blow to the American economy to secure his victory. He had come to power at the end of the Age of Optimism.

PART THREE

The Age of Anxiety

INTRODUCTION

During the Age of Optimism, globalization and American power underpinned the international system. Liberal internationalists were confident that the world of prosperity, freedom and stability was expanding, while the areas of poverty, dictatorship and anarchy were gradually being rolled back. All the real power still seemed to lie with the western world: the power of ideas, the power of money and – as a last resort – the power of the military. Yet although the Age of Optimism was a period of western dominance, the rising powers of Asia and Latin America had good reason to accept the international order. They were getting richer and had faith in the future.

The economic crash of 2008, however, has heralded a new Age of Anxiety. The United States, in particular, faces fundamental challenges to its global position. By the time Barack Obama took office, each of the five ideas that had underpinned American self-confidence during the Age of Optimism had taken a battering. The faith in the onward march of democracy had been shaken by the difficulties of exporting democracy to Iraq and Afghanistan, and by the rising confidence of authoritarian

China. The belief in the power of free markets took a terrible blow with the economic and financial crisis of 2008. The technological revolution no longer seemed the magical cure-all that it had promised to be, as problems as diverse as climate change and the mechanics of military occupation proved frustratingly impervious to a technological fix. The theory of the 'democratic peace' looked less persuasive, as Russia flexed its military muscles, almost overrunning democratic Georgia in August 2008. Finally, the belief in the unstoppable nature of American power that had animated the Bush administration looked much shakier with US troops bogged down in Afghanistan and Iraq, and the American economy reeling.

By 2010, with the intensification of the economic crisis within the European Union, it was clear that the world was witnessing not just a challenge to America's global position, but an erosion in the power of the western world as a whole. The western crisis is examined in Chapter 18.

With the underpinnings of the Age of Optimism shaken, four new forces are reshaping the international order. The first is the emergence of truly global political problems, such as climate change, terrorism and global economic imbalances. The second is the faltering and controversial drive for new forms of global governance to deal with these problems. The third is the new confidence of the world's authoritarian powers – in particular, China and Russia. The fourth is the threat of a new wave of failed states. The emergence of these new forces – combined with a weakening of American power – is replacing the win-win world of the Age of Optimism with a zero-sum world, in which the world's major powers are increasingly and dangerously at odds with each other.

The nature of the new global challenges is described in Chapter 19. In some ways, these problems represent the ugly, political side of globalization. In the Age of Optimism, the most ardent believers in the power of markets thought that if you let globalization do its work, it would ultimately solve the very problems in which it seemed to be implicated. So the solution to global poverty was to let markets rip and to encourage faster growth. The solution to global warming was to come up with some sort of market-based solution based around an international emissions-trading system. Failed states could be turned around if they could only be integrated into the global economy. The increased demand for natural resources like food and oil would simply encourage the market to find new supplies. The role of international politicians and regulators was to rip down barriers to trade and investment – and then to get out of the way and to let the markets do their work.

It is increasingly obvious, however, that there are many dangerous international political and economic problems for which there is no obvious market solution. The most logical response to the emergence of a set of global political problems would be to develop new forms of global governance – or 'world government', as its keenest advocates and most paranoid opponents would have it. There is certainly a possibility that the end of the Age of Optimism will lead to a massive increase in international co-operation and global governance, rather than to international conflict. This is the international vision closely associated with the European Union – and there are forces pushing in this direction. The most obvious is the formation of the G20 group of leading nations, in response to the global economic crisis. Chapter 20 discusses the drive for global governance in arenas such as the G20, the UN and the global climate-change talks. It shows why these efforts will fall short and will fail to break the emerging logic of the zero-sum world.

If neither the United States nor some form of 'world government' can provide the leadership to tackle the world's common political problems, a third alternative is the rise of an axis of authoritarianism, with China as its standard-bearer – and with Russia, Iran and Venezuela serving as the regional centres.

The authoritarians do not just reject the liberal assumption that there is an inevitable connection between political and economic freedom. They also reject the liberal belief that, in the modern world, the 'world community' should intervene to protect human rights, prevent mass atrocities and to restore order in failing states. On the contrary, the Russians and the Chinese are deeply suspicious of any such doctrine, fearing that it would give the West an excuse to meddle in their internal affairs.

The positions advocated by the Russians and the Chinese are gaining followers, even in some democratic nations. The Chinese have skilfully capitalized on resentment in much of the developing world at American dominance of the 'new world order'. For all Barack Obama's popularity, he has not been able to rely on the support of a world community on crucial international issues, such as Iran's nuclear programme or the Copenhagen climate-change talks. Even some of the biggest democracies in the developing world, including Brazil, Turkey, South Africa and Indonesia, have sided with the authoritarians on issues such as climate change and intervention in failed or oppressive states.

Diminishing American diplomatic, economic and military power will make it much harder for the US to intervene around the world over the next decade. And that may contribute to a rise in the number of failed states – a development dealt with in Chapter 22.

In these new international circumstances, the world's major powers are finding it harder and harder to co-operate. Zero-sum logic, in which one side's gain is another's loss, is increasingly dictating their approach to the world. Chapter 23 examines the growing economic and military rivalry between the United States and China – and shows how this competition is thwarting efforts to solve the world's most dangerous problems, from economic imbalances to climate change and the threat of nuclear proliferation.

The emergence of a zero-sum world carries a double danger. First, it means that the big global threats will not get solved – instead, they will get steadily more hazardous, increasing the chances of regional wars, a collapse in global trade, shortages of food and energy, environmental disasters and nuclear terrorism. Even if the worst outcomes are avoided, an inability to find co-operative ways of dealing with the big global issues will poison international relations, as the major powers clash, argue and manoeuvre for position.

In these new circumstances, it is increasingly urgent to break the zero-sum logic of the emerging international order. The final chapter of this book suggests new ways to revive international co-operation.

THE CRISIS OF THE WEST

The global financial crisis that broke in September 2008 undermined the two most fundamental underpinnings of the post-Cold War order: American power and free-market ideology. Barack Obama, elected to the White House on a ticket of hope and optimism, took over a country facing a profound economic crisis. The United States was also facing an intellectual crisis – questioning its place in the world and the ideas that had seemed so self-evident over the previous generation.

Just a couple of weeks after Obama had won the presidential election, I found myself in Bush country, at a conference that revolved around America's diminishing ability to shape the world. Texas A&M (which stands for Agricultural and Mechanical) was not the obvious place to pick for a conference dedicated to discussing the decline of America. The college sends more of its graduates straight into the military than any other civilian university in the US. Members of its officer training corps stride around the campus in crisply pressed uniforms and knee-high leather boots, greeting each other with brisk 'howdys'. George H. W. Bush, the president who was in charge when America won the

Cold War, has chosen A&M as the site for his presidential library and museum. The exhibition reflects a mixture of post-Second World War innocence and post-Cold War triumphalism. There is a replica of the red Studebaker in which the Bush family drove down to Texas in 1947 to start a new life. There are baby pictures of the young George W. Bush. And there is a sizeable chunk of the Berlin Wall, which fell in 1989, during President Bush's watch.

And yet in November 2008 – less than twenty years after America's triumph in the Cold War – Texas A&M was the site for an angst-ridden examination of a new American crisis. The conference was organized to discuss a new report on global trends until 2025, drawn up by America's National Intelligence Council (NIC), which co-ordinates the country's many intelligence agencies. The gloomy mood of the moment was captured by the opening address given by General Brent Scowcroft, who had been the first President Bush's national security adviser and closest confidant. The general, now in his mid-eighties, recalled that at the end of the Cold War, the United States had found itself in a position of unchallenged global power. 'We exercised that power for a while,' he mused, 'only to realize that it was ephemeral.'[295]

Some of the reasons for General Scowcroft's pessimism were reflected in the NIC's analysis. As the document frankly noted, 'the most dramatic difference' between the NIC report of 2008 and the one it had issued four years previously was that America's intelligence establishment now foresaw the end of the country's global hegemony. In 2004 America's spies had projected 'continuing US dominance' of international affairs. But now, looking forward to 2025, the NIC predicted 'a world in which the US plays a prominent role in global events, but the US is seen as one among many global actors'.[296]

What had caused this change of mood? In part, it was a growing awareness of what the NIC called 'the unprecedented transfer of wealth and economic power roughly from West to East';[297] and of the rise of China and India, in particular. America's bloody and inconclusive military involvement in Iraq and Afghanistan was also crucial. These were the places where the US had, in General Scowcroft's words, exercised its power, but then found it to be 'ephemeral'. The mighty American military machine had learnt that it could topple regimes in weeks. But, even after years of bloodshed, it could not ensure continuing peace and stability in an occupied land. All America's high-tech wizardry could not protect its troops from the simple roadside bomb. All the country's democratic evangelism and financial aid could not turn a broken, tribal territory like Afghanistan into a functioning nation.

The National Intelligence Council's research had been largely completed before the collapse of Lehman Brothers in September 2008. But the biggest financial crisis in America since the thirties added a new and deeper reason for the pessimism that was already reflected in the NIC report.

The vulnerability of the American economy and financial system had been largely unanticipated, even by those who were already convinced that the unipolar moment was coming to a close. The NIC report made only a glancing reference to financial instability. A widely read book by Fareed Zakaria, *The Post-American World*, which was published in 2008 and accurately reflected the new sense of limits at the closing of the Bush era, nonetheless had assumed that the American economy was basically sound. Zakaria had written: 'America's economic system is its core strength, its political system is its core weakness.'[298]

So the crash of 2008 was a huge shock. It undermined what was regarded as the very basis of American power and spread a new sense of American vulnerability. In the aftermath of the crash, America faced slower growth, higher unemployment and spiralling government debt. America's fiscal deficit for 2009 was around $1,500 billion – three times the previous record. The Peterson Institute for International Economics in Washington estimated that it was likely to remain close to an annual $1,000 billion for the next decade, pushing America's national debt to new and unprecedented levels.[299] Rather than a shiny new economic model, powered by high-tech and high finance, America looked in the mirror and thought it saw an artificial boom, built on credit and foreign borrowing. Francis Fukuyama, who had epitomized the sunny optimism of 1989, now took an altogether more gloomy view of the American system, lamenting, 'We have lost a lot of our manufacturing base, and the service economy that was supposed to supplant it is a mirage.'[300]

The belief that the world had changed fundamentally after the crash of 2008 was even more pronounced outside the United States. Just two weeks after the fall of Lehman Brothers, I was in China where I met Pan Wei, director of Beijing University's Center for Chinese and Global Affairs. Like many Chinese intellectuals, the professor was keenly aware of the projections by Goldman Sachs, the world's most powerful investment bank, that the Chinese economy would be larger than that of the United States by 2027. But, in the immediate aftermath of the Wall Street crash, he was wondering if Goldman hadn't been a little on the cautious side. 'My belief,' he said, 'is that in twenty years we will look the Americans straight in the eye as equals. But maybe it will come sooner than that. Their system is in chaos and they need our money to rescue them.'[301]

The sense that the crash of 2008 has accelerated the Chinese challenge to America hardened over the following year, as the US economy struggled and China bounced back to 8 per cent growth. Most shocking of all was the growing realization that the United States government was depending on the continued goodwill of Chinese lenders. In Barack Obama's first year in office, the US budget deficit soared to over 12 per cent of GDP. To fund the government, America needed foreigners to keep buying its debt. And in 2009 the Chinese were obliging by buying at least $20 billion worth of US Treasury bills a month.[302]

As many observers noted, the situation was uncomfortable for the Chinese as well as for the Americans. For if the Chinese stopped buying US debt, they might precipitate a collapse in the dollar, and so batter the value of the roughly $2.5 trillion in foreign reserves that China had amassed in the preceding years, most of it held in dollars. The Chinese were well aware of this particular dilemma. Visiting the country in 2009, I encountered a wild conspiracy theory that held that America was deliberately planning to destroy the economic strength of China by unleashing inflation, so undermining the value of China's dollar assets. Like a stern bank manager with a loose-living creditor, Prime Minister Wen Jiabao urged America to 'maintain its credibility, honour its commitments and guarantee the safety of Chinese assets'.[303] When in 2009 Tim Geithner, the US Treasury secretary, attempted to reassure an audience of Chinese students that the country's investments were safe in the US, he was met with derisive laughter.[304]

It has become a cliché that the relationship between American debtor and Chinese creditor is now so dependent that it represents a new form of 'mutually assured destruction' – a financial version of the nuclear balance of terror between the US and the USSR during the Cold War. It is clear that neither country's situation is entirely comfortable. But it is surely worse to be the debtor nation. Shakespeare warned, 'Neither a borrower nor a lender be.' But in international affairs, if you have to be one or the other, it is probably better to be a lender.

America's weakened economic position after 2008 undermined the country's power and influence in all its forms. It threatened its hard military power; and it weakened the soft power conferred by American prestige. Academics, looking at the long-term trends, signalled the retreat from the Age of Optimism. Stephen Cohen and Brad DeLong, economists at the University of California, captured the new mood with a book entitled *The End of Influence*, subtitled *What Happens When Other Countries Have the Money*. They bluntly predicted that one result would be that America would experience 'a loss of power to undertake unilateral foreign-policy actions'.[305] Harold James, a historian at Princeton University, was no more optimistic. He noted that 'traumatic financial crises usually... involve a new geography of power'[306] and predicted that 'After the financial crisis, the ability to supply new credit will translate

into political power.'[307] Indeed, senior members of the Obama administration were well aware of this point and made it publicly, before the
burdens of office forced them to become more circumspect.

Before taking office, Larry Summers, who became the chief economic adviser in the Obama White House, mused, 'How long can the
world's biggest borrower remain the world's biggest power?'[308] Campaigning for the Democratic Party nomination in 2008, Hillary Clinton
asked rhetorically, 'Why can't we get tough on China?' and answered,
'How do you get tough on your banker?'[309] As secretary of state in the
Obama administration, Mrs Clinton duly deliberately played down
America's traditional concerns about human rights in China.

American power in the unipolar moment rested on many things –
but the bottom line, as the world discovered after 9/11, was military
might. At the height of the Bush era, the United States was widely reckoned to be spending more on its military than the rest of the world
combined. This huge spending was intended to ensure that, as President George W. Bush's National Security strategy of 2002 made clear, no
rising power could threaten America's global dominance. US defence
spending made the country's military much more technologically
sophisticated than any plausible rival; so sophisticated, indeed, that
European allies increasingly found it difficult to fight alongside the
Americans. The Pentagon's budget also funded the string of military
bases around the world that gave America its global reach. During the
unipolar moment, there was no doubt that America could win a fight in
any part of the world where its strategic interests were at stake: the Gulf,
the Far East, Central Europe.

Robert Kaplan, a particularly enthusiastic journalist, delighted in
2005 that the US military had 'appropriated the entire earth and was
ready to flood the most obscure areas of it with troops at a moment's
notice'.[310] An overstatement, perhaps, but even American liberals felt
that it was a political necessity to pay tribute to the power and importance of the American military. Watching Barack Obama's confirmation

as the Democratic Party candidate for the presidency in Denver in August 2008, I was struck by the long parade of supportive generals that the Democrats felt it necessary to display on stage. It was true that America was at war at the time, and that the Democrats felt the need to bolster their patriotic credentials. But such an open display of militarism would have been unthinkable at a party conference in Britain – a country that was also at war and heir to a long military tradition.

By the time Obama took the nomination, however, the Iraq and Afghan wars had already undermined that belief that, in the last resort, America could always secure its goals through massive military might. It had become clear that the US could well quit both wars without achieving its goal of leaving behind secure and friendly regimes. As a result, it also became apparent that US dominance of the Middle East and South Asia could no longer be taken for granted.

The economic crisis has led to longer-term questions about American military dominance of East Asia and the Pacific. In the year that President Obama took office, the US was spending around 4 per cent of its GDP on the military. Historically, this is not a particularly high figure for the US and in normal times it would be eminently sustainable. But, over the next decade, there will be huge pressure on the federal budget. When the US is running budget deficits of 12 per cent a year – and much of the budget is eaten up by legally mandated 'entitlements'– the money spent on the military will come under pressure.

The situation must also look a little odd viewed from Beijing. The US and China like to say that they are partners, but they are also rivals and almost clashed over Taiwan in 1996. The two countries' military strategists plan for the possibility of American-Chinese wars. In recent years, the Chinese have been increasing their military spending by over 12 per cent a year, in an effort to narrow the military gap with the US. But China is also simultaneously funding continued American military dominance of the Pacific by helping to fund the US deficit, so making it easier to maintain the current level of American defence spending.

At present, US troops and warships are stationed all over East Asia and the Pacific – from the soldiers along the frontier between the two Koreas, to the huge US military base in Okinawa in Japan, and the forward naval and air base in Guam. Officially, China is not calling for an American military withdrawal from East Asia. Unofficially, some influential Chinese will tell visitors that it is unnatural for the US to have such a large military presence in Asia and that in the end this will change. There is even a strong current in Chinese thinking that holds that eventual war with the United States is inevitable. One American, who teaches at a Chinese university and is deeply sympathetic to the country, nonetheless told me in 2007 that he was 'disturbed by how many of the kids I teach have been taught that war with America is inevitable'.[311]

On his first visit to China, Barack Obama stuck doggedly to the mantras of the win-win world that he had inherited from Bill Clinton and George W. Bush. 'We welcome China's efforts to play a greater role on the world stage,' he declared. 'Power does not need to be a zero-sum game and nations need not fear the success of each other.'[312] And yet this is not entirely true. A more powerful China will inevitably threaten America's ability to play the role in Asia and the Pacific to which it has become accustomed.

Even before the crash of 2008, the military balance between China and the US was shifting. Aaron Friedberg of Princeton University noted in 2009 that China's sustained military build-up meant that 'Every one of the relative handful of bases on which the United States relies to sustain its presence in East Asia will soon be within range of bombardment by repeated salvos of precisely targeted Chinese conventional ballistic and cruise missiles.'[313] American aircraft carriers, the key to its Pacific strategy, are particularly vulnerable to new Chinese precision-guided weapons. Friedberg warned that 'Washington must find ways to counter China's evolving anti-access capabilities. If it does not, America's longstanding military dominance in East Asia will quickly disappear.'[314] He was not alone in his concerns. In an article on the 'Pentagon's

Wasting Assets' for *Foreign Affairs*, also in 2009, Andrew Krepinevich worried that 'East Asian waters are slowly but surely becoming a potential no-go zone for US ships'. Krepinevich pointed out that 'the US military's wasting assets are the direct consequence of the unavoidable loss of its near monopoly on guided weapons'.[315] China has also been working on its ability to knock out the communications satellites on which American high-tech warfare depends. When China blasted one of its own satellites out of the sky with a missile test in January 2007, the move was widely interpreted as an implied threat to American satellites.[316] This emerging power struggle is being followed closely around the world. In the aftermath of the financial crisis I was told by a senior British policymaker, 'Everywhere you go in Asia, you find questions about how long American military dominance can be maintained.'[317]

It is not just American military power that is threatened by the erosion in the country's economic position. America's ability to achieve its international aims in other ways is also undermined. The country simply has less money to throw about – and has to worry more about the views of its foreign creditors. Discussing America's ability to help failing states with a senior State Department official in 2009, I was told bluntly, 'We can't just do a Marshall Plan, we have to enlist others to help.'[318]

The prestige of the American system and of the ideas that America represents have also suffered a serious setback. Michael Mandelbaum, a scholar who chronicled the spread of American-inspired liberal economic and political ideas in his book *The Ideas that Conquered the World*, reflected in 2002 that 'An economic slump on the scale of the Great Depression would call into question the value of free markets, as it did in the thirties, and so shake the foundations of the international system.'[319] The world seems to have avoided a new Great Depression in the aftermath of the crash of 2008. But the deepest global recession since the thirties – originating, as it did, in a financial crisis in the United States – damaged the prestige of both free-market economics and of America itself. And that is a development that does indeed threaten to 'shake the foundations of the international system'.

The European Union, the other pillar of the western world, seems to be in even deeper trouble than the United States. The financial crisis caused debt levels to soar across the EU. During the Age of Optimism, from 1991 to 2008, European nations felt safely immune from the debt crises that plagued the likes of Argentina and Mexico. But in 2010 it became clear that Greece, with a national debt of around 115 per cent of GDP, could no longer borrow on the international markets. The threat that debt crises would spread across the Union, hitting countries like Portugal, Spain and Italy, forced the EU to create a massive bail-out fund of almost $1 trillion dollars that could be drawn upon by countries in an emergency.

The cost of the economic crisis to Europe was not just financial. Europe lost respect in the world and confidence in its own future, as the suspicion grew that the much-vaunted 'European social model' – with its well-funded social services and generous state benefits for the poor – was simply unaffordable. The climate of austerity and debt raised tensions both within and between European states. In Greece, one of the first countries to experience major cutbacks in wages and social benefits, there were deadly street riots in May 2010. From Spain to Britain, European nations contemplated a future of cutbacks and austerity, and worried about the social and political consequences.

As Germany's Chancellor Angela Merkel acknowledged, the crisis also threatened the future of the European Union itself. There was open speculation that Greece would be forced to leave the European single currency – and if Greece went, others would surely follow. Since the creation of the euro was the single most dramatic symbol of Europe's 'ever closer union', the potential disintegration of the single currency posed huge questions for the future of the EU itself. Yet one of the costs of keeping the single currency together, by loaning money to the weakest members of the currency union, was a major rise in tensions between EU nations. German newspapers reacted with disgust and alarm at the notion that

German taxpayers were effectively paying to fund the pensions of Greek civil servants. Reflecting on the bitter war of words that had broken out between the Greeks and the Germans, one much-respected former EU official told me in 2010 that 'this is as close to war as it gets in modern Europe. Two peoples have been set against each other.'

Talking to Asian and American officials who were observing this European debt crisis, I noticed a mixture of alarm at its global implications, mixed with something close to contempt for European weakness and vacillation.

But in the wake of the economic crash, the world's major powers also adopted a less respectful tone towards the United States. It was not just the Chinese, cheekily demanding that America support the value of the dollar. Even America's long-time allies spoke of the US and of the ideas that it championed with a new disdain. Yukio Hatoyama, who became prime minister of Japan after his Democratic Party won the election of 2009, startled the Obama administration when he wrote, shortly before winning office: 'The recent economic crisis resulted from a way of thinking based on the idea that American-style free-market economics represents a universal and ideal economic order.' For good measure, the new prime minister added, 'I also feel that as a result of the failure of the Iraq War and the financial crisis, the era of US-led globalism is coming to an end.'[320]

Hatoyama followed up his words with deeds. One of his first acts as prime minister was to demand that the US move one of its controversial military bases on the Japanese island of Okinawa – a demand that raised questions about the future of the fifty thousand or so American troops deployed in Japan. The US–Japan Security Treaty is fundamental to American strategy in the Pacific, so any doubt about its permanence raises immediate questions about the balance of power between America and China. The suggestion that Japan was tilting towards China was strengthened in December 2009, when Ichiro Ozawa, a leading figure in Hatoyama's party, led a delegation of over six hundred to Beijing, including 143 members of parliament. Hu Jintao, China's president, patiently posed for photos with each and every one of them. In Tokyo, shortly afterwards, I found western diplomats openly debating whether Japan, sensing a shift in the global balance of power, was beginning to realign itself away from America, and towards China. Hatayama's inability to deliver on his promise to close the marine base in Okinawa led to his resignation as prime minister in June 2010, but the questions he raised about Japan's place in the world will linger.

Japan was not the only traditional American ally seeking to distance itself from the wounded hyper-power. President Nicolas Sarkozy of France, who when he was elected in 2007 was referred to as 'Sarko l'américain' because of his frank and un-French admiration for the US, retreated to a more traditional Gallic position in the wake of the crisis, announcing grandly that 'The idea that markets were always right was mad... Laissez-faire is finished.'[321]

Sarkozy's remarks were just a taste of the international assault on the free-market beliefs that, to a great extent, all the world's major powers had subscribed to over the previous thirty years. The mantras of the Age of Optimism were deregulation, free trade, the abolition of capital controls and the encouragement of cross-border investment. But in the wake of the economic and financial crisis, the state was resurgent across the world, as governments stepped in to save their economies.

The extent of the intellectual reversal after the crash of 2008 was extraordinary. The collapse of Lehman Brothers sparked immediate fears of a global financial meltdown – and so prompted governments all over the world to pour money into their banks. For the previous thirty years, privatization had swept the world. But now nationalization was back. Analysts at the Bank of England calculated that over the following year, the total value of state interventions to prop up banks around the world was $14,000 billion.[322] Inevitably, the new state bankers swiftly wanted to set policy, urging the banks to start lending faster and, in the US, Britain and elsewhere, attempting to set limits on bankers' bonuses.

The new wave of nationalization did not stop with the banks. Politicians could not be seen to save the jobs of hated financiers, but to allow the jobs of blameless working men to disappear. So a new wave of state intervention, aimed at propping up the car industry, was unleashed. In the nine months after the fall of Lehman Brothers, international governments poured in over $100 billion in direct or indirect aid to keep car plants running.[323]

In extraordinary circumstances and facing extraordinary pressures, many of the assumptions about business and economics that had prevailed for the previous thirty years were tossed overboard. 'Shareholder value', the doctrine that companies should be managed above all in the interests of their shareholders, had been accepted business wisdom for decades. But suddenly, Jack Welch, the most revered American manager of his age and the foremost champion of shareholder value, popped up to announce that it was 'a dumb idea'.[324] The notion that the market should be allowed to set pay was abandoned. As it became conventional wisdom that the financial crash had been caused, at least in part, by incentives to take excessive risks, so governments all over the world moved to regulate bankers' pay. In the US and Britain, ideas derided as outmoded for the previous thirty years – such as the notion that the government should have an 'industrial policy' – made a comeback.

The return of the state was by no means confined to the western world. In fact, in China and in the oil-rich nations, the financial crisis merely accentuated a trend that was already in place. The pace of pro-market reforms in China had slowed, after Hu Jintao became president and party leader in 2002, with the government attempting to encourage the formation of state-controlled national champions in industries like oil, telecoms and aerospace. But these trends were accentuated by the global economic crisis. Prime Minister Wen Jiabao might have told a Davos audience that he was looking to Adam Smith for inspiration, but the Chinese state became more protectionist after the crisis – moving to block a foreign investment by Coca-Cola, harassing executives of Rio Tinto, which had fallen out with a Chinese state-owned company, and promoting a 'buy Chinese' policy for government spending intended to stimulate the economy.[325]

The Chinese, in turn, were following a trend that has been visible in the oil industry for some years, as privately owned western oil companies have been progressively squeezed out of the most promising markets by state-controlled national champions. As the political analyst Ian Bremmer noted in 2009, 'Governments, not private shareholders, already own the world's largest oil companies and control three-quarters of the world's energy reserves.'[326] By contrast, privately owned western 'multinationals produce just 10 per cent of the world's oil and hold just three per cent of its reserves'.[327]

Sovereign wealth funds (SWFs), which make strategic investments on behalf of cash-rich governments, are also increasingly big players in the global economy. What the NIC report called 'the transfer of wealth and economic power from West to East', means that the biggest SWFs are controlled by oil-rich nations, particularly in the Gulf, and by Asian nations such as China. The sovereign funds control more capital than private hedge funds; according to Bremmer, by 2009 they already accounted for one-eighth of global investment, and the figure is rising.[328] Although SWFs routinely claim that they make their investments on purely economic grounds, as major investors they have political influence if they choose to use it. This should come as no surprise to the West, where it has long been routine to use investment – or disinvestment – as a political weapon. Think of the sanctions campaigns against South Africa in the eighties and against Iran today.

Some of this revival of state economic power was a temporary reaction to an emergency. The American government clearly had no desire to own large chunks of the automobile and financial industries in perpetuity. But, in the aftermath of the financial crisis of 2008, conventional assumptions about the proper role of the state in the

economy are likely to have shifted for decades. And that has implications for globalization – and for the international system that has been
built around globalization.

Think back to the assumptions of the Age of Optimism. In an age of
free trade, shrinking states and steadily rising global prosperity, it was
much easier to believe in a win-win world. All the major powers would
get richer together by letting market forces rip. They would co-operate
and avoid conflict. This was a world in which there was plenty of everything to go around – plenty of economic growth, plenty of oil, plenty of
scope to pump carbon dioxide into the atmosphere.

But international economics – and therefore international politics –
look very different in a post-crash world. The relationships between
nations and national economic interests look a lot more zero-sum. It is
no longer clear that the most important economic relationship in the
world – that between China and the United States – is still mutually
beneficial. The Americans worry about their trade deficit with China
and argue that an undervalued Chinese currency helped to create the
credit bubble that blew up in 2008. The Chinese call such charges
absurd – and worry about the safety of their dollar assets. Both sides toy
with ideas that could be profoundly damaging to the other side: the
Americans think about raising tariffs, the Chinese flirt with a sell-off of
dollar assets.

With the resurgence of state control of the economy, it is also increasingly tempting for nations to use their strategic economic stakes for
national goals – and that, in turn, threatens globalization and the
assumption of shared interests that underpin it. The aftermath of the
economic crisis threw up many examples, large and small, of this
process at work. President Sarkozy asked French companies in receipt
of state aid to close their factories in other parts of Europe – and save
those in France. When Chancellor Merkel attempted to arrange a state
bail-out of Opel, it was under similar conditions: close Opel car factories
elsewhere in Europe; save German jobs. American legislators took a

similar line. Wall Street banks in receipt of government funds were told to hire American graduates.

State intervention in the management of the economy is once again respectable and that indirectly threatens many of the internationalist assumptions that governed world politics during the Age of Optimism. This will be all the more the case with governments around the world increasingly anxious about the security of the supply of crucial commodities – in particular, food and oil. If the market cannot be relied upon to provide these crucial products, the implication is clear – the state will intervene. That will probably mean more agricultural protectionism, as governments pursue 'food security'. Asian and Middle Eastern nations, in particular the Saudis and Gulf Arabs, have also begun leasing large tracts of land in Africa, in an effort to grow food that is reserved for their own nations. Some of these efforts have become highly controversial; Daewoo of South Korea was rebuffed in an attempt to buy a large chunk of Madagascar in 2008.[329]

The state-sponsored pursuit of resources is already very visible when it comes to the global struggle to secure and control access to energy. US foreign policy in the Middle East is closely related to its search for reliable supplies of oil. Chinese foreign policy is also increasingly driven by the country's ever-growing energy needs, which has led the Chinese government to cultivate close relationships with unstable or unsavoury regimes in countries such as Sudan and Iran.

Slower economic growth will also make it harder to smooth over tensions in the international system. A favourite cliché of national politicians is that it is better to make the economic pie bigger, rather than to argue over how best to cut it up. The same is true of the world economy; with rapid growth, there is more wealth to go around – with a slower world economy, distributional conflicts are more likely to break out. The world economy was, in fact, growing at its fastest rate for decades in the years immediately before the crash, and the American economy, the world's largest, was crucial to global growth. But the United States now looks set for a long period with a weaker economy, as consumers pay down debt and the government wrestles with its fiscal deficit. The European Union is also facing an age of austerity. Slower growth in the US and Europe would mean slower growth for the world as a whole. Even if the BRICs (Brazil, Russia, India and China) manage successfully to decouple their economic fortunes from those of the United States and to forge ahead without the need for strong American demand, the world economy will still feel very different. With the US and the European Union growing much more slowly than developing nations, it will be harder to make the case that this is a win-win world, in which all major powers are getting richer together, and all have an incentive to co-operate and to keep their markets open.

The temptation to turn away from globalization is likely to be particularly pronounced in the rich world. For while the American government has been a champion of an open global economy, the American people have been far less convinced. This was evident well before the crash. When the Pew Global Attitudes survey polled forty-seven countries in 2007, the US came absolutely last in its support for free trade.[330] So if President Obama maintains America's traditional support for an open, global trading system, he will be doing so in the teeth of deep public scepticism.

Indeed, as the Obama administration attempts to maintain the stability of the global system that the US has dominated since the end of the Cold War, it faces two big new obstacles. The first is a sharp fall in America's relative power. The second is a loss of faith in the ability of markets to provide order and prosperity to the world system – and to create common interests between nations. And yet that sense of common interests has never been more vital. For it is increasingly apparent that economic globalization has helped to create a set of urgent global political problems that demand solutions.

A WORLD OF TROUBLES

The United Nations is in the middle of Manhattan, but many Americans have long regarded it as hostile territory – a platform for foreign despots to take a free shot at the United States, while accepting American hospitality and hand-outs. The line-up of speakers at the opening of the UN General Assembly meeting in New York on 23 September 2009 had the pundits on Fox News fulminating with rage and scorn. It included Mahmoud Ahmadi-Nejad, the president of Iran, Hugo Chavez from Venezuela and Muammar Gaddafi of Libya.

But the main attraction on that September day was Barack Obama, the president of the United States, still lightly covered in star-dust after his historic election the previous November. The United Nations had got used to being scolded and ignored by George W. Bush. But Mr Obama was determined to woo the world body. He had appointed Susan Rice, one of his closest campaign aides, as American ambassador to the UN and had given her a place in the cabinet. In his first address to the UN General Assembly, Obama set out to charm the assembled world leaders.

The new president's approach to the UN reflected his temperamental preference for 'engagement' rather than confrontation. But it was also based on two core beliefs about the world he had inherited. First, that the Bush years had conclusively demonstrated that unilateral American action could no longer achieve the most important goals of US foreign policy. President Bush's decision to invade Iraq without a UN mandate was the ultimate test of an American policy of 'ourselves alone'. The Obama team were determined not to repeat that approach, with all the costs and traumas that it had brought in its wake.

President Obama's second insight was that many of the most troubling issues facing his administration were global in nature. No single country, acting alone, could hope to solve them. In his UN speech, he set out these problems: 'Extremists sowing terror in pockets of the world. Protracted conflicts that grind on and on. Genocide and mass atrocities. More and more nations with nuclear weapons. Melting ice caps and ravaged populations. Persistent poverty and pandemic disease. I say this not to sow fear, but to state a fact; the magnitude of our challenges has yet to be met by the measure of our action.'[331]

Critics on both the right and the left would dispute some of the items on the president's list. Conservatives are sceptical about climate change. Liberals express doubts about the war on terror. Yet, in certain respects, it does not matter whether all of the fears and problems listed by President Obama turn out to be justified. What matters is that most of the world's major powers agree that these problems are real – and demand action. Every major government – from Beijing to Brussels, Moscow to Delhi – is committed to the idea that climate change is happening and they are all participating in the UN-sponsored negotiations to limit emissions of greenhouse gases. The United States under President Bush took the lead in the war on terror – but Russia, India and Britain have all been more recent victims of major terrorist attacks. Poverty, pandemic disease, nuclear proliferation, peacekeeping and genocide are all firmly on the UN agenda.

Obama was also right to argue that there is now a whole set of political, economic and environmental problems that can only be fixed by international agreement. It is telling that many of the toughest issues facing the world's governments now routinely have the word 'global' added to them as a prefix: the 'global financial crisis', the 'global war on terror', global warming. America's traditional sense that the oceans that lie between the United States and the world's other major powers provide some protection could be easily refuted by the citizens of New York. Since the turn of the millennium, the city has been the place where global crises have announced themselves. The global war on terror began on the southern tip of Manhattan on 9/11. The global financial crisis had its epicentre a few blocks north of that, on Wall Street. And a little further north, in Midtown Manhattan, the United Nations itself has been the forum for agonized debate on critical issues, such as the Iranian nuclear programme, climate change and international efforts to save Afghanistan and Iraq.

Indeed, far from being alarmist, Obama's list of global problems was arguably a little on the short side. The US president chose to highlight terrorism, war, genocide, the proliferation of nuclear weapons, global warming, global poverty and the threat of pandemics. To that list could be added global economic tensions, shortages of food, water and energy, failed states, international crime and uncontrolled mass migration.

All of these issues are problems of globalization. Some have been created or worsened by the process of global economic integration that has defined international politics since 1978. None of them can be solved without a significant degree of international co-operation. And yet the world lacks the international political structures needed to fix global problems. That will be the central dilemma of international politics for the next decade or more. To understand the dilemma better, it is worth looking at these problems issue by issue.

The great recession

The global financial crisis arrived in the United States in mid-September 2008. Initially, Europeans and Asians hoped that they would be spared the consequences of bad lending by US-based banks. But it swiftly became apparent that the problem was global in nature. In the twelve months after the crisis broke, the world economy as a whole shrank for the first time since 1945.

When economists searched for the origins of the crisis, many decided that it had an inescapable international dimension. The emergence of 'global economic imbalances' became a favoured explanation, especially in the United States. The idea was that China, in particular, had accumulated billions of dollars through running trade surpluses with the United States. This money had then been recycled through the purchase of American assets, creating excess liquidity in the US and leading to a boom in reckless consumption and lending. The only way to fix the fundamental causes of the bust, according to this analysis, was for China to consume more and the US to consume less. And that must mean China allowing its currency to rise against the dollar. While this analysis was widely accepted in America, it was often scornfully rejected in China, where the theory of 'global economic imbalances' was denounced as an effort by Americans to export the blame for their own dangerous extravagance. And yet even the Chinese recognized that there was an inescapable global aspect to the crisis. Hence their repeated demands that the United States support the value of the dollar and keep its markets open.

The other popular scapegoat for the crisis was loose regulation of financial institutions and a culture of excessive risk-taking in investment banks. When the world's political leaders attempted to deal with this issue, they once again found themselves facing a set of problems that were inescapably global in nature. There was clearly a mismatch between international financial institutions, such as Lehman Brothers and AIG, and national regulators.[332] This regulatory mismatch was part of the origins of the crisis – and it also made it much harder to fix matters. Politicians everywhere were itching to get tough on bankers by regulating their pay and bonuses, and by forcing financial institutions to hold more capital. But they had to tread carefully. Any government that acted alone risked seeing investment banks move offshore to more loosely regulated environments – taking jobs and tax revenues with them.

In an ideal world, the major economic powers and financial centres would act co-operatively to resolve global imbalances and to regulate global, financial institutions. In the real world, global economic problems are more likely to be a source of tension than of co-operation. China, in particular, has resisted any suggestion that it should let its currency float freely against the dollar – and that, in turn, is almost certain to be the source of continuing trade tensions with the US.

Climate change

Climate change is the most perplexing example of a crisis that can only be solved on a global basis. There is little point in a single nation cracking down on greenhouse gases, if the rest of the world does not follow suit. Since 'clean energy' is currently more expensive than the alternatives, a country that acted alone would risk making all its industries uncompetitive, without having any lasting impact on the problem of global warming. In his last year in office as Britain's prime minister, Tony Blair took to telling visitors ruefully that he had been informed that he could shut down the entire British power industry – only to find that China had added the equivalent amount of generating capacity in just one year.

The problem of climate change is intimately related to globalization. The globalization of manufacturing and of western consumption patterns has dramatically increased the release of climate-changing gases. In 2008 China overtook the United States as the largest emitter of carbon dioxide in the world.

To many western eyes, it seems obvious that the pain and costs of controlling greenhouse gases must be shared equally around the world. But that is not how things look in China and the developing world. The developing nations make two powerful points. First, the scientific consensus is that what matters is the overall stock of greenhouse gases in the atmosphere – and most of that has been put there by rich western nations that industrialized hundreds of years ago. The rest of the world is currently paying the environmental price for the wealth the western world has accumulated over centuries, so it is the West that should bear the burden of cutting back emissions.

The second point is that while China may now emit more carbon dioxide than the United States, it still emits far less per person because its population is four times that of America. Levels of energy consumption are closely connected to levels of wealth and comfort – think of all those cars in American driveways, air-conditioned homes and tumble-driers. So the Chinese, Indians and other developing nations argue that it is morally unsustainable for western nations to insist on maintaining their energy-intensive lifestyles, while trying to cap the per capita consumption of poorer Asians.

The Chinese attitude is complex. There is little doubt that the governing elite, packed with people with a scientific background, takes climate change seriously. They know that a country with as little water as China is seriously threatened by global warming, and point to the fall in the level of the Yangtze and Yellow rivers as a danger sign. Yet their attitude to the western consumerist lifestyle is decidedly ambivalent. In Beijing in 2008 I was gravely informed by a Chinese official that 'Your western way of life is unsustainable.' Then I walked out into streets lined by new shopping malls and choked with new cars, all of which would soon be able to drive on the thousands of miles of new motorways that the Chinese government is constructing.

The Chinese have been willing to commit to ambitious-sounding national targets to make their energy use less carbon-intensive.[333] But, as became clear at the disastrous UN conference on climate change in Copenhagen in December 2009, the Chinese are unwilling to accept binding international commitments to reduce emissions. Their stubbornness reflects a powerful mix of economic self-interest, genuinely felt emotions about 'global equity' and a deep reluctance to concede national sovereignty to an international legal regime. India is similarly ambivalent: sometimes decrying western consumerism, but reacting with rage at any American suggestions that rising energy consumption in Asia is part of the global warming problem.

As for the Americans themselves, faced with foreign suggestions that America's love affair with the open road would have to be modified, President George W. Bush was fond of replying that 'the American way of life is not negotiable'. Barack Obama might not be that blunt, but he too knows that it would be electoral suicide to impose huge new environmental costs on the American economy, while apparently giving China a free pass.

It was this impasse that helped to cause the Copenhagen climate talks to fail. There will be efforts to revive a global climate deal, but they all risk falling foul of the same zero-sum economic logic. Most of the proposed global deals on climate change envisage the US and Europe essentially bribing the developing world to cut carbon emissions by funding the transfer of technology. But any such deal will be very tough to sell politically in the US, with America running record budget deficits and China sitting on over $2 trillion worth of reserves.

Even if some sort of global climate deal is reached, it will just be the first of many such negotiations, as both global warming and technology advance. The trouble is that agonizing global negotiations are likely to deliver an agreement that falls well short of what scientific advice deems to be necessary – and any such deal will, in any case, prove to be almost impossible to monitor and enforce. That, in turn, will ensure that climate change continues to be a major source of tension within the international system.

Resource shortages

In the year before the financial crisis hit, international leaders were worrying about a different sort of global economic crisis – the soaring price of commodities, in particular oil and food. This crisis is likely to return, because it is intimately linked to the economic growth in Asia unleashed by globalization. The demand for natural resources is rising. That is leading to a spike in prices and jostling between the world's major powers to secure access to supplies of energy, food and water.

There is a lively debate between experts about whether the world has reached 'peak oil' – the moment when oil reserves peak and then decline. Believers in 'peak oil' point out that, while the number and size of new oil discoveries has been falling since the mid-eighties, global demand is rising steadily. The International Energy Agency projects that, to keep pace, 'Some 64 million barrels per day of additional gross capacity – the equivalent of almost six times that of Saudi Arabia today – needs to be brought on stream between 2007 and 2030.'[334] James Schlesinger, a well-respected former US energy secretary, predicts that 'We are heading for a crucial moment as the nations of the world face a time, the first time since we had major economic development, of an inability to increase the supply of oil.'[335]

These projections sound alarming, but critics point out that dire predictions that the world was about to run out of oil were also fashionable in the seventies – and were then disproved by new finds and new technology. Alternative sources of fossil fuel are already emerging. The US is beginning to capitalize on its large reserves of natural gas produced from shale; the world has plentiful supplies of coal that can be converted into liquid hydrocarbons at a reasonable price. And new discoveries of fossil fuels are likely to be made underneath the Arctic.

But whatever the real situation, the world's major powers are increasingly behaving as if their supply of energy is anything but assured. Chinese oil consumption doubled between 1994 and 2003, and doubled again in the seven years after that. The country's energy needs are now forcing China to adopt a more expansive foreign policy. Until 2000 China was essentially a regional power without a major footprint outside Asia. But that has changed with the burgeoning Chinese relationship with the African continent, driven above all by the country's search for oil and other raw materials. China has forged controversial relationships with the despotic governments of Sudan and Angola, which are both major oil producers. Chinese troops have been stationed in Africa to protect the country's workers and interests in unstable places like Sudan and Ethiopia.[336]

The Chinese are far from alone in finding their foreign and defence policies increasingly shaped by their energy needs. The motivations for America's invasion of Iraq remain controversial. But at least one well-informed observer, Alan Greenspan, believed that the Iraq War was 'largely about oil'.[337] Even if that is a false charge, no American government would deny that the Arabian Gulf region is an area of crucial strategic importance, protected by a huge deployment of US military power. And, in this case, 'strategic importance' is essentially shorthand for the fact that the Gulf is home to two-thirds of the world's known oil reserves. The biggest foreign policy dilemma of the EU also revolves around energy, and a dangerous reliance on Russian gas.

It is not just 'energy security' that is exercising the world's political leaders. 'Food security' is also back on the agenda. The world's population is rising, the emerging middle classes of Asia are eating better and that, in turn, is forcing up the price of food. In 2007, the year before the financial crisis hit, the world price of basic foodstuffs rose by 50 per cent.[338] Several countries were shaken by riots over rising food prices, including Mexico, Indonesia and China. Indeed, Hillary Clinton claimed in 2009 that there had been food riots in more than sixty countries over the previous two years, adding that 'Massive hunger poses a threat to the stability of governments, societies and borders.'[339]

Ever since Thomas Malthus first predicted in the eighteenth century that a rising population would cause famine, gloomy predictions about food shortages have always eventually been confounded by technological advances, which have ensured that supply has kept pace with demand. Over the long term, that may well prove to be the case again. But, over the next decade, a resumption of global economic growth – combined with uncertain weather linked to climate change – is likely to provoke further destabilizing spikes in food prices. Poor countries, where as much as 80 per cent of household budgets are spent on food, will be hit particularly hard and could well be destabilized. As big food importers, Egypt and the Philippines are especially vulnerable, but they are far from isolated cases. Meanwhile, rich countries, worried about their 'food security', may increasingly resort to protectionism and defensive attempts to buy farmland in Africa and elsewhere.

A scarcity of water is also increasingly a source of international disputes. Rapid economic growth, urbanization, industrialization and more intensive farming are all straining water supplies. Indeed, the biggest threat to the Chinese and Indian economic miracles may be a shortage of water. One Beijing-based political analyst predicts that renewed political unrest in China will come 'the day that people turn on their taps in Beijing and find that there is no water coming out'.[340] The unresolved border dispute between China and India – which flared up again in 2009 – is also closely connected to both countries' concern about their water supplies. The Indians are acutely aware that they are dependent on water flowing from rivers in Chinese-controlled Tibet. Brahma Chellaney, a leading Indian strategic thinker, predicts that 'The battles of yesterday were fought over land. Those of today are over energy. But the battles of tomorrow will be over water.'[341] The threat of a struggle between India and China over water sounds dramatic. But there are areas where conflict is already being driven by water shortages, including the Horn of Africa, Darfur and the occupied Palestinian territories, where Israeli settlers use 7.5 times more water than the Palestinians.[342]

Many of these problems are, of course, linked. Concern about the rising price of oil convinced the US to encourage farmers to produce bio-fuels made from grain. But the surge in the production of bio-fuels exacerbated the rise in the price of basic foodstuffs. Water shortages are, in turn, worsened by the irrigation required to increase food supply.

The struggle for energy, food and water is a source of tension between the world's major powers. It also threatens dramatically to worsen the plight of the world's poorest people.

Poverty and population

It is generally accepted by economists that globalization has pulled hundreds of millions of poor people out of poverty. But, in recent years, there has also been a growing realization that a large part of the world is being left behind. The plight of the 'bottom billion' – a phrase made famous by Paul Collier, an Oxford academic – is now high up the list of global political problems. There are both moral and practical reasons for this. The vision of a billion people struggling to survive in a world of plenty is morally offensive. It is also dangerous.

Collier's work demonstrates that there is a close connection between poverty and conflict in Africa. As he points out, 'Civil war is much more likely to break out in low-income countries: halve the starting income of the country and you double the risk of civil war.'[343] Once civil war breaks out, a country can get locked into a vicious circle, as war destroys the economy, worsening the poverty that had helped create the fighting in the first place. Civil conflict also has a way of spilling across borders – look at the way that the Rwandan civil war contributed to the tragedy in neighbouring Congo, or at the way in which the fighting in Afghanistan has destabilized neighbouring Pakistan. There are many reasons for the difficulties and dangers of stabilizing Afghanistan, but the fact that it is now the world's fourth poorest nation is surely a major contributory factor.

In the Age of Optimism it was hoped that globalization would allow the world's poorest countries to trade their way out of poverty. That hope remains for some countries – particularly those African nations that can benefit from the boom in commodity prices, provoked by resource short-ages. But there are still many countries that are left behind – those that are landlocked, drought-stricken, run by crooks or locked into civil wars are especially at risk. And, once again, all these conditions seem to be linked. Recent research has suggested that conflict is 50 per cent more likely to break out in an African nation in a year in which drought has led to food shortages – a further reason to fear the impact of climate change.[344]

Images of starvation in Africa have been familiar to western television viewers since at least the mid-eighties, when the Live Aid concerts of 1985 mobilized popular concern about the Ethiopian famine. But, for the world's rich nations, the fate of the 'bottom billion' should now provoke not just compassion, but fear.

In a globalized world, the suffering of the poor is not always going to be walled off from the West. The world population is growing rapidly. It was 2.5 billion in 1950, reached 6.6 billion in 2008 and is projected by the UN to hit over nine billion by 2050. Most of this population growth will be in the poorest parts of the world. The citizens of rich nations will make up a smaller and smaller proportion of the world's people. That will cause tensions within rich societies, as they struggle to assimilate seemingly unstoppable flows of immigrants from poor nations. And it will cause tension between regions as the richer parts of the world try to tighten border controls to keep the poor out.

But even bottling the poor up in their home countries will not spare the West from the instability and violence caused by poverty. There is a close link between poverty, state failure and security threats. After the *Financial Times* ran an article on efforts to combat Somali pirates preying on international shipping passing through the Gulf of Aden, Jeffrey Sachs, a development economist, wrote an acid letter to the *FT*, complaining, 'You discuss the Somali crisis in conventional foreign policy and security categories...without even a single word about Somalia's extreme poverty, hyper-aridity and water stress, extreme vulnerability to drought and climate change, massive illiteracy, unconscionable disease burdens, and bulging population growth rates resulting from the

extreme poverty. When people are starving to death, our diplomats…
invariably treat the unrest as signs of extremism… Somalia is of no
interest to the West, as long as it doesn't block the sea lanes.'[345]

Failed states

America rediscovered the threat of failed states on 9/11. But the problem
was not exactly a new one. The Clinton administration's humiliating
experiences with Somalia and Haiti underlined the sheer difficulty of
propping up collapsing states. Under the administration of George W.
Bush, there was a backlash against the very idea of nation-building.
Donald Rumsfeld, Bush's first defence secretary, famously said that the
US military 'did not do nation-building' – and this was an attitude that
persisted right up to the invasions of Iraq and Afghanistan. Nation-
building was reluctantly put back on the agenda only when it became
clear that the inability to establish stable governments in Iraq and
Afghanistan threatened many of the gains that America had made on
the battlefield. The counter-insurgency strategies adopted in Iraq under
Bush and then Afghanistan under Obama were intended precisely to
buy the time and space to establish functioning governments. Meanwhile, in Afghanistan, a military surge was to be followed by a 'civilian
surge', aimed at helping to foster economic growth and civil institutions.

But the rediscovery of counter-insurgency and nation-building was by
no means a complete answer to the problems of failed states. It was
simply too costly in lives, money and political energy to be a solution
that could be applied to all the potential candidates. Somalia replicated
some of the more alarming circumstances of Afghanistan before 9/11,
with a strong rebel movement linked to al-Qaeda, and cross-border spill-
over in the form of rampant piracy. Yet, faced with this situation, the
international community chose to hover off the coast of Somalia in a
vast international flotilla aimed at the pirates. Nobody had the stomach
for military intervention on the ground. The same cautious hands-off
approach applied to Yemen, whose role as a new base for al-Qaeda was

highlighted after a failed attempt to blow up a plane over Detroit on Christmas Day 2009.

The problem was all the more alarming because the list of potential failed states seemed only to be growing – particularly in the aftermath of the Great Recession. Some of the nations on the watch-list were big countries of obvious strategic importance. The US Defence Department caused massive offence in Mexico with a leaked assessment that America's southern neighbour was in danger of becoming a failed state.[346] If the implication was that Mexico might turn into Afghanistan or Somalia, that was clearly absurd. And yet, if a failure to control territory and to exert the rule of law is one important mark of a failed state, Mexico clearly fitted the description to some extent. Drug-related violence was rampant across the country in 2008 and 2009, fed, the Mexicans complained, by gun exports from the US and by America's voracious appetite for drugs. The United States felt the backwash from Mexico's drug wars. In 2008 criminal activity linked to the Mexican cartels meant that there were more drug-related kidnappings in Phoenix, Arizona than in the whole of Colombia.[347]

The country whose fate caused most sleepless nights in Washington was Pakistan. In the weeks before his inauguration, Barack Obama told confidants that this was 'the most frightening country in the world'.[348] Unlike its neighbour, Afghanistan, Pakistan has a strong military, civil society and private sector. But for many years the Pakistani government also let terrorist and jihadist groups flourish relatively unmolested in the tribal areas along the border with Afghanistan. That policy only appeared to change when the Pakistani state itself became obviously threatened by jihadist terrorism – with the assassination of Benazir Bhutto, the former president, in December 2007 and repeated terrorist attacks in major cities, such as Lahore and Islamabad.

A visitor to Pakistan is left in no doubt of the country's status as a nuclear-weapons state. Large stone monuments bearing the nuclear symbol stand at the entry to each of the major cities. The thought of such a country entering the ranks of failed states was the ultimate nightmare for Washington and the western world.

Terrorism and nuclear proliferation

In some eyes, the Bush administration's insistence on the dangers of the links between terrorism and weapons of mass destruction – and the subsequent failure to find WMD in Iraq – has permanently discredited the idea that nuclear proliferation and the war on terror should be central concerns of the American government, or the world at large.

The Obama administration, however, does not take the relaxed view – and nor do the senior international civil servants charged with policing the issue. Mohamed ElBaradei, the former head of the International Atomic Energy Agency and a man who clashed repeatedly with the Bush administration, has insisted that nuclear terrorism is 'the most serious danger the world is facing'.[349] President Obama, after a long hesitation, decided to send many more troops to Afghanistan, citing the need to prevent the establishment of terrorist safe-havens as the principal justification. Rather than ending President Bush's war on terror, Obama was, in effect, betting his own presidency on the very same issue.

In his first year in office, Obama also launched a major diplomatic initiative to combat nuclear proliferation – holding out the eventual prospect of a nuclear-free world. Efforts to prevent Iran gaining nuclear weapons were also placed at the very centre of American diplomacy.

In taking these steps Obama sided with the nuclear alarmists – those who argue that the spread of nuclear weapons is one of the biggest threats facing the world. The optimists could make the case that – despite President John F. Kennedy's prediction that there could be up to twenty-five nuclear-weapons states by 1964 – the nuclear club has remained reassuringly small.[350] The Nuclear Non-Proliferation Treaty, although a little tattered, appears to be doing its job.

The pessimists' response is that this is dangerously complacent. North Korea, one of the world's poorest and most isolated states, has manufactured nuclear weapons, so the Treaty is clearly in trouble. If Iran, the leader of a radical anti-western bloc, goes nuclear, then much of the Middle East could follow suit. And if Pakistan collapses, then the nightmare of terrorists with nuclear weapons could indeed come true.

Searching for global solutions

Surveying all these problems, Obama concluded that only unprecedented levels of international co-operation could solve them. He was not alone in his thinking. Across the world, intellectuals grappling with the problems of international politics were coming to similar conclusions. In Singapore, Kishore Mahbubani lamented that 'All 6.5 billion inhabitants of Planet Earth sail on the same boat. Nevertheless we do not have a captain or a crew for the boat as a whole… None of us would sail into an ocean or on a boat without a captain or a crew to sail the boat, but that is exactly how we expect our globe to sail through the twenty-first century.'[351] In the United States, Jeffrey Sachs argued that 'The paradox of a unified global economy and divided global society poses the single greatest threat to the planet'[352] and concluded that planetary survival demanded that 'Global co-operation will have to come to the fore. The very idea of competing nation-states that scramble for markets, power and resources will become passé.'[353] The World Economic Forum responded to the new conventional wisdom by launching a grandiose new Global Redesign Initiative, promoted at the annual forum in Davos in January 2010.[354]

But where were these inspiring new examples of global co-operation to be found? In Washington, Francis Fukuyama came up with a surprising answer. Reflecting on his 'end of history' thesis in 2009, twenty years after the publication of the original article, Fukuyama mused that one respect in which he might have gone wrong was that 'I kind of assumed that American power would be used wisely.' In the aftermath of the Bush administration, that no longer seemed a safe assumption. And the man who twenty years earlier had been seen as the very epitome of American triumphalism argued that 'The End of History was never about Reaganism, you know...the true exemplar of the End of History is the European Union, not the United States, because the European Union is trying to transcend sovereignty and power politics; it's trying to replace that with the global rule of law, and that's what ought to happen at the end of history.'[355] In Brussels, capital of the EU, there were plenty of people who did indeed see the global economic crisis as a unique opportunity to push a distinctively European view of the world.

GLOBAL GOVERNMENT:

The World as Europe

The idea that the European Union might represent the culmination of world history is depressing. Brussels, the capital of the EU, is a comfortable but dull city. The Union is administered from a bunch of uninspiring office blocks, strung along either side of a busy road, the Rue de la Loi. The 'European quarter' of Brussels has no real landmarks or historic sights. When EU leaders wanted to gather somewhere for a minute's silence in the days after 9/11, they ended up convening on a traffic island – the Rond-point Schuman.

Efforts to inspire loyalty to the Union among the nearly five hundred million 'citizens of Europe' generally backfire. When European leaders wrote a constitution that attempted to capture the spirit and powers of the Union in uplifting language and to endow it with an anthem and a flag, things went badly wrong. The proposed constitution was decisively rejected in 2005, after referendums in France and the Netherlands, two of the founder nations of the EU. Unwilling to abandon the project, European leaders simply rewrote the constitution in deliberately obscure and bureaucratic language, and pushed it through national parliaments. The whole exercise was fairly shoddy and embarrassing.[356]

And yet for those who believe that the world will only prosper (or even survive) in the twenty-first century if it can develop new forms of global government, the European Union is genuinely inspirational. For the Union is by far the most advanced example in the world of 'supranational government' – that is, of laws and governing structures whose authority crosses international boundaries and transcends the principle of 'national sovereignty', on which international politics has been based ever since the Peace of Westphalia ended Europe's wars of religion in 1648.

The 'European project' has progressed remarkably since its origins in 1951 as a coal and steel community. By 2008 a European Union of twenty-seven nations had been established, with a queue of aspirant members stretching from Turkey to Iceland. The EU long ago established the vital principle that European law – administered by the European Court of Justice in Luxembourg – has supremacy over the national laws of its member-states. Europe now has a single currency covering seventeen of its members. Border controls have been largely abolished within the EU. The Union negotiates as a bloc in international trade negotiations. And its members are committed to providing loyal support to a common foreign policy. There are some important areas where the Union still largely leaves the individual nations to set their own policies – in particular, direct taxation, health and education. But in other areas it is European law that dominates – in particular, anything touching competition policy, trade within Europe, monetary policy (for euro members) and environmental legislation.

Jean Monnet, the founding father of the EU, believed that European unity was 'not an end in itself, but only a stage on the way to the organized world of tomorrow'.[357] His successors in Brussels make no secret of the fact that they regard the Union's brand of supranational governance as a global model. Some American intellectuals who believe that the world badly needs new forms of international government, such as Strobe Talbott, the head of the Brookings Institution, and Jeffrey

Sachs of Columbia University, also regard the EU as a model and an inspiration.

So could the European model go global? There are moments when it seems that it might. When I attended the G20 summit in Pittsburgh in September 2009, I found the surroundings and the atmosphere strangely familiar. It felt like I was back in Brussels, and this was just a globalized version of an EU summit. It was the same drill and format. The leaders' dinner the night before the summit; a day spent negotiating an impenetrable, jargon-stuffed communiqué; the setting-up of obscure working groups; the national briefing rooms for the post-summit press conferences.

All these procedures are deeply familiar to European leaders – but rather new to the Asian and American leaders whom they are carefully enmeshing in this new structure. As a result European leaders often seemed much more alive to the potential significance of what they were negotiating than their new partners from countries unfamiliar with supranational politics, such as Indonesia or Saudi Arabia.

The fate of the G20 matters a great deal to the future of international politics. It is an international organization that brings together around one table the leaders of all the world's major powers, including the US, China, India, Japan, the European Union, Brazil and Russia. Together, the nations represented at G20 summits represent around 90 per cent of the world's economic output, 80 per cent of trade and two-thirds of the world's population. If the world is to find the 'global solutions to global problems' that President Obama calls for, it will be the leaders represented at G20 summits that have to strike the deal.

The establishment of regular G20 summits was the single most important international political development to emerge directly from the global economic crisis of 2008–9. The organization had come together during the Asian financial crisis a decade earlier, but – until 2008 – it had only been for finance ministers. In response to the near meltdown of the international financial system, President Bush abandoned his instinctive unilateralism and convened the first ever G20 summit for world leaders, which met in the columned splendour of the National Building Museum in Washington on 15 November 2008. Kevin Rudd, the Australian prime minister, captured the grim mood of the moment when he told the assembled leaders that they were facing a financial crisis, which would turn into an economic crisis and then into an unemployment crisis and then into a social crisis, before finally mutating into an international political crisis.[358]

At the first G20 summit, the assembled leaders solemnly promised to forswear all future acts of protectionism and to complete the Doha round of world trade talks. And yet, by the time they met in London the following April, seventeen of the countries involved had passed protectionist legislation of some description – and the Doha round remained uncompleted. Yet it was at the London summit that it became apparent that, for all the backsliding, something important and worthwhile was going on. The assembled leaders managed to patch over a dangerous disagreement over whether governments should respond to the economic crisis with large-scale deficit spending. In response, the world's stock markets appeared to turn a corner.

The appearance of international unity probably mattered as much as anything concrete that the leaders agreed to in London. At a time when many observers were worried that an international economic crisis would lead to international conflict, the leaders of the world's major powers were sending a message that – as Bill Clinton liked to say of globalization – 'We're all in this together.'

By the time the G20 reassembled in Pittsburgh in September 2009, the organization had momentum. It announced that from now on, G20 summits would displace the summits of the old G8, which was a club of western nations, plus Japan and Russia. It had taken a global economic crisis to force the world's leaders to acknowledge the realities of globalization. World leadership no longer resided exclusively in North America, Europe and Japan. If the world was to have any chance of sorting out the problems of globalization, the major emerging powers had to be represented at the top table.

Formally speaking, the shift from the G8 to the G20 represented a dilution of European power. And yet, as I noticed in Pittsburgh, there was something distinctly 'European' about the new organization's aims and methods. European leaders were also seriously over-represented around the conference table. Huge nations such as Brazil, China, India and the US were represented by one leader each. The Europeans managed to secure eight slots for Britain, France, Germany, Italy, Spain, the Netherlands, the president of the European Commission and the president of the European Council. Most of the key international civil servants present were also Europeans: Dominique Strauss-Kahn, head of the International Monetary Fund, Pascal Lamy of the World Trade Organization, and Mario Draghi of the Financial Stability Forum.

At his closing press conference, President Sarkozy was fizzing with excitement at the possibilities the G20 had opened up. 'Banking secrecy, that's all over,' he cackled, lauding a G20 agreement on tax havens. This was a 'historic occasion'; the atmosphere between the G20 leaders was 'superb'. There would be many more achievements to come at future G20 summits.

President Sarkozy sometimes fits the stereotype of the excitable Frenchman. But he is not alone in seeing huge possibilities in the G20. It is true that the organization has started modestly, but then the modern-day European Union also started, quite deliberately, with baby steps. The famous Schuman Declaration of 1950 announced that 'Europe will not be made all at once, or according to a single plan. It will be built through concrete achievements, which first create a de facto solidarity.'[359] Jean Monnet believed that Europe would be built through 'the common management of common problems'[360] – and this is exactly how the G20 is starting as well.

If the G20 develops as its keenest supporters hope, its first major step could be the development of a system of global financial regulation for the financial institutions that crashed so nastily in 2008. Then the G20 would agree on some sort of common approach to 'global economic imbalances', smoothing out excessive trade and current-account deficits and managing the rise and fall of currencies in a more stable manner. The anti-poverty programmes that were trumpeted by the G8 would be adopted by the G20 and made much more effective. And the G20 leaders would finally give some impetus and energy to world trade talks, so saving the open trading system that underpins globalization.

Once they have secured agreement on economics, the G20 leaders could move on to the trickier political issues. Freed from the chaos of UN-sponsored negotiations they would, of course, hammer out a deal on climate change. And they would recognize that all the world's biggest economies – whether democracies or autocracies – are threatened by terrorism, failed states and nuclear proliferation. Building on the group goodwill established by earlier successes, G20 leaders would agree common rules and principles for intervention in failed states – and create new resources for pursuing terrorists and deterring nuclear proliferation. As they develop mutual trust, the G20 leaders would develop the confidence to delegate more powers to institutions such as the International Court of Justice, the International Criminal Court and the International Monetary Fund. Meanwhile, the G20 itself would establish a small secretariat of international civil servants – based somewhere uncontroversial, like Canada – that would develop the ideas that the leaders agree on at their summits and flesh them out into proper proposals. In time, the G20 secretariat would look a bit like a global version of the European Commission – the Brussels bureaucrats who have pushed forward the process of 'ever closer union' in Europe. Of course, nationalists and conspiracy-theorists in the United States, China and elsewhere would scream that a sovereignty-denying world government had been formed. But the leaders of the G20 would brush these concerns aside.

It is certainly conceivable that the G20 might develop in this way. But it is also unlikely. There are at least three major obstacles to the development of some sort of global version of the European Union. They lie in the United States, China and the ranks of nations excluded from the new organization.

The first problem is to do with the G20's uneasy legitimacy. The Pittsburgh summit of September 2009 took place just after the UN General Assembly. It was clear that many of the G20 leaders were pleased to leave the circus of New York, where they could be harangued by the likes of Colonel Gaddafi, and to reconvene in a smaller and more businesslike environment. But the countries that did not make the cut were distinctly disgruntled to find themselves excluded from the G20. Anders Aslund, a leading Swedish economist, raged that 'the G20 has usurped power over global financial governance. It has made decisions that it expects 160 other countries to obey.' Aslund worried that 'the rule of the big powers over the rest is in danger of becoming unjust and reactionary'.[361] The danger that the G20 might be 'reactionary' is sharply increased by the fact that its membership necessarily includes autocratic governments such as Saudi Arabia and China. You cannot have a proper economic discussion without the Chinese and the major oil producers at the table. But the G20 will struggle to tackle the tough international political issues when its core members are divided over basic values.

While Anders Aslund and others worry that the G20 is too small and exclusive, in some respects it is already too big. There are so many states and organizations that are desperate to secure an invitation to the world's top table that there were actually far more than the advertised twenty participants at G20 summits. The Spanish and the Dutch have gatecrashed successfully, as have numerous international organizations, from the Association of South-east Asian Nations to the International Labour Organization. All told, I counted thirty-three participants in Pittsburgh. The larger the meeting, the harder it will be to move beyond formulaic statements. So the G20 – for all its early successes – may be stuck in no-man's land. It is too small to be legitimate and too large to be effective.

Even if G20 leaders do succeed in hammering out agreements on the difficult global issues, their troubles will not be over. In fact, the more far-reaching the deals, the more likely they are to run into political difficulties back home. Unlike the countries of the European Union, the United States and China still think and behave as traditional nation-states that zealously guard their sovereignty.

Many Americans are deeply resistant to the idea that their country can be bound by anything but the United States constitution – and this is an attitude that has deep roots in American history. Congress rejected American membership of the League of Nations after the First World War. Although the US went on to play a crucial role in setting up the major international institutions after 1945, the traditional suspicions of 'world government' are now reasserting themselves – particularly on the conservative right.[362] The US Congress still regularly exercises its right to reject international treaties agreed by the president. The Kyoto treaty on global warming was rejected 95–0 in the US Senate – and Congress might well do the same to any new climate-change treaty agreed by the Obama administration. Congress's earlier refusal to ratify the Comprehensive Nuclear-Test-Ban Treaty posed a serious problem for President Clinton's efforts to make progress on nuclear disarmament. The United States, unlike the countries of the EU, has refused to adhere to the International Criminal Court. All this means that any US president is going to have to be extremely careful about what he or she agrees to – at the G20, the UN or any other international forum. The difficulty of getting the US Senate to ratify new international treaties – the 'League of Nations' syndrome – is a huge obstacle to ambitions for more far-reaching global governance. Voluntary international deals may be all that US politics can stand at the moment. But, by their nature, voluntary deals are impossible to enforce.

China, like the US, is a big country with a long tradition of doing things its own way. As an authoritarian country, under constant pressure over its human rights record, China also has a particular extra reason to be wary of anything that looks like an infringement of the principle of national sovereignty. At the United Nations, the Chinese, along with the Russians, are always suspicious of western efforts to put pressure on countries that are violating their citizens' human rights, whether in Zimbabwe, Sudan, Iran or Sri Lanka. The Chinese do not want to set a precedent or to crimp their freedom to pursue their national interests by striking deals with other authoritarian governments. China's opposition to international action is not absolute and unvarying. The authorities in Beijing did agree to mild, targeted sanctions against Iran over its nuclear programme. And China has become an increasingly important participant in UN peacekeeping missions – unlike the US, which is still unwilling to see its troops placed under the command of a foreign general. But, in most other areas, the Chinese remain very wary of new international treaties and obligations. The Beijing government's refusal to accept binding targets on the emission of greenhouse gases was a major contributory factor to the failure of the Copenhagen climate talks. And China – like the US – has refused to accept the jurisdiction of the International Criminal Court.

China and the United States are the two countries that are most likely to prevent the G20 turning into an effective new instrument of international government. But that opens the way to an alternative. If the G20 cannot do the job, how about a G2 of the United States and China? In some ways, the idea is attractive. Rather than getting bogged down in the paraphernalia of international conferences and multilateral treaties, why not just get the world's two biggest powers to sort things out between them? There are subjects where agreement between the US and China would probably be decisive. Their trading relationship is so important to the balance of the world economy that any US-Chinese agreements on currency management would force global adjustments. If the two countries could reach an agreement on climate change, that would set the stage for a global deal, since together they account for some 40 per cent of greenhouse gas emissions.

And yet there are subjects where even an agreement between America and China would not be enough. There would be no point in striking a new deal on nuclear non-proliferation without the active participation of a major nuclear power like Russia – and the agreement, reluctant or otherwise, of aspiring nuclear powers like Iran. The success of the world trade talks absolutely demands the agreement of India, which has been one of the toughest negotiators in the Doha round.

It is not even clear that either China or the United States would welcome the idea that they should try to solve the world's problems together through an informal G2. In many ways, it still suits China to insist on its status as a 'developing country' with a great many poor people. That makes it easier to avoid the burdens of global leadership when they look too difficult or costly. The Chinese eagerly anticipate the day when they will look the Americans in the eye as equals, but they also know that the US economy and the US military are still much bigger than those of China. This is not yet an equal relationship, so a G2 might not always be comfortable for China. For its own reasons, the US is also very wary of the idea of a Chinese-American G2 trying to run the world. The Americans know that any such talk will antagonize and even destabilize vital American allies such as Japan and the EU. The Obama administration also sees a strategic benefit in trying to include fellow democracies – whether in Europe or Asia – in negotiations with China. Above all, direct Chinese-American negotiations risk hitting deadlock again and again, since the two nations' assessment of their vital national interests are so much at variance. From climate change to global economic imbalances, the two countries are increasingly locked into a zero-sum logic, in which one country's gain is the other's loss.

If the G20 and the G2 cannot do the job of dealing with Mr Obama's alarming list of global problems, the world's major powers will find themselves heading inexorably back to the United Nations. For all its faults, the UN has two vital assets – the legitimacy that comes from having a universal membership and the power to make law. The international legal system, such as it is, dictates that it is UN Security Council resolutions that determine whether a war is legal or illegal – and whether a 'rogue state' should be placed under international sanctions. The UN has unique powers to authorize peacekeeping missions and to pull together the military forces needed to make them work. UN bodies like the World Health Organization do important work, monitoring pandemics and combating disease.[363]

At times, the United States has warmed to the idea of a more powerful UN. When the first President Bush spoke of a 'new world order', he was thinking mainly of the idea that the UN Security Council might finally transcend the divisions of the Cold War and actively tackle global security problems. President Harry Truman, who was present at the creation of the UN, used to carry around a copy of Alfred Tennyson's poem 'Locksley Hall', which waxed lyrical about the vision of a 'Parliament of man, the Federation of the world'.[364] Even Ronald Reagan once endorsed the idea of a standing UN military force, ready to intervene in conflicts around the world – a notion that would get many modern-day Reaganites heading for their local gun store.

Today's reality, however, is that the United States has found the UN a frustrating and sometimes an enraging place to do business. In the face of Russian and Chinese opposition, the US has found it very hard to press for tough action against Sudan and – most important of all – for sanctions that are powerful enough to contain Iran. Even the advent of the Obama administration has not really changed things very much. Meanwhile, many years of clashes with the UN over money and over Israel has eroded the image of the United Nations in the eyes of many Americans.

The trouble is that the UN has a double legitimacy problem. While many Americans regard it as a forum for America-bashing, and are frustrated by its inaction over Iran (and, before that, over Iraq), much of the rest of the world regards the UN as unfairly biased towards the interests of the West. The General Assembly, in which all countries are represented and America-bashing is rife, is relatively powerless. Colonel Muammar Gaddafi of Libya was not alone in comparing it to Speakers' Corner in London, in which everybody is free to speak – but nobody listens. The real power resides with the Security Council – and that still reflects the power balance of 1945. There are only five permanent veto-wielding Council members – the US, Russia, the UK, France and China. Shifts in international power since the end of the Second World War mean that it would now clearly be logical to add India, Japan, Brazil, an Islamic country and, perhaps, Germany to the Council. But all efforts to reform the Council to make it more representative of the realities of the twenty-first century have excited fervent opposition from somebody – and so failed. China blocks Japan and is lukewarm about India. Latin America resists the notion that it should be represented by Brazil. The Islamic world cannot agree on a single candidate. The Germans are opposed by the Italians and the Spanish. The French and the British pretend to be in favour of reform – but are desperate to hang on to their anachronistic privileges.

The result is that the Council remains unreformed and so, increasingly, under attack. The Iranians and Venezuelans regularly bitterly attack its legitimacy– and their protests enjoy more sympathy than America and its allies like to believe. Major emerging powers such as Brazil and India also decry the unfairness of the Security Council system. One senior UN official describes the failure to reform the Council as a 'cancer in the system'.[365] The irony is, however, that adding new members to the Security Council would not necessarily make it work better. In recent years, the Council has often been deadlocked on the most contentious issues brought before it – Iran's nuclear programme, Sudan's war in Darfur, Zimbabwe, Burma. If more countries were given a vote and a veto, the UN might seize up even further.

The most dangerous demonstration of the dysfunctional nature of the UN system was the failure of the UN-sponsored climate talks in Copenhagen at the end of 2009. With almost two hundred countries represented, the talks swiftly degenerated into a mixture of political grandstanding and procedural deadlock. Leaders like Hugo Chavez of Venezuela and Mahmoud Ahmadi-Nejad of Iran used their turns at the rostrum to denounce western capitalism. Small, developing countries dug in their heels on procedural issues and blocked discussion of the substantive issues.[366] In the end, the world's leaders left Copenhagen with a feeble text that was not even legally binding. The obvious conclusion was that the UN was simply incapable of delivering a meaningful climate deal.

All this talk of G20s and G2s, Security Council reform and rows at the General Assembly fascinates diplomats but can seem abstract and dull to everyone else. However, deadlock in the world's most important international organizations has real and dangerous consequences. It means that those 'global problems' identified by President Obama are likely to get worse, rather than better.

The outlook on four of the most important issues – climate change, nuclear weapons, trade and failed states – illustrates the point, and the dangers of international deadlock.

The unpleasant truth about the global negotiations on climate change is that even 'success' – hard as it is to achieve – will probably represent failure. Even if the countries involved in global negotiations manage to strike a deal, setting a global cap on emissions, it is likely to be too weak actually to solve the problem.

Here, the European Union – so often held up as a model by believers in global governance – offers a very discouraging example. For as the economic crisis unleashed in 2008 progressed, so one of Europe's signature projects – the euro – ran into deep trouble. The threat of a sovereign default in Greece, and of debt crises to come in Spain and Italy, raised questions about whether Europe's single currency will even survive. The crisis stoked ill-feeling and recriminations within the countries of the Union, as members like Germany accused the Greeks of lying about their economic statistics and flouting the EU's rules.

The crisis has exposed one of Europe's nasty secrets. The EU's high-sounding commitments are sometimes ignored or thrown overboard in a crisis. The Greeks had lied for years about their economic statistics before the global economic emergency exposed the reality of their situation. Other European rules are simply massaged away or ignored, if they become too inconvenient. Well before the Greek crisis, the EU rules limiting budget deficits had been almost defined out of existence when they became too tough for France and Germany to accept.

But it is Europe's efforts to deal with its dwindling fish stocks that offers the most precise and alarming analogy with the world's climate talks. EU ministers have developed an elaborate system of 'fish quotas' allocated to each member of the Union – and similar, in principle, to carbon-emissions quotas. The trouble is that Europe's fish quotas are – for political reasons – much laxer than the scientific advice demands. They are also very hard to monitor and enforce and are regularly violated and ignored by national fishing fleets. The result is that Europe's fish stocks are nearing collapse and the continent's fishing fleets are busy pillaging off the coasts of Africa and Latin America.

Reaching a global agreement on climate change – which affects the entire world economy – will be much harder than reaching a limited deal on European fishing fleets. But even if the deal is done, it is likely to emulate the European fish problem by being weaker than scientists have recommended and wide open to violation by its signatory states. That in itself will become a source of international tension. There is now a sizeable group of economists and climate scientists who have concluded that the whole notion of a global deal to limit greenhouse gases is fatally flawed – and that it would be much more realistic for nations to reach a looser deal that all the major economies will impose national carbon taxes.[367]

The efforts to strike an international deal to patch up the nuclear non-proliferation regime are also consuming a great deal of time and energy. But, as with global warming, success in striking an international deal and genuine success in tackling the problem is not necessarily the same thing. The fact that North Korea, one of the world's poorest and most isolated states, was apparently able to manufacture nuclear bombs is a graphic illustration of the weakness in the international nuclear regime. The world's failure to rein in the Iranian nuclear programme is also very ominous. Indeed, the Iranian story could well end with the ultimate failure of the international system – war.

Even those bits of the international system that have worked relatively well over the last thirty years are now looking pretty threadbare. The formation of the World Trade Organization in 1995 was a great expression of the 'globalization consensus' that replaced the Cold War. International agreements to open up trade express a belief in a win-win world in which all countries can prosper together. So it is a bad sign that the members of the WTO have repeatedly failed to complete the Doha round of world trade talks. The failure of the WTO talks is by no means an isolated example. The Kyoto treaty on global warming did not achieve its goals. The ambitious targets for the reduction of poverty and disease by 2015, agreed by the 192 nations that endorsed the UN's Millennium Development goals, also seem likely to be missed. As Moisés Naím, former editor of *Foreign Policy* magazine, points out, 'Since the nineties, the need for effective multicountry collaboration has soared, but at the same time multilateral talks have inevitably failed.'[368] The Copenhagen climate summit was just the latest depressing example of a well-established trend.

And then there are the world's war zones and failed states. Here again, hopes that the world will find a more co-operative and effective way of dealing with political violence are dwindling. The number of UN peacekeeping missions has increased markedly over the last decade – but many of the worst situations, such as the wars in Darfur and the Congo, have continued to fester. American hopes that the UN or Nato or a new alliance of democracies would take on some of the burdens of being the world's policeforce have also been largely dashed. The surge of new US troops sent into Afghanistan by President Obama means that the war there is increasingly being run and fought by Americans. There were forty-three nations represented in the Nato force in Afghanistan at the end of 2009, which sounds like an impressive display of international commitment and solidarity. But, after the Obama surge is completed, some two-thirds of the fighting troops will be American, executing a plan conceived and run by American generals.

At the height of the Age of Optimism, liberal internationalists at the UN and elsewhere came up with their own idealistic vision of a 'new world order'. It was of an international political system in which the world's major powers would co-operate to suppress wars and would intervene to prevent mass atrocities – even within states. The notion that an international community has a 'responsibility to protect' abused populations at risk of genocide might strike many people as uncontroversial. But it was, in fact, a major departure from the international norms, based on national sovereignty, that have governed relations between states for centuries. And yet, in a rare moment of unity between rich and poor, democracy and autocracy, the United Nations agreed in 2005 on a new doctrine of an international 'responsibility to protect' abused peoples from genocide, ethnic cleansing, war crimes and crimes against humanity. Controversially, this suggested that international intervention, even military intervention, is justified to prevent mass atrocities of the sort that shocked the world in Rwanda and Bosnia in the nineties.

Once again, however, there proved to be a difference between securing an agreement on paper and achieving real change on the ground. The fact that the world is now theoretically committed to a 'responsibility to protect' (known colloquially as R2P) has not led to any actual interventions.[369] Wars involving large-scale civilian casualties have broken out in Gaza, Sri Lanka, Sudan and Somalia – but the world has proved unwilling or unable to intervene.

During the Age of Optimism, when American power reigned

supreme and the European Union was expanding steadily, it was possible to believe that liberal ideas had developed an unstoppable international momentum. Democracy, free markets and the international rule-of-law would advance on all fronts. But liberal ideas are now on the retreat in international forums. Research by the European Council on Foreign Relations (ECFR) shows a steady 'erosion of support for western positions on human rights' in the UN General Assembly. The authors of an ECFR report in 2008 pointed out that 'In the later 1990s, EU positions on human rights were backed by over 70 per cent of votes cast at the General Assembly. In the last two years, the level of support has fallen to around 50 per cent.'[370] Since European and American positions on human rights issues are usually the same, this represents a general setback for 'the West'.

The European Union believes that its ideas of international co-operation and the global rule of law represent the best model for the twenty-first century. For the moment, however, the rest of the world does not seem to agree. In fact, with China now commanding unprecedented respect and influence on the international stage, the world's liberal democracies are now themselves giving ground to a new axis of authoritarianism.

AXIS OF AUTHORITARIANISM:
The World as Russia and China

B y the end of his time in office, President George W. Bush was extremely unpopular in much of the world. But Georgia, a small, democratic state bordering Russia and the Black Sea, was an exception. Landing in the capital Tbilisi in April 2008, I discovered that the airport road was named in his honour – George W. Bush Avenue.

There was a good reason why Georgia and George W. Bush liked each other so much. When the US president was struggling to rescue his 'freedom agenda' from the morass of Iraq, Afghanistan and the Middle East, events on the fringes of the former Soviet Union had provided him with some hope. Between 2003 and 2005, the 'colour revolutions' in Georgia, Ukraine and Kyrgyzstan overthrew authoritarian or corrupt administrations and installed democratic, pro-western governments in their places. Mikheil 'Misha' Saakashvili, the youthful, multilingual new president of Georgia, was the poster child of the colour revolutions – adored in Washington and loathed in Moscow.

For Saakashvili, the support of the United States was crucial to maintaining the independence that Georgia had won back from Moscow in

1991. Over a lunch on a sunny hotel terrace in Tbilisi that April, he told me, 'The whole history of Georgia is of Georgian kings writing to western kings for help, or for understanding. And sometimes not even getting a response.'[371] Bush, it seemed, was a different sort of western king. A few weeks earlier, the American president had tried and failed to persuade Nato to put Georgia firmly on the path to membership of the western military alliance. 'Bush really fought for us at this Nato summit,' Saakashvili recalled. 'When I went into the room he looked like he was back from the OK Corral – red-faced, very tired, exhausted.'[372]

Despite the setback at Nato, the Georgian president was still in an ebullient mood. After lunch, he invited me to join him on a forty-five-minute helicopter ride to a military base in the middle of the mountains, where he inspected some commandos who had just graduated from a one-year intensive training course run by Israeli advisers. There were salutes, anthems and speeches. The message was that Georgia was a proud member of the club of western democracies.

Four months later, many of those commandos were almost certainly dead. A long period of skirmishing and mutual provocation between Georgia and Russia ended when Russian tanks rolled into Georgia and briefly threatened to go all the way to Tbilisi. The Georgian commandos were on the front line, fighting a much more powerful military force, and took heavy casualties.

The war in Georgia broke out on 8 August 2008 – the very same day that the Olympics were opening with an awe-inspiring ceremony in Beijing. News channels in the West switched from one event to the other. It was strangely reminiscent of another split-screen experience almost twenty years earlier – when the Tiananmen Square massacre in Beijing and the first free Polish elections had taken place on the same day, 4 June 1989.

But the message of the two split-screen days was very different. In 1989 the world was witnessing the crumbling of Russian control of Central Europe and a Chinese regime clinging to power through a

desperate resort to violence. A generation later, the Chinese Communist Party – now very firmly back in control – used the Olympics to
proclaim the power and confidence of a resurgent nation. Russia, which
had refrained from sending troops into Poland in 1989, was once again
using military force to intimidate a neighbour.

The Saakashvili government survived the war of August 2008 – but
Georgia's hopes of joining Nato were put on indefinite hold and the
world was put on notice that a rich, angry Russia was intent on reasserting a 'sphere of influence' in its immediate neighbourhood. The
implications for fragile democracies in Georgia, Ukraine and even the
Baltic states were not encouraging.

The colour revolutions had marked a high-water mark for the global
democratic resurgence that had begun in Western Europe in the mid-
seventies with the fall of authoritarian regimes in Spain, Portugal and
Greece. Shortly after the colour revolutions, the democratic tide had
begun to recede. In early 2009 the authoritative report on *Freedom in the
World* issued by Freedom House, the US think-tank, noted that '2008
marked the third consecutive year in which global freedom suffered a
decline. The setback was most pronounced in sub-Saharan Africa and
the non-Baltic former Soviet Union, although it affected most other
regions of the world.'[373] Jennifer Windsor, the executive director of Freedom House, noted that in the new climate 'Democracy's antagonists are
increasingly assertive and its supporters are in disarray.'[374]

Talking to high government officials in Moscow or Beijing in the
years after the colour revolutions, I could see that new assertiveness on
full display. A few months before visiting Georgia, I had met Dmitry
Peskov, Vladimir Putin's spokesman, in his office in the Kremlin. While
Putin has a habit of unsettling visitors with sharp remarks and mirth-
less smiles, Peskov was a much more welcoming character. He spoke
fluent American-accented English and the jumble on his desk suggested
a man completely at home with the West: a new Apple iPhone, an invitation to the Kremlin film club's showing of *The Graduate*. He also

exhibited a slightly dark sense of humour. The screensaver on his computer was a series of revolving quotations from Orwell's 1984 – 'Big Brother is watching you', 'war is peace', 'freedom is slavery'. It was quite funny until you remembered that Stalin had administered the Soviet gulag from the same building.

Yet for all his affability, Peskov's message was tough and nationalistic. The West had taken advantage of a period of Russian weakness in the nineties by expanding Nato right up to Russia's borders in violation of previous agreements.[375] Russia was richer and more stable now. It was not going to be pushed around any more. On issue after issue – Kosovo, Georgia, missile defence, Iran, the investigation into the murder in London of the Russian dissident Alexander Litvinenko – Russia intended to stand up for itself. Peskov's boss, Vladimir Putin, could be even blunter. In a television address to the nation, he complained that, in the nineties, 'We showed ourselves to be weak, and the weak get beaten.'[376] Buoyed by a high oil price, the Russian economy had boomed during the Putin years. After almost going bankrupt in 1998, Russia had built up the world's third largest foreign reserves by 2008; GDP per head had more than quadrupled over the same period and stood at almost $9,000. Income tax was set at a flat rate of 13 per cent.[377]

The same mixture of pride and defiance, co-operation and confrontation was on display in Beijing. The smoother diplomats from the Chinese foreign ministry liked to talk the language of globalization, peaceful co-existence and mutual dependence. But, sometimes, one got a glimpse of something much harsher. Visiting the Chinese Ministry of Defence with a group of Americans and Europeans in January 2007, we were confronted with an array of braided generals and told bluntly, 'Taiwan independence would mean war.' China would not be intimidated by threats of American intervention.

The new mood of the Russians and Chinese was not just about a more assertive foreign policy. The official elites in Moscow and Beijing were also more confident in their rejection of western liberalism. At best, they seemed to think that western lectures on human rights and political freedom were naïve and arrogant. At worst, the West was deliberately accused of attempting to undermine the stability of Russia and China by sowing chaos. In neither country is there an outright rejection of democracy. Indeed, Peskov insists that Russia is a democratic country, albeit with flaws like other democracies. Hu Jintao, the Chinese president, has said that democracy is the aspiration of all mankind. But nonetheless, in both countries there is an emphasis on the rights of the group rather than the individual, and on the importance of order as a prerequisite for development.

It is perhaps no surprise if the rhetoric of Putin's Russia sounds rather like the kind of thing one hears in Beijing – for the Russians looked to China for lessons in the aftermath of their near economic collapse of 1998. For all the similarities, Russia is simultaneously a freer and a more lawless place than China. The country has multi-party elections, although they are carefully managed – and Russian intellectuals can get away with saying things about their government that would be unacceptable in China. The Russian authorities simply ensure that these modern-day dissidents never get on to prime-time television. Both Russia and China display a marked ambivalence to their totalitarian pasts. There have been moves to rehabilitate Stalin in Russian history textbooks and Mao's portrait still appears on the Chinese currency. But the modern authoritarianism of both countries is still miles away from the state terror of the Soviet and Maoist eras. In normal circumstances, in modern Russia and China, only those people who directly challenge the state need fear repression. Meanwhile, the apolitical middle classes are kept happy with the promise of steadily rising living standards.

The lack of a middle-class push for democracy in Russia and China is a challenge to the prevailing western assumptions of the Age of Optimism. The standard argument was that economic liberalism would inevitably lead to political liberalism. Middle-class people who had got used to freedom and choice in their personal lives would eventually demand freedom and choice in politics as well. As Nicholas Kristof of the *New York Times* once put it, 'No middle class is content with more choices of coffee than of candidates on the ballot.'[378] But, so far, it does not seem to be happening like that. In countries with recent memories of horrors such as the Cultural Revolution and, less traumatically but more recently, the mass job losses and currency collapse of Russia in the nineties, the promise of a government that can keep order and promote prosperity must seem pretty good. The Chinese and Russian middle classes must also know that they are outnumbered by poorer compatriots, who might attack the privileges of the middle classes in a more genuinely democratic system.

Finally – and worryingly for the West – the governments of both Russia and China have found an alternative source of legitimacy to that offered by free elections: nationalism. Opinion polls suggested that the Georgian war of 2008 was very popular among the Russian public. Chinese nationalism is also easily stirred up – either into popular demonstrations, or outbursts of violent, nationalist comments on the internet. Recent displays of patriotic anger were provoked by Chinese resentment at pro-Tibetan demonstrations in the West in 2008 and by the visits of Japanese leaders to Tokyo's Yasukuni shrine dedicated to Japan's war dead. At times, the Chinese leadership has even seemed discomfited by the strength of nationalism among the population at large. But there is little doubt that fostering a sense of national pride and strength has its uses for ruling elites in Moscow and Beijing.

The increasingly confident rejection by Russia and China of western political values is matched by a loss of confidence in the United States about the whole project of exporting democracy – reflecting the harsh lessons learnt in Iraq and Afghanistan. At their most hubristic, Bush administration officials seemed to believe that simply toppling Saddam Hussein and the Taliban would be enough. 'Freedom' was a natural condition that would set in, as soon as American troops toppled the statues of the dictators and were 'greeted with flowers' by a liberated population. The lessons learnt in Central Europe, where democracy had flowered relatively easily after 1989, were transferred unthinkingly to much poorer and more traumatized societies. But the democratic wave began to recede when it crashed against the rocks of some of the most broken countries in the world.

In the wake of the Afghan and Iraqi debacles, western politicians are more inclined to accept strictures from sociologists and political scientists who have long made the point that it is very hard to establish a lasting democracy in a very poor country. As long ago as 1959 Seymour Martin Lipset, a celebrated sociologist, noted that 'the more well-to-do a nation, the greater the chances to sustain democracy'.[379] Contemporary academics have fleshed out this claim. They have calculated that democracies very rarely fail in countries with a GDP per capita of more than $6,000.[380] But democratic governments rarely survive long in countries with a per capita GDP of less than $1,500. The Chinese government has been eager to weigh in on this debate. When the Kenyan elections of late 2007 provoked violent clashes between rival ethnic groups, the *China People's Daily* commented that 'western-style democracy simply isn't suited to African conditions, but rather carries with it the seeds of disaster'.[381]

The idea of a $6,000 threshold before democracy becomes sustainable should, in some ways, be reassuring for those who continue to believe in the inevitable advance of democracy. For all the visible wealth in its major cities, average income in China is still below that level. As the country gets richer it may yet democratize, as western liberals have long hoped and predicted. The trouble is that the $6,000 threshold is just an indicator – not a reliable guide. India has managed to sustain free elections, a lively press and an independent judiciary with a GDP per capita below $1,500. But Russia's GDP per capita had reached over $8,000 by 2008 – and the country has grown significantly more authoritarian in recent years.

In the United States, the democratic evangelism of the Bush years has given way to something much more cautious. The Obama administration made it quite clear that it was determined to 'press the reset button' in relations with Russia – downplaying arguments over Georgia, missile defence, the expansion of Nato and democracy, and searching for areas of agreement. Secretary of State Hillary Clinton struck a similarly cautious note on her first visit to Beijing, deliberately putting political and civil rights to one side.[382]

With the US still reeling from the Great Recession and drained by the wars in Iraq and Afghanistan – and with the Chinese and Russian governments much more confident – it is now possible that the forces of autocracy will go on the offensive across the world in a way that has not been seen for at least thirty years. There is still plenty of mutual suspicion between Russia and China. The Russians fear that China's powerful economy and huge population may ultimately pose a threat to Russian control over sparsely populated, resource-rich Siberia. But the two countries share an approach to the world based on an absolute insistence on the importance of national sovereignty. In 2005 China and Russia staged joint military exercises for the first time since 1969, under the auspices of the Shanghai Co-Operation Organization – a regional body that brings together Russia, China and four Central Asian countries and that is utterly committed to the principle of absolute respect for national sovereignty. Robert Kagan, the American neoconservative intellectual, paints a stark picture of the potential power of a Russian-Chinese axis. As he pointed out in 2008, before the economic crash further darkened the outlook for the West, 'Two of the world's largest nations, with more than a billion and a half people and the second- and third-largest militaries between them, now have governments committed to autocratic rule and may be able to sustain themselves in power for the foreseeable future.'[383]

An axis of authoritarianism now also has powerful outposts in the rest of the world. Iran has become the focus for resistance to a US-led world order in the Middle East. Venezuela plays the same role in Latin

America. Both countries hold elections, but are fundamentally authoritarian. The façade of Iranian democracy suffered irreparable damage with the rigged elections of June 2008 and the subsequent repression of popular protest. The Venezuelan government of Hugo Chavez has won several elections. But it has also been increasingly brazen in its harassment of opposition, taking control of the courts, the armed forces and all independent regulatory agencies, as well as launching criminal investigations of opposition politicians and clamping down on opposition in the media.

Nonetheless, both Iran and Venezuela could protest with some justice that there are other more authoritarian regimes in the world that do not attract nearly as much western criticism. (Saudi Arabia is an obvious example.) For the international order, however, the significance of Iran and Venezuela is their willingness to become a focal point for regional opposition to the United States and to the liberal world-view associated with the advance of globalization.

The Iranian government has become a sponsor of radical Islamist militias, such as Hezbollah in Lebanon and Hamas in Palestine. Its influence is palpable in Iraq and is feared across the rest of the Gulf region and the Middle East. Iran's efforts to press ahead with its nuclear programme, in the face of threats from America and its allies, has also become a symbol of resistance to the US-led global order.

After the wave of democratization and free-market reform that took hold in Latin America in the eighties, recent years have seen a revival of leftist, anti-American sentiments across the continent, with Hugo Chavez's Venezuela at the core of the ideological movement. There is a group of countries that Moisés Naím, a former Venezuelan minister, has called 'the Axis of Hugo'. The core of that axis is formed by Venezuela, Bolivia, Ecuador and Nicaragua. Chavez's relative youth, his flamboyant anti-American rhetoric and his oil money have all enabled him to displace Fidel Castro's Cuba as the international face of Latin American radicalism.

Chavez's mishandling of the Venezuelan economy and a fall in the oil price have threatened the stability of his country and government. But, for all its internal frailties, the 'Axis of Hugo' has developed international as well as regional significance. At the Copenhagen climate summit, the most vociferous denunciations of the deal that the Danish hosts attempted to broker came from Latin American radicals, who claimed that it institutionalized an unjust global order. In the end, they may have borne the greatest responsibility for the talks' ultimate failure. As the *Financial Times* reported, 'Four countries – Venezuela, Bolivia, Cuba and Nicaragua – were implacably opposed to the accord, meaning that it could not be formally adopted as a decision of the UN meeting.'[384]

Chavez has repeatedly demonstrated that he has international ambitions that extend well beyond his own nation. He has been vociferous and threatening in his denunciation of Colombian military ties with the United States. Venezuela has also established an important place in an informal global axis of authoritarians. Iran and Venezuela have signed some three hundred co-operation agreements covering everything from energy to agriculture, manufacturing and mining. In November 2009 President Ahmadi-Nejad of Iran capped off a Latin American tour with his fourth visit to Venezuela, where he was warmly embraced (literally) by President Chavez, who praised the Iranian leader as a 'gladiator of the anti-imperial struggle'. In the US, some Venezuela-watchers are worried that Chavez will help the Iranians evade UN sanctions – and that there might even be nuclear co-operation between the two nations.[385]

Worried by the idea of growing co-operation between the world's authoritarian powers, some American voices have called for much deeper and more formal ties between the world's democracies. John McCain, the Republican presidential candidate in 2008, called for the formation of a global alliance of democracies, reflecting the thinking of Robert Kagan, one of his main foreign-policy advisers. Kagan, for his part, has written that 'In a world increasingly divided along democratic and autocratic lines, the world's democrats will have to stick together.'[386]

He proposed the formation of a 'global concert or league of democracies'[387] that, if necessary, could circumvent a blocked and divided United Nations to provide an alternative source of legitimacy for international interventions.

There were sympathizers to the notion of some sort of 'concert of democracies' in the ranks of the advisers of Barack Obama.[388] But, in the end, the Obama administration steered clear of the idea. In large part, this was because the notion of a 'concert of democracies' sounded like an invitation to a new Cold War – and ran counter to the new president's emphasis on the need for 'engagement' with governments such as Iran and China.

But there was also a wider problem. If the Obama administration inspected the list of global political problems that defined its foreign-policy agenda, it became apparent that they demanded genuinely global co-operation. But very few of the political or economic issues pitted democracies against non-democracies in a straightforward manner.

On climate change, democratic India and authoritarian China had formed an informal alliance as the world's two biggest developing nations in order to resist binding restrictions on their emissions of greenhouse gases and to insist on the primary responsibility of the rich nations of the West. When President Obama attempted to stage a last-minute meeting at the Copenhagen summit with the Indians, he was told that the Indian prime minister had already flown home – only to discover that Manmohan Singh was, in fact, quietly meeting China's prime minister, Wen Jiabao.[389]

On nuclear proliferation, the need for binding UN sanctions on Iran meant that the US government felt that it was crucial to cultivate co-operation with the Russians and the Chinese. When it comes to energy security, there is no getting around the fact that America's biggest suppliers of oil are authoritarian states, including Venezuela. Global economic imbalances could not be tackled co-operatively without close co-ordination with China. One of the biggest divisions on economic management was between countries that were amassing large current-account surpluses and others that were running big deficits – but this too did not divide the world neatly into democracies and autocracies. After China, the two most significant members of the 'axis of surplus' were Japan and Germany. When it comes to the war on terror, Russia and China are, if anything, even more insistent on the need to be ruthless with Islamist militancy – and will tolerate methods that make the US feel distinctly squeamish. As for stabilizing Afghanistan and Iraq, the tacit co-operation of neighbouring Iran will ultimately be crucial.

Dividing the world into autocracies and democracies was, therefore, not a helpful way of finding the 'global solutions to global problems' that President Obama insisted he was after. And there was a further problem. In the aftermath of the Great Recession, a sense of American weakness and renewed Chinese strength meant that even countries that America would hope to regard as reliable, democratic allies began to sound distressingly neutral in their attitudes to arguments between the United States and the axis of authoritarianism.

President Lula of Brazil cut a lucrative oil deal with China in 2009, congratulated President Ahamdi-Nejad of Iran on his electoral 'victory' of June of that year, warmly welcomed him to Brazil a few months later and then opposed UN sanctions on Iran in June, 2010. Lula also positioned himself as a neutral arbiter between the US and Chavez's Venezuela – indeed, at times, he has seemed to endorse Chavez's rule.[390]

Post-apartheid South Africa has proved even more of a disappointment to liberal opinion in the West. When the South Africans gained a non-permanent seat on the UN Security Council in 2006, they frequently blocked western-backed resolutions on human rights:[391] Zimbabwe, Iran, Uzbekistan – they all enjoyed South African protection at the UN. Questioned about their foreign policy, South African officials argued that western strictures on human rights were hypocritical when the world order was so heavily weighted towards the west.

Turkey is another example of a large, democratic nation in a strategically crucial part of the world that is taking an increasingly distant attitude towards the US and the European Union. During the Cold War, Turkey was a vital member of the western alliance. And when President Bush declared a global war on terror, Turkey was once again seen as a crucial player – this time as a model of a secular, democratic, Muslim country. However, Turkey's refusal to co-operate with the invasion of Iraq in 2003 signalled that the country was not as loyal an ally as the US had hoped. Ever since the Iraq War, opinion polls in Turkey have regularly demonstrated very high levels of anti-American sentiment. Frustrated by the slow progress of the country's ambitions to join the European Union, Turkey's mildly Islamist AKP party seems increasingly to be reorienting the country's foreign policy towards the Middle East and Asia and away from the West.

This discouraging pattern for the US and the West was already well established by the end of the Bush years. Many Americans hoped that the election of Barack Obama would help win back some of its old friends. But while hostility to the United States, as measured by opinion polls, diminished sharply around the world in the wake of his election, there was not much evidence of a rallying of developing-world democracies towards more pro-American positions on the big global issues. In Latin America, the Middle East and Africa, crucial strategic players such as Brazil, Turkey and South Africa continued to follow a policy of equidistance between the West and the world's authoritarian powers.

Why is this happening? The broad answer seems to be that the Brazilian, South African and Turkish identities as democracies are balanced – or even trumped – by their identities as developing nations that are not part of the white, Christian world. All three countries have ruling parties that see themselves as champions of social justice at home, and a more equitable global order overseas. Or – to put it another way – the United States may not have fully realized how much resentment there is in the developing world at American dominance of the global order. Now that that dominance is under challenge by China, a country that still styles itself as part of the developing world, there are other rising nations that are just as likely to identify with China as with the US. At the UN climate talks, China carefully positioned itself as the head of the G77, the biggest UN grouping of developing nations.

All of this matters because, even if the authoritarian powers do not always co-ordinate their actions and sometimes disagree, they share a distinctive approach to the world that contrasts sharply with the liberal attitudes that were advancing steadily during the Age of Optimism. Perhaps the two most important characteristics shared by this informal axis of authoritarians are an innate suspicion of American power and an insistence on the importance of national sovereignty in the conduct of international affairs. So the attitude of large democracies in the developing world like Brazil, Turkey and South Africa matter a lot. In votes at the UN and international diplomacy in general, these are the swing states. If they choose to side with the authoritarians, the authoritarian world-view gains ground.

A world in which the authoritarian powers wield considerably more influence looks very different from the years 1991–2008, when the world order was informally based on two central facts – American power and globalization. A more authoritarian world order will make it much harder for the US and its allies to intervene overseas – either to slap down perceived enemies, such as Iran, or to combat mass atrocities in places like Kosovo or Sudan. On the contrary, there would probably be a deliberate push-back against American influence around the world – in particular, US military influence in East Asia, the Gulf and Latin America. Countries such as Colombia in Latin America and Bahrain in the Gulf – which play host to the US military – will be encouraged to think twice.

There is also likely to be an attempt to take on the symbols of American economic power. Iran and Venezuela have often talked of changing the way in which oil is priced, so that it is no longer automatically quoted in dollars. This would be an important symbolic move, although its practical effect is questionable. China has also spoken with increasing urgency of the need to find an alternative global reserve currency to the dollar. Any such move is likely to be the work of many years. But China's growing importance as a market, customer and source of cash is already increasing its global influence. The Beijing government's willingness to extend aid to African nations without imposing the political conditions that western nations liked to insist on has made China a favoured partner for a range of African governments from Zimbabwe to Sudan and Angola. The largest Sovereign Wealth Funds, which mobilize the capital of nations for overseas investment, are almost all controlled by undemocratic countries – the sole exception is the Norwegian fund. As a result, an America that is already struggling with the military and financial burdens of global leadership will find itself increasingly checked in global politics, in ways that have become unfamiliar over the past generation.

This informal axis of authoritarians, however, is not yet in a position to mount a coherent or co-ordinated challenge to the American-led global order of the Age of Optimism. In particular, there is a crucial distinction between the strength of China and the relative weakness of other members of a putative axis of authoritarianism. China is now the world's second largest economy and it has built its wealth on the back of a broad-based manufacturing revolution. There are legitimate questions about the political and economic stability of China that will be discussed in the final chapter of this book. But the other leading members of the axis – Russia, Iran and Venezuela – are much more obviously fragile. The Iranian theocracy has been tottering in the face of public protests, triggered by the rigged re-election of President Ahmadi-Nejad in June 2009. All three are petro-economies that are very vulnerable to a collapse in the price of oil. Russia also has severe problems with public health and fertility that mean that its population is currently shrinking at an alarming rate – by about seven hundred thousand a year.

The authoritarian powers cannot ultimately provide a complete alternative to the American-dominated order of the Age of Optimism for two main reasons. First, an inability to project power globally; second, the lack of a convincing alternative vision of how the world should be run.

In different ways, all of the four major authoritarian powers rely on international trade and so are committed to globalization. When it comes to international politics, the authoritarians will continue to push back against anything that looks like a threatening infringement on national sovereignty – such as western military interventions, even on humanitarian grounds; or efforts to impose sanctions on countries that abuse their own populations, such as Sudan and Zimbabwe. But the authoritarians' attitudes to the big global political problems, such as failed states, climate change or nuclear proliferation, are essentially based on opposition to America 'throwing its weight around'. There is no alternative Chinese-Russian view of how to deal with these problems – other than to insist on the importance of national sovereignty and to suggest that America is making too much of a fuss or has dangerous, ulterior motives.

In the Age of Optimism, the United States was often able to press ahead with its own view of what should be done – even if the Russians, the Chinese, the Iranians and the Venezuelans objected. This was the case in Kosovo and Iraq. But in the Age of Anxiety, there are likely to be many more financial and political constraints on American activism around the globe. The world's policeman will not go home. But he is likely to spend a lot more time inside the police station, doing his paper-work – and rather less time out on patrol.

A less activist US would have important implications for international order. During the Age of Optimism, the world order was defined by American power and globalization. The bipolar world of the Cold War was replaced by a single world system, ordered around the spread of international capitalism and American might. The world's zones of prosperity and order seemed to be expanding and the zones of anarchy seemed to be shrinking.

Economic changes that began to reverse globalization would weaken one of the pillars of the global order. An American pull-back in response to economic weakness and challenges from authoritarian powers would undermine the other.

The American military remains the only force with a global reach. If America becomes much warier of foreign entanglements in the wake of Iraq, Afghanistan and the Great Recession, there is no co-ordinated global force prepared to move into the vacuum. Each of the authoritarian powers is likely to become more assertive in its backyard. China will continue its military build-up and might increase the pressure on Taiwan. Venezuela will continue to use its oil money to build the 'Axis of Hugo' and might clash with Colombia. Iran will continue its pursuit of nuclear weapons and its sponsorship of regional surrogates. Russia might take another whack at Georgia. This is not a pretty picture. But it is also not a co-ordinated challenge to the US-led global order of the last twenty years. It is more like a spreading rot, eating away at the structure of world order. The result will be a less prosperous, less predictable and more violent world – a fractured world.

22

Fractured World:
The World as Pakistan

To visit Peshawar in 2007 was to see a city poised between the globalized world and anarchy. Its shops stocked the big international brands, there were internet cafés and satellite dishes. It had smart, westernized hotels with business centres and twenty-four-hour cafés. But the hotel manager at the Pearl Continental was in a state of near despair. After a spate of suicide bombings, very few guests were passing through the city.[392]

The few women on the street shuffled along in all-encompassing veils and the American consulate was an armed fortress surrounded by barbed wire, checkpoints and blast walls.

Peshawar is just three hours' drive from the Pakistani capital, Islamabad, but it borders the lawless tribal areas along the frontier with Afghanistan. My travelling companion in the city, Phillip Gordon of the Brookings Institution,[393] had agreed to give a talk on American foreign policy at the University of Peshawar – a bold decision given that the city is sometimes referred to as 'the birthplace of al-Qaeda'.[394] While Phil took to the rostrum, I positioned myself carefully at the back of the room, as near as possible to the door, and listened. The mood of the students was angry and fearful. The speaker was harangued about the iniquities and inconsistencies of American policy, yet there were female students in the audience who had chosen not to wear the hijab and young men who had not grown the full beards that were a mark of Islamist devotion. These students were critical of the West, but terrified of the Taliban. 'I am from Peshawar,' said one young man, 'but I am a secular person, and soon it may no longer be safe for me to live here.'

By the time I returned to Pakistan, eighteen months later, I was strongly advised against returning to Peshawar, which was now being hit by several bombings a month. During 2008, while Barack Obama closed in on the American presidency, the forces of violent Islamism had gained ground in both Pakistan and Afghanistan. Benazir Bhutto, Pakistan's most charismatic politician, was assassinated and the Marriott, Islamabad's leading hotel was destroyed by terrorists. By 2009 the Swat Valley, a tourist area just two hours from the capital, had fallen under the control of the Pakistani Taliban – it was only won back after a long and bloody assault by the Pakistani army. Shortly before he took office, Obama received a four-hour intelligence briefing devoted entirely to Pakistan. He emerged shaken and convinced that Pakistan was the most dangerous international problem facing the United States.[395]

It was worries about the stability of Pakistan – a nuclear-armed nation of 180 million people – as much as concerns about Afghanistan itself that persuaded Obama to send over fifty thousand more American troops to fight the Taliban in Afghanistan.[396] And yet even as he announced the second and largest part of the American surge, in a speech at West Point in December 2009, Obama signalled that there were limits to the costs that the United States could be expected to bear. He explained that 'In the wake of an economic crisis too many of our friends and neighbours are out of work and struggle to pay the bills, and too many Americans are worried about the future facing our children. Meanwhile, competition within the global economy has grown more fierce. So we simply cannot afford to ignore the price of these wars...

Our prosperity provides a foundation for our power. It pays for our military... That is why our troop commitment in Afghanistan cannot be open-ended.'[397]

Visiting some of the newly arrived American forces in Afghanistan in early 2009, I certainly did not get the sense of a war being fought on the cheap. The US military was startlingly better equipped than its Nato allies. While the British fretted about a lack of helicopters, the Americans had no shortage of air power. Colonel David Haight from the 10th Mountain Division, whose troops had just installed themselves in Logar province about forty miles south of Kabul, told me that all the Afghans wanted an American-run 'Provincial Reconstruction Team' (PRT) because the US had so much more money to spend than the Europeans. 'Getting a US-run PRT is like winning the lottery,' he joked. And yet this impression of boundless American resources was an illusion. With the US running a massive budget deficit, the war in Afghanistan was being paid for with a Chinese credit card. In 2008 China bought roughly $300 billion of US Treasury bills, while the annual Pentagon budget was a little over $600 billion.

Obama's reference to limited resources was an acknowledgement of the growing financial constraint on American global power. A cautious estimate is that by 2011 the US will have spent $2 trillion on the Afghan and Iraq wars.[398] But Obama's decision to soldier on in Afghanistan was also a reflection of the importance of the struggle to American security. For one of the consequences of globalization is that there is nowhere that is so far away that the rich world can afford to forget about it.

In many ways, Afghanistan is about as remote as it gets in the modern world. Colonel Haight in Logar province found himself nostalgic for the modernity and sophistication of his previous posting – Iraq. He talked wistfully about Baghdad's high levels of literacy and skilled labour. Some 80 per cent of the population in Logar was illiterate; there were no reliable supplies of electricity; no paved roads apart from the ones the Americans had built themselves. 'It's biblical out there,' said the colonel, gesturing towards the dusty countryside. And yet even Afghanistan is plugged into the modern world. As the West discovered after 9/11, young men could travel easily between terrorist training camps in Afghanistan and Pakistan and the major cities of the West. Flying into Afghanistan in 2009, I was struck that there were four scheduled flights a day between Dubai and Kabul, as well as several other daily flights to Baghdad and Peshawar.

Obama's decision to expand the war in Afghanistan may yet succeed in stabilizing the country. And yet the prospect for the next decade is that, globally, the zone of international anarchy and danger referred to collectively as 'failed states' is still likely to expand.

There are two main reasons for this. The first is that – after Iraq and Afghanistan and with government spending out of control – America's appetite for further bloody and expensive foreign military engagements will be severely diminished. It is true that US military intervention overseas has sometimes helped to cause state failure rather than remedy it – Cambodia in the seventies is an obvious example, and Iraq may yet repeat this sorry pattern. And yet some of the most rigorous studies of failed states have concluded that foreign military interventions are often critical to turning the situation around. Paul Collier is a bearded, left-wing Oxford professor – not a neoconservative – but he has concluded that in saving failed states, 'military intervention, properly constrained, has an essential role, providing both the security and the accountability of government to citizens that are essential to development'.[399]

America has unrivalled military resources, and yet the country is clearly wary of further entanglements overseas. Opinion polls released in the same week that Obama announced the surge into Afghanistan showed isolationist sentiment in the United States at its highest level for almost half a century. A Pew survey found that the number of Americans agreeing with the proposition that the 'US should mind its own business and let others get along with their own' had risen to 49 per cent, up from 30 per cent in 2002, and the highest level of support recorded since the question was first asked in 1964.[400]

There is no ready replacement for the United States as a global policeman. The European Union lacks the resources and the will. The Russians and the Chinese will react fiercely to security threats within their borders and flex their muscles in their immediate neighbourhoods – but they have no stomach for military policing missions overseas. It is possible that an expanded UN peacekeeping role can fill some of the gap, as it did in the nineties. But with the UN Security Council often deadlocked and with most contributing nations increasingly aware of the costs of deployment, it is unlikely that the UN will be able to keep pace with the demand for military interventions. And some jobs are just beyond the UN. By 2009 the Democratic Republic of Congo was the location for the largest ever UN peacekeeping operation – but the country continues to slide backwards. The peacekeeping deficit means that, over the next decade, more parts of the world are likely to join the list of failed states and fall into disrepair and despair.

A second reason why the number of failed states is likely to rise is that the rapid global economic growth that preceded the crash of 2008 is unlikely to resume for some years. The prospect that globalization would offer jobs and opportunity to some of the poorest people in the world was the best hope of combating the root causes of state failure. There is a close connection between poverty and war in failed states. Basically, the poorer a country is, the more likely it is to degenerate into civil war.

Perhaps the most dispiriting aspect of the struggle to turn around Afghanistan is that 'success' would entail making the country look and feel more like neighbouring Pakistan: richer, with a stronger central government, an army that could fight without foreign help and a functioning civil society and private sector. And yet, by most standards, Pakistan is in a pretty desperate and dangerous state. The government is nearing bankruptcy; there are power cuts across the country that can last up to eight hours a day; all of the biggest cities have been subject to major terrorist attacks; and the rural, tribal areas remain largely beyond the control of the central government and are the main global haven for al-Qaeda.

The danger for the world in the wake of the Great Recession is that more of the world will begin to look like Pakistan. Listing potential failed states has become almost an academic cottage industry. The Brookings Institution produces it own index of weak states, which runs to 141 countries.[401]

Predicting exactly where lightning is likely to strike is an imprecise science. Some countries that appear hopelessly malfunctioning can stumble on for decades, more or less under control – Bangladesh perhaps falls into this category. Others that have been held up as beacons of successful development, such as Kenya and Ivory Coast, can deteriorate suddenly and alarmingly. 'State failure' is, in any case, a very sweeping term that can cover many very different problems.

But to understand the potential dangers, it is worth looking at three countries in closer detail: Somalia, Mexico and Egypt. Their situations are not the same – the Mexicans would be rightly outraged at a direct comparison between their nation and Somalia. (Mexico comes in at 123 on the Brookings list of weak states, while Somalia tops the rankings, followed by Afghanistan.) However, in their different ways, each country is threatened by political or social turmoil that threatens the control of central government in ways that endanger the international system.

Foreign troops have got sucked into Somalia on several occasions in recent years. The Americans withdrew after a bloody engagement in the early Clinton years. More recently, Ethiopia invaded with American encouragement in 2006 – and then retreated. The country is in a state of near anarchy, with much of it under the sway of an Islamist militia linked to al-Qaeda and with pirate fleets disrupting the vital waterways of the Gulf of Aden that link the Middle East to Asia. The anarchy of Somalia threatens to infect the stability of neighbouring, pro-western nations such as Kenya and Ethiopia. Somalis have also moved across the world as refugees. Some 0.5 per cent of the population of London is now said to be of Somali origin – and several of the suspects in a failed terrorist attack in the British capital in 2005 were Somali. And yet still the West hangs back. The United States occasionally fires missiles at Islamist militants from a safe distance, and has even sent special forces into Somalia to hunt down and kill particular people.[402] But strikes like these have little chance of stabilizing the country. And there is no western stomach for involvement in yet another bloody and inconclusive war in one of the wildest and poorest parts of the world.

The worries about Egypt and North Africa are more about the future than the present. Egypt is regarded as a close ally of the US and a force for moderation in the Middle East, so its autocratic government is not only tolerated, but heavily funded by America. But what happens when President Mubarak, now well into his eighties, goes, for there are clearly political and social pressures that make the country a pressure cooker? The population is growing rapidly and youth unemployment and inflation are high. Political Islam in the shape of the Muslim Brotherhood is gaining strength, despite repression by the state. It is not hard to imagine that, after Mubarak, Egypt's autocracy will be swept away by an Islamist-influenced revolution.[403] The pressures visible in Egypt are replicated across North Africa: elderly authoritarian leaders, young and growing populations, economies that are not growing fast enough to provide hope and opportunity. Meanwhile, sitting across the Mediterranean, an ageing, wealthy, largely Christian European Union needs migrant labour – but fears and resents the social impact of Muslim immigration from across the sea.

Mexico risks turning into North America's version of North Africa. The country is a democracy, has a functioning market economy and no ideological equivalent of Islamist radicalism. But the Mexican economy is failing to provide enough jobs for its people, fuelling mass emigration to the US.

Mexico has also become sucked into a violent drugs war that has

worrying security implications for its northern neighbour. In 2008 a
Pentagon study upset the Mexicans by pairing the country with Pakistan
as a state at risk of a 'rapid and sudden collapse'. Michael Hayden, President George W. Bush's departing CIA chief, claimed that Mexico could
become 'more problematic than Iraq'.[404] This may sound like hyperbole.
But, in fact, the level of civilian deaths in Mexico was actually higher
than in either Iraq or Afghanistan in 2009. Some two and a half thousand civilians were killed in the fighting in Afghanistan in that year,
whereas more than six and a half thousand Mexicans died in the country's drugs war. There were over fifteen thousand drug-related killings
in the three years after President Felipe Calderón took office in December 2006 – and Mexican drugs gangs now operate in all of the major
American cities.[405]

The raw numbers suggest that Mexico fully deserves to be put into
the basket of failed states alongside Afghanistan. But, in fact, if you visit
the two countries within months of each other – as I did in 2009–10 –
it becomes obvious how misleading statistics can be. Afghanistan is
one of the poorest countries in the world and the security situation is so
terrible in Kabul that most westerners barely venture out on the
streets alone. Mexico City is a vast, bustling and fairly wealthy city –
full of foreigners who move around it freely, at least during the daytime.
The level of violence in Mexico is dreadful, but most of the killings
are between drugs gangs, and random acts of terrorism are almost
unknown.

So does it make sense to describe the country as a potential failed
state? Unfortunately, it does, in ways that underline the dangers Mexico
poses to the US. The reason President Calderón unleashed his 'war on
drugs' is that he realized that parts of his nation are out of the control
of government and are, instead, effectively controlled by organized criminal gangs. As a result, Mexico faces a deeply unpleasant choice. It can
continue to take the fight to the drugs gangs and risk years of violent
anarchy. Or it can reach a tacit accommodation with the cartels that

would have huge implications for the Mexican state – and for the rest of the world. Mexican gangs are now so rich and powerful that they have the money to subvert governments as far away as West Africa.[406]

The fact that this dangerous situation has gripped Mexico is an example of the disappointment of some of the high hopes that were once invested in globalization. The conclusion of Nafta in 1994 was one of the signature acts of the Age of Optimism, linking the economies and fates of Mexico, the US and Canada – countries that were at very different stages of development. In some ways, Mexico has made progress since then. It has joined the Organization of Economic Co-operation and Development, a rich-country club, and is a member of the G20. There has been a manufacturing boom along the Mexican frontier with the US. And yet, until the recession struck, some half a million Mexicans a year were crossing into America in search of work. The political effects of the opening up of Mexico are also ambiguous. The coming of democracy to the country during the Age of Optimism boosted the legitimacy of the government. But, by disrupting the old top-down one-party state, it may also have weakened the central government's ability to control Mexican territory. The drugs gangs have expanded into the vacuum.

The threat is not that the state of Mexico will collapse. The Central Bank is not about to be stormed by Kalashnikov-wielding drugs gangs. But where Mexico does resemble truly failed states is that there are parts of the country where the law does not reach – or can be beaten back by organized violence. In a fractured world, such areas of lawlessness and zones of anarchy are likely to increase, providing more areas in which terrorists and organized criminals can operate.

If the rich world is unable to control the threats emanating from failed states by intervention overseas, the pressure will grow to do it another way – by closing borders and cracking down on immigration. This trend is already visible in both the United States and the European Union. Enlargement was the great achievement of the European Union in the decade after 1995. But high unemployment and a fear of Muslim immigration has largely persuaded Europe to call a halt. The prospects of Turkey fulfilling its longstanding ambition to join the EU seem to be receding year by year, as European politicians shrink from the implications of adding a Muslim nation of some seventy million people to their Union.

Anger about illegal immigration continues to rise in the US, which is thought currently to play host to over twelve million illegals. That anger is reflected in the popularity of the anti-migrant campaigns of Lou Dobbs, the former television host, and in books such as Pat Buchanan's *State of Emergency: The Third World Invasion and Conquest of America*. More practically, fear of illegal migration has led to efforts to build a huge, new fence along the frontier with Mexico.

This European and American retreat from engagement with poorer neighbours reflects a more general retreat from the ideas that ordered the world during the Age of Optimism. After a long period in which all of the world's major powers have felt that they benefited from the international system, competition and rivalry is returning to international politics.

ZERO-SUM WORLD

Throughout the Age of Optimism, it looked like the world was going America's way. The Soviet Union collapsed. The Japanese challenge faded away. China embraced capitalism. India opened up to trade and investment. Democracy and free markets spread across the globe. American technology remade the world. The United States enjoyed a long economic boom. The post-Cold War world was, in the words of Tom Friedman, the *New York Times*'s chronicler of globalization, 'a great era in which to be an American'.[407]

The spread of American ideas was so powerful that for many people the notions of 'Americanization' and 'globalization' somehow fused. American brands like McDonald's, Apple, Microsoft and Nike became the symbols of global capitalism. Starbucks even opened an outlet inside the Forbidden City in Beijing, although it was eventually closed after a nationalist backlash in China.

Even those American commentators who realized that rapid economic growth in Asia must mean a relative shift in power away from the US tended to argue that the spread of western ideas would more than compensate. Fareed Zakaria, in his influential book *The Post-American*

World, reassured his audience that 'The power shift…is good for America, if approached properly. The world is going America's way. Countries are becoming more open, market-friendly and democratic.'[408] But in the aftermath of the Great Recession, the post-American world looks a less reassuring place. A shrinking economy and a rising China have changed the way that America thinks about the world.

In these new circumstances, it is much harder for Americans to believe that globalization is leading to a win-win world. And it is not just American attitudes to globalization that are changing. The European Union – subject to many of the same economic pressures – is also turning inwards. The enlargement of the EU, which was the signature European project of the Age of Optimism, has stalled. European leaders talk increasingly of their desire to 'protect' their populations from the harsh challenges of the outside world.[409]

More protectionist and defensive attitudes in the West will, in turn, spark a counter-reaction in Asia and much of the developing world. Emerging powers such as China, India, Brazil and South Africa will be confirmed in their suspicions that the US and Europe are not ready to accept the rise of non-western powers. That, in turn, will create new international tensions and rivalries.

Over the coming decade, there will be three main sources of zero-sum thinking in the international system. The first is slower economic growth. The second is growing rivalry between the United States and rising powers – in particular, China. The third will be the clash of national interests, as the world looks for solutions to the big global problems: climate change, global economic imbalances, nuclear proliferation, resource shortages and failed states.

The economic pressures created by the Great Recession will play out in several ways. There is a rising pressure for protectionism, particularly in the US and Europe. There is a risk of a radicalization and polarization of domestic politics across the world that could lead to the rise of nationalist and xenophobic forces. Finally, there is a growing fear that the Great Recession is more than a serious cyclical downturn. If the environmental movement is even half right, the world may need to rethink its attitude to economic growth. A shortage of natural resources, global warming and a rising population would all stoke competition between nations.

The most gloomy environmentalists argue that, over the long run, global warming will cause droughts, famines and wars, as mankind struggles over shrinking supplies of food and habitable land.[410] An alternative to this Hobbesian vision of 'war of all against all' is that mankind might actually succeed in reining in carbon emissions. But this could just be an alternative route to the same end – an international struggle for a fixed or diminishing 'pie' of economic wellbeing. My colleague at the *Financial Times*, Martin Wolf, has written eloquently on this last point and the dangers of a 'zero-sum world economy'. Wolf argues that 'the biggest point about debates on climate change and energy supply is that they bring back the question of limits... For if there are limits to emissions, there may also be limits to growth. But if there are limits to growth, the political underpinnings of our world fall apart. Intense distributional conflicts must then re-emerge – indeed, they are already emerging – within and among countries.'[411]

Since politicians everywhere tend to prioritize short-term political survival over long-term planetary survival, it seems unlikely that the world's major powers will sacrifice the elixir of growth on the altar of environmentalism. That, indeed, seems to be the lesson of the failure of the Copenhagen climate summit. Instead, there will be an effort to return to economic growth as usual – combined with inadequate efforts to limit emissions of greenhouse gases. This failure to tackle global warming will, in itself, turn into a major and continuing source of international tension. Fairly quickly, it is likely to merge with more traditional complaints about foreign economic competition.

The American public has long been more sceptical than the country's policymaking elite about the benefits of free trade and the free flow of capital. An opinion poll taken a year after the fall of Lehman Brothers asked whether free-trade agreements are good for the US: 43 per cent of the public thought so, compared to 88 per cent of members of the Council on Foreign Relations (CFR), which brings together members of the academic and policymaking elite. In a similar vein, 85 per cent of the public believed that protecting American jobs should be a top priority of US foreign policy – but just 21 per cent of CFR members concurred.[412]

In the aftermath of the crash of 2008, however, even senior US officials and top economists began openly to question America's economic relationship with China – the most important trading relationship in the world. Timothy Geithner, Obama's first Treasury secretary, provoked a diplomatic row by suggesting in his Congressional confirmation hearings that China 'is manipulating its currency'.[413]

China's ferocious reaction ensured that Geithner largely dropped this kind of language in public. But there were plenty of influential commentators willing to make the point for him. The argument was essentially that China had piled up trade surpluses with America by deliberately suppressing the value of the Chinese currency – and refusing to let it float freely on the world's currency markets. The Chinese had then recycled their dollar surpluses into the US by buying American assets. This had depressed US interest rates and so fed the credit boom that had popped in 2008. Meanwhile, American and European workers lost their jobs because Chinese goods were kept artificially cheap by currency manipulation.

China angrily rejected this line of argument. Desperate to maintain growth in the wake of a collapse in demand in the months after the fall of Lehman Brothers, the last thing the Chinese wanted to do was to raise the cost of their exports by letting their currency rise. But Chinese resistance was more than a knee-jerk reaction to an emergency. Many Chinese policymakers believe that the Japanese economic miracle effectively ended when, during the eighties, the government in Tokyo succumbed to American pressure to let the yen rise against the dollar, permanently damaging the competitiveness of Japanese industry.[414]

As it became clear that the Chinese would not respond to the Great Recession by letting their currency rise, so calls for protectionism became more mainstream in the United States. In September 2009 President Obama imposed punitive tariffs on Chinese tyres, provoking howls of anger from China. But the tyre tariffs may just be a foretaste of what is to come. There are increasingly powerful voices in the US and Europe who regard China as essentially a protectionist country. Paul Krugman, a winner of the Nobel Prize for Economics, wrote in late 2009: 'In normal times, I'd be among the first to reject claims that China is stealing other people's jobs, but right now it's the simple truth… Beggar-thy-neighbour policies by major players cannot be tolerated. Something must be done about China's currency.'[415] A couple of months later Krugman became more specific. He argued that high unemployment in America meant that 'the usual rules don't apply' and that 'the victims of mercantilism have little to lose from a trade confrontation'. In a prediction that verged on a recommendation to the American government, the Nobel Laureate argued that if China did not adapt its policies, 'the very mild protectionism it's currently complaining about will be the start of something much bigger'.[416]

Most mainstream economists still adopted a 'more in sorrow than in anger' tone when discussing the possibility of western trade protectionism as a counter to Chinese 'exchange-rate mercantilism'. But some were prepared to break the taboo and openly advocate tariffs. Robert Aliber of Chicago University, the traditional bastion of free-market economics, was one. He argued that 'Americans have been patient – too patient – in accepting the loss of several million US manufacturing jobs because of China's determined pursuit of mindless mercantilist policies.' His solution was simple and brutal – 'a uniform tariff of 10 per cent on all Chinese imports'.[417]

It is likely that China will attempt to head off some of these pressures by allowing a modest appreciation of its currency. But concessions by the government in Beijing may well be too weak to head off an anti-China backlash in America, fuelled by high unemployment and a growing sense of geopolitical rivalry.

The anti-Japanese backlash in the US in the eighties was ultimately limited by the fact that Japan is an ally of America and a democracy. No such constraints apply when it comes to China. Instead, the fact that China has so far failed to fulfil liberal predictions by turning into a democracy as it becomes richer has also fed the argument that American workers have been sold the virtues of free trade on a false prospectus. James Mann, a former Beijing correspondent for the *Los Angeles Times*, complains that 'US policy towards China since 1989 has been sold to the American people on the basis of a fraud... Across the United States, factories have closed and millions of Americans have been put out of work as the result of our decision to keep our markets open to Chinese goods. Meanwhile, the American people have been informed repeatedly that...free trade was going to lead to political liberalization.'[418]

For the last thirty years, protectionism has come second only to communism as the world's most unfashionable economic idea. No respectable participant at the World Economic Forum in Davos could ever admit to being a protectionist. It was an idea that ran completely counter to the spirit of the age – and also seemed to fly in the face of history. America's Smoot–Hawley tariffs of the thirties are still remembered as the turning point that helped create the Great Depression by shutting off American markets and sending world trade into a downward spiral. When, in 1993, the then vice-president Al Gore staged a television debate with Ross Perot about the virtues of a North American Free Trade Area, he even presented his opponent with a photograph of Messrs Smoot and Hawley. It was a very effective putdown, which some felt turned the whole debate.

Rehabilitating a discredited idea like protectionism is politically difficult – but not impossible. High unemployment in America and fear of a rising China help to create the background conditions. But the clinching argument may be provided by climate change. Whatever the details of the interim agreements reached, tensions are likely to persist between America and China. There is simply too much of a gap between the Chinese position that it is the rich world that must bear the brunt of cutting greenhouse gases and the American insistence that China is now the world's leading emitter and must play a much bigger role. The price that Congress is likely to insist on for raising the 'carbon price' inside America – either through taxes or a cap-and-trade scheme – could well be a 'carbon tariff' on goods from countries that are deemed to be delinquent on climate change. In this way, protectionism would be repackaged – rather than being a defensive and selfish move, it could be presented as part of an effort to 'save the planet'.

Protectionism is the economic form of nationalism. So a souring of the trade relationship between the US and China would not take place in a political vacuum. It would both reflect and stoke a radicalization of domestic politics in both nations.

The United States is, in many ways, psychologically ill-prepared for the end of American hegemony. Economists and America's National Intelligence Council may regard the emergence of a multi-polar world as inevitable. But, given the highly polarized nature of American politics, there will be many Americans who attribute any erosion in US power to weakness and failure by Washington politicians – and to nefarious schemes by foreigners. The rise of the Tea Party Movement in the US reflects the resurgence of radical anti-government sentiment. In the aftermath of the financial crisis and the election of Barack Obama as president, the US Department of Homeland Security even warned in an internal report of the possibility of a resurgence of far-right extremism in the US, arguing that 'The economic downturn and the election of the first African-American president present unique drivers of right-wing radicalization and recruitment.'[419]

Even if warnings about a resurgence of American domestic terrorism are not vindicated, the atmosphere of mainstream politics could become increasingly polarized – particularly against a background of persistently high unemployment, a failure to secure a clear victory in Afghanistan and spiralling federal budget deficits.

Americans have no monopoly on nationalism. If the US moves towards protectionism, or manages to force China to revalue its currency in some other way, the nationalist reaction in China is liable to be ferocious. Many Chinese have long suspected that America is out to thwart their country's rise – and react neuralgically to anything that appears to confirm these suspicions. The usually emollient Prime Minister Wen Jiabao has said that he believes that America intends to 'preserve its status as the world's sole superpower and will not allow any country the chance to pose a challenge to it'.[420] Clashes over trade and currency only re-enforce these suspicions. Indeed, Wen has angrily denounced pressure over China's currency and 'brazen trade protectionism against China' as a deliberate 'restriction on China's development'.[421]

The most potent displays of Chinese nationalism in recent years have come on the streets of Beijing, rather than in government offices. The huge street demonstrations provoked by America's (inadvertent) bombing of the Chinese embassy in Belgrade in 1999 are a reminder of the depth of potential anger against the United States that could easily flare up, if relations between the two countries deteriorate. Nationalist books have also become regular bestsellers in China. *Currency Wars*, published in 2007, argued that America had deliberately engineered the end of the Japanese economic miracle and the Asian financial crisis – as well as arguing that the western financial system is controlled by the Rothschilds.[422] In 2009 *Unhappy China* hit the top of the charts. Its authors argued that 'With Chinese national strength growing at an unprecedented rate, China should stop self-debasing and come to recognize the fact that it now has the power to lead the world.'[423]

Since China and the United States are now the world's two largest economies and geopolitical rivals, a rise of nationalist politics in either nation will shake the international system. But they are not the only two countries susceptible to political radicalization in hard economic times.

European politics also threatens to be polarized in response to perceived threats from the outside world. Europe accounted for 25 per cent of the world's population in 1900, but the figure is just 11 per cent now – and that could fall to 6 per cent by 2060. While the indigenous population of Europe is stagnating, the neighbouring Arab world is going through a population boom. Between 1980 and 2010 the region's population doubled from 180 million people to 360 million.[424] But youth unemployment in the Arab world is at least 20 per cent. The obvious solution has been for young Arabs (and Africans) to move to the richer pastures of the EU – legally or illegally. But high levels of Muslim immigration have provoked a fierce counter-reaction in Europe, which is only likely to increase as growth slows and unemployment rises. Anti-immigration parties have made serious headway in several European countries including France, Austria, Italy, Switzerland, Denmark – and, most spectacularly, the once famously liberal Netherlands.

European Union leaders have responded to a more fearful public mood by increasingly portraying the outside world in threatening terms – railing against cheap Asian goods and illegal immigrants. Both President Nicolas Sarkozy of France and Chancellor Angela Merkel of Germany have called for a 'Europe that protects'. A European Union that more than doubled in size between 1995 and 2004 is now much more cautious about further expansion.

But while the Europeans may look anxiously at the outside world, the real threat to the vaunted 'European model' may lie within. Like the United States, the EU was already facing a daunting fiscal challenge as the baby-boomers aged and retired. But that problem was gravely compounded by the fiscal consequences of the crash of 2008. The West successfully avoided a Great Depression at the cost of a near doubling of public debt. It was like a family that responded to unemployment by living off its credit card. That way of life cannot go on for ever. And in

Europe, as in the US, there is a fear that a long period of austerity and slower growth beckons, as governments struggle to control spending.

In fact, it could be a lot worse than mere austerity. Governments that fail to rein in spending in a controlled way could lose the confidence of the markets and be forced into chaotic cuts that cause political and social turmoil. In the years after the crash, Greece had to slash public spending in ways that provoked social unrest. Hungary and Latvia had to apply to the International Monetary Fund for loans and also experienced wrenching periods of domestic austerity. Unemployment hit nearly 20 per cent in Spain – and nonetheless, the government was forced to cut wages in an effort to balance the books.

The worries for Europe are now twofold. First, that a serious economic crash in one member of the European Union will have a contagion effect that will threaten the European single market, the stability of the single currency – and even the survival of the European Union itself. The second danger is that one of the EU's bigger nations – Italy, Spain or even Britain – is forced down the Irish and Greek roads of savage cuts in public spending. Serious political or social instability in one of the EU's big six (France, Germany, Italy, the UK, Poland and Spain) would have worldwide ramifications. It would certainly place huge strain on the European Union and further hamper Europe's already quixotic efforts to promote global governance on the European model.

Both the United States and the European Union are increasingly likely to see the outside world as presenting threats, rather than opportunities. That suggests a more defensive attitude to trade, to immigrants, to neighbouring states like Mexico and Egypt and to rising powers like China and India. Over time that will threaten the very system of globalization that underpinned the Age of Optimism.

Historians point out that there have been previous periods of globalization in world history, most of which ended badly. Harold James of Princeton University points to the Roman imperial period, the

Renaissance and the nineteenth century as periods when international trade expanded rapidly and notes, bloodcurdlingly, that 'All of these previous globalization episodes came to an end, almost always with wars that were accompanied by highly disruptive and contagious financial crises.'[425] The First World War, it is frequently pointed out, broke out despite a long period of international economic expansion and the development of deep commercial ties between Britain and Germany. Kevin O'Rourke of Trinity College, Dublin, writes that 'Globalization can seem an irresistible force... History, however, suggests that globalization is as much a political as a technological phenomenon, which can be easily reversed.'[426] O'Rourke's research suggests that historically 'the pattern of trade could only be understood as being the outcome of some military or political equilibrium between contending powers'.[427] In other words, globalization in general – and the surge in Chinese-American trade, in particular – could only take place in a benign international political environment. If the environment changes – and a major shift in power between the US and China certainly represents a change in the environment – then globalization could well fall victim.

Of course, not all episodes of globalization are the same. Modern technology has arguably created a global community that will be much harder to disrupt than in previous eras. Protectionist trade barriers cannot dismantle the internet.

But even if technology ensures that modern globalization is different from previous eras – and much harder to reverse completely – a rise in tensions between the world's major powers is still highly likely in the new economic and political climate created by the Great Recession.

As in the Cold War, nuclear deterrence should ensure that those tensions do not culminate in a war between major powers. But international rivalries will increase. And the advent of a zero-sum world will probably make it impossible to find the 'global solutions for global problems' that President Obama has pleaded for.

Properly understood, the big global problems – climate change, global economic imbalances, nuclear proliferation, terrorism, resource shortages, poverty and failed states – are ripe for win-win solutions. Solving these problems is clearly in the interests of all of the world's major powers. But the end of the Age of Optimism is making it less and less likely that these issues will be solved co-operatively.

Phrases like 'failed state' or 'nuclear non-proliferation' can sound bland by the force of constant repetition – the kind of problems that are fit for a sleepy university seminar, but that need not trouble ordinary people. This is a dangerous misconception. Left unsolved, each of these big global problems could lead to a major disaster.

The most immediate dangers are posed by the nuclear issue. With the world collectively unable to persuade Iran to rein in its nuclear programme, a new war in the Middle East is becoming increasingly likely. Israel or the United States may well choose to bomb Iran's nuclear facilities, in an effort to stop or stall the drive to an Iranian bomb. Iran would almost certainly retaliate against Israel or American troops in the region or the oil traffic in the Gulf. There would then be a belt of conflict across the greater Middle East – with America sucked further into conflicts in the neighbouring states of Iraq, Iran and Afghanistan. The alternative would be to accept the possibility of an Iranian bomb – but that might only defer the danger of conflict. A newly confident nuclear Iran might seek to increase its influence in Syria, Lebanon and Palestine – provoking an arms race in the Middle East.

Iran presents the most dramatic nuclear challenge. But it is not the only one. North Korea, a nuclear-armed state, is near collapse and openly threatened war with its southern neighbour in 2010. And the security of Pakistan's nuclear weapons remains a constant headache for the West, in a state that is threatened by Islamist radicalism.

The nuclear issue inevitably merges with continuing concerns about terrorism and failed states. American foreign policy is no longer centred on terrorism – as it was in the years after 9/11 – but the danger of new terrorist attacks has not disappeared. New plots are regularly uncovered in both Europe and the United States, while India and Russia have been recent victims of major attacks. Another terrorist spectacular in the US or Europe could once again cause turmoil in international politics. And while the West's security services have undoubtedly become more effective in the years since 9/11, events in the developing world are moving against them. The emergence of more failed states, with both globalization and US power in retreat, will create more lawless areas from which terrorists and organized criminals can operate. A particular concern is the fate of Afghanistan – and therefore of Pakistan – in the wake of an American withdrawal. A spate of terrorist attacks inside India is also increasing the dangers of war between Pakistan and India, two nuclear-armed neighbours.

The dangers of climate change have been amply rehearsed. If the United Nations' International Panel on Climate Change is correct, there is a serious risk in the coming decades of desertification, crop failures, the flooding of coastal cities and mass migration by displaced people – with war and conflict following in the wake of environmental disaster. Even many of those who are sceptical about the UN-endorsed science on climate change accept the need for international action to curb greenhouse gases – if only as an insurance policy against catastrophe.

The failure to address global economic imbalances will, as outlined above, probably lead to a rise in protectionism. That too would have dangerous real-world consequences – leading to a longer and deeper economic crisis, with higher unemployment, slower growth and accompanying social, political and international tensions.

In the nuclear era the chances of an all-out war between major powers has, thankfully, diminished sharply. But if Chinese-American relations become more hostile, the chances of conflict by miscalculation will rise, particularly as China flexes its new military muscle in the Pacific – an ocean that the US has got used to treating as an American lake. China's increasingly vigorous efforts to secure its supplies of oil, energy, food and water are another potential flash-point. Niall Ferguson argues that as China seeks to diminish its dangerous dependence on the American market it will adopt an 'imperial' strategy, based on investments in Africa and the cultivation of trade links with Asia. Ferguson even reaches for a disturbing historical parallel: 'Imagine a re-run of the Anglo-German antagonism of the early 1900s, with America in the role of Britain and China in the role of Germany. This...captures the fact that a high level of economic integration does not necessarily prevent the growth of strategic rivalry and, ultimately, conflict.'[428]

The United States is not the only major power with which a rising China risks clashing. India is uneasy about growing Chinese influence in its immediate neighbours, Sri Lanka, Burma and Pakistan. The Indians and Chinese went to war in 1962 and still have an unsettled territorial dispute that has heated up in recent years. Both countries are hungry for energy and water, which increases the tensions between them. Over the long-term, the Russians worry that sparsely populated, energy-rich Siberia might become a target for Chinese expansionism.

The leaders of the world's major powers can see the logic of striving for co-operative international solutions to the political, environmental and economic problems of the world. Every G20 statement contains promises for new international agreements. And yet while they strive to find win-win solutions to the big global problems, the world's leaders are increasingly trapped in a zero-sum logic that prevents agreement. On every one of the big global issues, a mixture of national interests and ideological disagreements blocks the chances of an international deal.

When it comes to the Iranian nuclear programme, the Chinese have hard commercial interests that make them very reluctant to agree to significantly tougher sanctions – the 'crippling' measures that Hillary Clinton once called for. Iran is a major oil supplier to the Chinese economy. But there are also issues of principle at stake. The Chinese are very wary of the use of international economic sanctions to achieve political ends. China itself experienced mild economic reprisals in the aftermath of the Tiananmen Square massacre of 1989 and regards sanctions as a preferred American tool for imposing its political preferences on sovereign nations. Russia is also deeply suspicious of American use of the UN, following the experiences of the Iraq and Kosovo wars. The Americans and Europeans argue that stopping the Iranian nuclear programme is a global interest that should concern all the world's major powers. The Chinese and Russians see it in zero-sum terms.

The same mix of hard economic interests and genuine principles often block efforts to intervene in failed states or to put pressure on oppressive regimes. China has energy interests at stake in both Burma and Sudan. But it also has an ideological objection to western efforts to put pressure on sovereign governments. China and America co-operate to moderate North Korean behaviour – but there is a tacit rivalry that limits this co-operation. For China fears that a re-unified Korea would provide a base for US troops right on the Chinese border.

The efforts to stabilize the world economy reflect the same rise of zero-sum logic. In the immediate aftermath of the financial crisis, there was a realization from the world's major powers that they would sink or swim together. That led to the formation of the G20, where genuine efforts have been made to advance international co-operation in the interests of all nations. But when the G20 gets close to the really hard issues, zero-sum logic takes over. Fearful that it will be put under pressure to revalue its currency, China has effectively prevented all serious discussion of 'global economic imbalances'.

National interest and ideology also turn a potential win-win situation over climate change into a zero-sum game. In principle, all nations have an overriding shared interest in stopping global warming. But, in fact, all governments treat climate change as an argument about sharing out economic pain – a lose-lose situation. Politicians often speak hopefully about the potential economic gains from 'green growth' – all those jobs insulating houses and producing hybrid cars. But the truth is that cutting emissions of greenhouse gases will carry a heavy economic cost, at least in the short term. So national governments do their utmost to pass the cost on to other nations – and live in fear that they will be attacked at home for naïvely taking on too much of the burden. As the *Wall Street Journal* pointed out during the ill-fated Copenhagen climate conference, 'The argument between the US and China reflects the two countries' broader contest for economic power in the decades ahead.'[429]

This pragmatic battle for economic advantage is then overlaid by a battle of principle. The argument between rich and poor countries – and between the US and China – swiftly descends into an argument about the morality of the international economic order. The developing nations argue that the bulk of the carbon dioxide in the atmosphere has been put there by the rich nations. Both the Chinese and the Brazilians are fond of comparing the western nations to a rich man who has gorged on an expensive meal, invites his poorer neighbour in for coffee and then suggests that they split the bill. Not only that, but the West continues to consume far more energy per head than the developing world. How dare the Americans and Europeans insist on their right to consume energy at much higher levels than Asians and Africans? The Americans respond that China has got rich by feeding the western consumption patterns that it now denounces as unsustainable. How dare the Chinese, the world's largest emitters of greenhouse gases, refuse to assume their planetary responsibilities? And so the win-win logic that should push nations towards international co-operation on global warming is replaced by a zero-sum battle that prevents agreement.

Throughout the Age of Optimism, all the world's major powers felt pleased with the way the world was going. Globalization truly seemed to have created a win-win world. But the economic crash, the rise of China and the weakening of American power and the emergence of a set of intractable global political problems have changed the logic of international relations. A win-win world has been replaced by a zero-sum world.

24

SAVING THE WORLD

Most of my career has been spent reporting on a world where things were steadily improving. I started work in London during the Thatcher boom of the mid-eighties. At the BBC World Service, we followed the spread of democracy around the world, from Latin America to South-east Asia. I first visited Moscow during the Gorbachev years, as the long Soviet nightmare was coming to a close. I was in Madison Square Garden to see Bill Clinton accept the Democratic Party nomination in 1992, while the crowd danced to 'Don't Stop Thinking About Tomorrow'. I spent the next five years reporting on Asia, witnessing the way that rapid economic growth was transforming people's lives for the better from Bangkok to Bangalore. Based in Brussels from 2001, I followed the reunification of Europe, as countries like Poland and the Czech Republic joined the ranks of free and prosperous nations. I was in London when Tony Blair won his first electoral victory in May 1997, swept along by a campaign anthem that seemed to capture the spirit of the age: 'Things can only get better'.

It doesn't feel that way now. My friend Charles Grant, the head of one of Britain's leading think-tanks, recalls that, when he launched his

Centre for European Reform in 1995, 'The big issues were whether Britain should join the euro and how fast Poland should join the European Union… Most of the problems that worry us now – climate change, energy security, how to handle a more assertive Russia, the rise of China and terrorism – were scarcely on the agenda then.'[430] In Washington, my contemporary, Andrew Sullivan, seems to feel the same way. 'It feels like the late seventies,' he wrote at the end of 2009, 'but with no cheerful Ronald Reagan waiting in the wings… I've never experienced such widespread gloom in the 25 years I've lived here.'[431]

For some Americans the Age of Optimism ended on 9/11. But, in fact, the underpinnings of the win-win world survived the attacks on Washington and New York. Both globalization and America's global hegemony remained intact. All the world's major powers still had good reason to believe that the international system was working in their favour. That has changed in the aftermath of the crash of 2008. The world economic system is now creating disagreement and discord between nations. New rivalries are emerging with the decline of American power. The world's major powers are finding that they cannot solve the big global problems that threaten them all: climate change, nuclear proliferation, terrorism, failed states, energy and food security.

The crash of 2008 has been a disorienting experience for people who have spent the last thirty years arguing for the virtues of free-market economics, globalization and western democratic values. I count myself among them. Throughout the period, both of the publications I've worked for – *The Economist* and the *Financial Times* – were energetic chroniclers and promoters of globalization and of the spread of free-market and democratic ideas.

The economic crisis that was unleashed in 2008 has led to a backlash against some of the ideas that underpinned the Age of Optimism. But the economic and political gains made between 1978 and 2008 were not a mirage. The spread of democratic government around the world ensured that hundreds of millions of people were able to lead freer lives.

The years 1978–2008 did see big reductions in poverty in the developing world, above all in China, and a long, economic expansion in the West. Violent conflict around the world has fallen sharply since the end of the Cold War. All of these gains were real.

So what went wrong? The problem is that the market for ideas is a bit like the market for shares. In both cases, a long run of success can lead to a period of 'irrational exuberance' and an overshoot. After a generation of success, the promoters of free-market economics and democratic politics succumbed to intellectual arrogance and hubris. They pushed their ideas to their logical conclusions and then well beyond them. A faith in markets degenerated into allowing global investment banks to bet billions of dollars on unregulated securities. A faith in democracy promotion moved from peaceful support of human rights in Eastern Europe in the eighties to the invasion of Iraq in 2003.

Yet while some of the ideas that underpinned the Age of Optimism have taken a severe pounding, the alternatives are not particularly attractive. A backlash against free trade, globalization and democracy promotion is likely to worsen international conflict and to lead to a less prosperous, less free world.

So how should we react to the emergence of a zero-sum world and the backlash against liberal economic and political ideas? For Americans and Europeans, I think there should be three basic guidelines. The first is, to borrow a British slogan from the Second World War, 'keep calm and carry on'. The world did look unusually bleak in the aftermath of the global economic crisis. But the past century has proved the resilience of liberal democracy and free-market economics.

The second guideline is not to accept that rivalry between nations will inevitably dictate international relations. In previous chapters, I have explained why many of the biggest global issues have got trapped by zero-sum logic. But creative leadership should be able to identify new ways for the world's major powers to co-operate – gradually rebuilding the win-win logic of the last thirty years.

Finally, the success of the United States and the European Union in defending their interests and values in the rest of the world will depend crucially on their ability to rebuild and strengthen their own economies and societies.

An injunction to 'keep calm' might sound bland, or even complacent, in the face of declining national power and rising global threats. But those gripped by the idea of the inexorable decline of the United States – or indeed the Western world – should remember that we have been through phases of 'declinism' before. During the thirties, and then again during the early Cold War, there were many in the West who believed that the Soviet system was working better than western democracy. By the late eighties, the United States was transfixed by the rise of Japan. Yet the Soviet challenge collapsed and the Japanese challenge faded away.

Western capitalism is going through its biggest crisis since the thirties. But the capitalist system recovered from the Great Depression. Over the long term, it will prove its resilience again.

When it comes to politics, the long-term trends highlighted by Francis Fukuyama in 1989 remain impressive. As Fukuyama argued, 'The growth of liberal democracy... has been the most remarkable macropolitical phenomenon of the last four hundred years.' In 1975 there were still just thirty electoral democracies around the world; by 1990, after the collapse of the Soviet empire, there were sixty-one.[432] The democratic wave continued for another decade, toppling one-party states across Africa and Asia. It peaked and then began to recede with the colour revolutions of 2003–5 on the fringes of Russia. There is, for the moment, a confident group of authoritarian powers. But the global move towards democracy has taken place over centuries. Progress will eventually resume.

It could happen quite soon. In Russia, President Dmitry Medvedev has begun openly to challenge some of the authoritarian thinking associated with his mentor and predecessor as president, Prime Minister

Vladimir Putin. The Iranian theocracy is clearly highly unstable. A resumption of the trend towards democracy might help change the logic of a zero-sum world. It is true that some of the assumptions of 'democratic peace' theory are a little naïve. Democratic nations can fall out bitterly – and they certainly do not always line up with each other on the big international issues, such as climate change. But, as a general rule, shared democratic values do help countries to get along.

The big question hanging over the international system, however, is the future of China. It is certainly far too soon to write off the idea that China will become democratic. Even the Singaporean academic Kishore Mahbubani, a longstanding critic of what he regards as western complacency, argues that 'China cannot succeed in its goal of becoming a modern developed society until it can take the leap and allow the Chinese people to choose their own rulers.' As Mahbubani tells it, 'China's present leadership is acutely aware that eventually China will have to move towards democracy.'[433] The country's GDP per capita is just approaching the $6,000 figure that political scientists say makes it likely that a democracy will survive.

A democratic China would not necessarily be more internally stable. It might even be more nationalistic. But the probability is still that political liberalization in China would help to stabilize the international system. One reason why there is little speculation that a rising India will clash with the United States is that both nations are democracies. An authoritarian China inevitably looks more threatening to the United States – and feels more threatened by America.

But while it may be likely that China will eventually become more democratic, the turning point could still be many years off. One reason for the decline in western optimism in recent years has been the gradual realization that confident predictions that one-party rule in China would soon come to an end have, so far, not been vindicated. The theory, after 1989, was that China would quite quickly have to choose between authoritarianism and economic success. But China has kept powering relentlessly forward and shows little sign of genuine political reform. As James Miles, *The Economist*'s Beijing bureau chief, put it recently, 'It is becoming increasingly possible to imagine that when China puts a man on the moon and surpasses the output of America's economy, it will still be a one-party state that brooks no organized opposition.'[434]

For the moment, the US and the European Union must assume that they will continue to deal with a China that is getting steadily richer, more powerful and more globally influential – but that is still authoritarian. That, naturally, makes Americans nervous. But there are some signs that Americans may now be making the same mistake that they made with the USSR and Japan – exaggerating the strengths of its scariest rival. The Pew survey of 2009 that discovered that US isolationism was at record levels also showed that a majority of Americans now believe that the Chinese economy is larger than that of the United States.[435] This is plain wrong. At the time the poll was taken, the Chinese economy was around half the size of America's.[436]

A comparison between the Chinese and Japanese challenges is telling. In some ways, China is a less plausible rival to the US than Japan was in the late eighties. Japan is a wealthy, homogeneous, developed nation with a stable political system. China is, in many respects, just what its leaders always insist it is – a developing nation. Although some western intellectuals have lauded China's ability to plan for the long-term, the country's political system is inherently unstable. The actions of China's government often suggest that its leadership remains very nervous about its power and legitimacy. When President Obama first visited China, his hosts went to some lengths to prevent his spontaneous remarks being broadcast live on national television. China's angry insistence on the unity of the nation also betrays deep anxiety about separatist challenges in Tibet and Xinjiang. President Hu Jintao was so spooked by the riots in Xinjiang in July 2009 that he flew home early from a G8 summit in Italy.[437] Despite the rapid economic growth that China achieved in the aftermath of the Great Recession, it is also not yet clear that the country has found an alternative to its over-reliance on the US market.

So China lacks both the inherent stability of Japan and its established prosperity. But in other, more important, ways, China is a much more serious challenger to American hegemony than Japan ever was. The most obvious point is demographic. The population of China is four times that of the United States, whereas Japan's population is less than half that of the US. Japan was (and is) also a democracy, an ally of the United States and the base for some fifty thousand American troops. China is, by contrast, a geopolitical rival. And, unlike the USSR, China has an economic system that works. Pundits have been predicting the end of the 'Chinese miracle' almost since it began in the late seventies – but China has kept growing at double-digit rates. There is still tremendous scope for internal development in China, so the odds must be that the country will continue to grow fast for some years, even if it experiences disruptions and occasional recessions along the way.

The geopolitical significance of the crisis of 2008 is that it has made people realize that the 'China challenge' is not something for the distant future – it is happening here and now. While the date at which the Chinese economy is larger than that of the United States is probably still fifteen years or more away, in some important respects China is already the world's biggest player. It has the world's largest currency reserves. It is the world's largest exporter. It is the largest producer of steel and of greenhouse gases. It is the biggest market for motor vehicles. It is now the largest trading partner of other major emerging economies, such as India and Brazil.

For all the courtesies that the US and China are still careful to pay towards each other in public, theirs is an increasingly difficult relationship. On all of the big global problems – economic imbalances, climate change, nuclear proliferation, interventions in failed states, energy and food security – the US finds itself bumping up against an obdurate Chinese leadership that is able to rally considerable support for its positions from other authoritarian powers, and from the developing world.

The leaders of America and China continue to make genuine efforts to work together in international forums such as the G20, the UN and the climate-change talks. But they usually fail to reach meaningful agreements because increasingly they find their interests are at odds with each other. There is therefore an urgent need to find some non-trivial topics on which America and China can work together – and rediscover the win-win logic that prevailed during the Age of Optimism. A better Chinese-American relationship might then serve as a foundation for breaking free from the zero-sum logic that is afflicting international relations as a whole.

Global warming is one area where China and America could still work together constructively. This might sound improbable, given the bitter Chinese-American haggling at the Copenhagen climate negotiations of 2009. Curbing greenhouse gases is a classic example of a subject where zero-sum logic kicks in. It is all about the distribution of economic pain. However, if, as seems increasingly likely, the world's efforts to curb greenhouse gases are inadequate, the pressure to find new technological solutions to the threat of climate change will become increasingly urgent – and that is where there is scope for greatly intensified international co-operation, with a Chinese-American agreement at the heart of the deal.

The American government has shown in the past that it is capable of sponsoring pioneering science, from the Manhattan Project that produced the atomic bomb to the space programme. Why not apply the same energy, urgency and financial backing to scientific research into global warming – but this time make it an international effort? The secrets of the bomb and the space programmes were kept closely guarded for reasons of national security. But climate change is a question of international security. An international project, mobilizing the scientific and engineering talents of China and the United States, could do crucial research on a range of subjects from renewable energy to geo-engineering. It should also incorporate scientists from India, Europe and the rest of the world. If a global climate research project received high-level backing from the leaders of the US and China, it would provide a valuable example of the two nations co-operating on a vital topic of shared interest.

Nuclear-arms negotiations provide another opportunity for the world's major powers to break free from zero-sum logic. Here the two key players are the US and Russia, who still hold 95 per cent of the world's nuclear warheads between them. In the aftermath of the Russian-Georgian war of 2008, US-Russian relations were at their chilliest for many years. But the Obama and Medvedev administrations identified a mutual interest in nuclear-arms reductions and pursued it tenaciously.

Cutting the nuclear arsenals of the world's major powers will not solve the more directly threatening problem of nuclear-arms proliferation. International efforts to stop the Iranian nuclear programme have so far proved futile. But charges of double-standards and hypocrisy levelled at the world's nuclear-weapons states have made it much harder to rally support to crack down on those countries that aspire to join the nuclear-weapons club. In the past, progress on nuclear-arms reduction has made it easier to secure new international deals on non-proliferation.[438] So if a nuclear-arms deal between Russia and the United States is ratified and acted upon, it could have positive effects throughout the international system.

It is certainly crucial to find some way of defusing the gathering crisis over Iran's nuclear programme. Much of President Obama's initial emphasis on the need for a policy of international engagement and on reaching out to the Muslim world was driven by a desire to head off conflict with Iran. The first fruits of Obama's approach to Iran were disappointing. The rigged Iranian presidential elections of June 2009 made it much harder to make the case for negotiations with a discredited Iranian leadership. They have also thrown internal Iranian politics into turmoil, making the country even harder to read as a potential negotiating partner. If anything, internal turmoil seems to have persuaded the Iranian leadership to take an even harder line on its nuclear programme. But this has not helped President Obama with his Plan B – which is to persuade China and Russia to go along with much tougher sanctions on Iran.

Yet it remains the case that a diplomatic solution to the Iranian nuclear issue would dramatically change the international climate for the better. The much-discussed 'Grand Bargain', in which America and its allies trade economic engagement and diplomatic recognition for Iran, in return for abandonment of the Iranian weapons programme, is still worth pursuing – if only because the alternatives are so appalling. It would help hugely if China recognized a self-evident truth – that its reliance on Gulf oil means that it too has a major interest in avoiding another Middle Eastern war.

United Nations peacekeeping is another area where the world's major powers can improve co-operation in ways that are both urgent and mutually beneficial. Agreeing on the mandate for a UN operation can be politically fraught – particularly when sensitive questions of state sovereignty or national interest are at stake. Nonetheless, UN peace-keeping activities have actually expanded enormously since the end of the Cold War and have contributed to the sharp drop in deaths in warfare. Between 1999 and 2009, the number of UN peacekeepers deployed around the world increased eightfold to around one hundred thousand troops. The threat that the number of failed states will rise is only likely to increase the demand for peacekeeping troops.

As the US seeks to control military costs, the UN will be an increasingly attractive option as a tool for peacekeeping. Susan Rice, Obama's ambassador to the UN, has pointed out that for every dollar the US spends on an equivalent military deployment, the UN will spend 12 cents.[439] UN peacekeeping also offers another chance to break from zero-sum logic in relations between America and China. It is one area where

China has been willing to use its expanded international reach in ways that the US and its allies could find helpful, rather than threatening. In recent years, China has gradually moderated its suspicion of UN interventions and sharply increased its participation in peacekeeping operations. By 2010 it was the thirteenth largest contributor to UN peacekeeping operations, with over two thousand troops deployed, mainly on African missions, such as those in Liberia and Sudan.[440] The US, by contrast, was the seventy-fourth largest contributor – reflecting America's refusal to put its troops under UN command.[441]

If the world's major powers are to reverse the dangerous logic of a zero-sum world, the most important question of all is the preservation of the international economic system that underpinned globalization and the Age of Optimism. In the wake of the economic crash of 2008, legitimate questions have been raised about the stability of the international economic system and the extent to which the world's major powers all still benefit from globalization. Yet a breakdown of the system would slow the world economy in ways that would damage the livelihoods of ordinary people all over the world. Trade wars would also embitter international relations and strike directly at the commercial and investment ties that have created a web of shared interests between the world's major powers over the last thirty years. It is clearly not true that international trade and shared economic interests make war impossible. But commerce surely makes conflict less likely.

All the world's major economic powers bear responsibility for keeping intact the system that benefits them all. China needs to let its currency rise in value against the dollar – and not just by token amounts – to ward off protectionist sentiment in America. It should also recognize that a stronger currency, whose value is determined by the market, reflects an increase in the nation's wealth that will make ordinary Chinese richer in a very direct way. The Indians, who have played a particularly obstructive role in the Doha round of international trade talks, need to recognize that they have been among the biggest beneficiaries of globalization – and have a huge stake in preserving and extending the system. Europe's baroque system of agricultural subsidies – long an embarrassment – has also now become a major impediment to a new deal at the World Trade Organization. Calling for 'completion of the Doha round' has become a tiresome cliché of international diplomacy. It is the equivalent of praising motherhood and apple pie. But, while cynicism about the Doha round is certainly justified, its completion would be really valuable. For if the world's leaders could agree to a new round of trade opening, they would send a vital signal that they still believe that a win-win world is possible.

The European Union, which has long regarded itself as a model of international co-operation, is now struggling to contain tensions within its ranks. A big and visible failure for the European project would send dangerous signals to the rest of the world about the resurgence of nationalism and the decline of globalism. The travails of the euro have been a major blow to the morale of the European Union. There is however, one obvious (if politically difficult) way for the EU to rediscover its spirit and élan – and that is to recommit to the enlargement of the Union. The expansion of the European Union was arguably the single most successful exercise in the promotion of democratic values and free-market economics during the entire Age of Optimism. The political difficulties of expanding the European Union to take in Ukraine and Turkey – and, who knows, maybe eventually Russia and parts of North Africa – are formidable. But it would be the biggest single contribution Europe could make to defeating the logic of a zero-sum world.

It is unavoidable that a special responsibility will fall on the United States. The US is the core of the world economy and the international security system, and the foremost exponent of democratic and free-market values. Its actions remain uniquely important. For all his domestic difficulties, the global popularity of President Obama provides a vital base on which the United States can build. America cannot be sure of winning all the arguments in international diplomacy – far from it. But at least it now knows that the world is once again listening.

Indeed, as the world looked for political leadership from President Obama in his first year in office, there was a certain amount of frustration. Why was he spending so much of his time and energy on endless domestic battles about stimulus packages and health-care reform, when the whole world was looking to him for a lead – even to the extent of awarding him a Nobel Peace Prize when he had barely got his feet under the Oval Office desk?

In fact, there is a vital connection between Obama's efforts to revive the American economy and repair the country's social safety net, and his administration's ability to defend globalization. With US unemployment in double-digits, it is increasingly difficult to persuade Americans of the joys of unfettered global economic competition. With the budget deficit soaring, it is also much harder to convince Americans that it is worth paying the costs that come with global leadership. It is only when Americans once again feel optimistic and secure that they will once again accept that globalization really can create a win-win world.

The fate of the American economy and political system also matters to the rest of the world as a demonstration of the power of democracy and capitalism. The United States ultimately prevailed in the Cold War not by defeating the Soviet Union on the battlefield, but because it won the war of ideas. After the last great crisis of US capitalism, in the thirties, it was similarly crucial that America showed that it had the energy and the ideas to overcome a terrifying economic downturn. President Obama's success in passing health-care reform was an important demonstration that the American political system – so often attacked as hopelessly dysfunctional – is still capable of delivering real social reform.

As President Obama struggles to revive the American economy, he should recall the words of John Maynard Keynes, in an open letter to President Roosevelt in 1933: 'You have made yourself the trustee for those in every country who seek to mend the evils of our condition by reasoned experiment within the framework of the existing social system. If you fail, rational change will be gravely prejudiced throughout the world, leaving orthodoxy and revolution to fight it out.'[442]

Eighty years after the Great Depression, a strong, successful and confident America remains the best hope for a stable and prosperous world.

NOTES

PROLOGUE: DAVOS, 2009

1   'Kapital Gains', *The Times*, 20 October 2008.

2   Quoted in Gideon Rachman, 'November 2012: a dystopian dream', *Financial Times*, 17 February 2009.

3   Quoted in Martin Jacques, *When China Rules the World: The Rise of the Middle Kingdom and the End of the Western World* (London: Penguin, 2009), 349.

4   Derek Chollet and James Goldgeier, *America Between the Wars: From 11/9 to 9/11* (New York: PublicAffairs, 2008), 152.

5   Quoted in Geoff Dyer, 'China flexes its diplomatic muscle', *Financial Times*, 1 February 2010.

6   Kishore Mahbubani, *The New Asian Hemisphere: The Irresistible Shift of Global Power to the East* (New York: PublicAffairs, 2008), 14–15.

7   Quoted in John Kampfner, *Freedom for Sale* (London: Simon and Schuster, 2009), 260.

8   David Hale, 'The Best Economy Ever', *Wall Street Journal*, 31 July 2007.

9   Gideon Rachman, 'How the bottom fell out of old Davos', *Financial Times*, 1 February 2010.

10 'Greek deputy PM says Nazis "wrecked German economy"', *BBC News*, 25 February 2010.

11 Barack Obama, 'Responsibility for Our Common Future', address to the United Nations General Assembly, 23 September 2009.

12 Chollet and Goldgeier, *America Between the Wars*.

Part One: The Age of Transformation, 1978–91

CHAPTER 1: CHINA, 1978:
DENG'S COUNTER-REVOLUTION

13 Nicholas Kristof and Sheryl Wudunn, *China Wakes* (New York: Times Books, 1994), 368.

14 Ibid., 431.

15 Jonathan Fenby, *The Penguin Modern History of China: The Fall and Rise of a Great Power, 1850–2008* (London: Allen Lane, 2008), 475.

16   Ibid., 531.

17   Ibid., 536.

18   Jonathan D. Spence, *The Search for Modern China* (New York: W. W. Norton, 1990, 1999), 621–3.

19   Ibid., 622.

20   Ibid., 623.

21   'The second Long March', *The Economist*, 11 December 2008.

22   Fenby, *The Penguin Modern History of China*, 558.

23   Ibid., 554.

24   Nicholas Lardy, *China's Unfinished Economic Revolution* (Washington DC: Brookings Institution Press, 1998), 1.

25   Ibid.

26   Interview with the author. Hum does note, however, with some pride, that the British did spot the importance of the agricultural reforms being carried out by Zhao Zhiyang in Sichuan – and even arranged for Zhao to visit Britain. Zhao later became a key reformist ally of Deng and, by his own account, the author of many of the most important reforms. The two men later fell out over the suppression of the Tiananmen Square uprising of 1989.

27   'Man of the Year 1978, Teng Hsiao-p'ing', *Time*, 1 January 1979.

28   Ronald Reagan, *An American Life* (New York: Simon and Schuster, 1990), 368.

29   'The second Long March', *The Economist*, 11 December 2008, argues that 'Party officials, preferring their heroes to be larger than life, have massaged their history to imply that the meetings 30 years ago were a clarion call for reform and opening. They were not... The word "opening" did not even appear in the communiqué issued on December 22, 1978... Reform was mentioned only once.'

30   James Kynge, *China Shakes the World* (London: Weidenfeld and Nicholson, 2006), 14.

31   Ibid., 16.

32   Quoted in 'The second Long March'.

33   Quoted in Francis Fukuyama, *The End of History and The Last Man* (London: Penguin, 1992), 98.

CHAPTER 2: BRITAIN, 1979:
THATCHERISM

34   Quoted in Richard Roberts and David Kynaston, *City State: A Contemporary History of The City of London and How Money Triumphed* (London: Profile Books Ltd, 2001), 117.

35   Andrew Marr, *A History of Modern Britain* (London: Pan Macmillan, 2007), 365.

36   Margaret Thatcher, *The Downing Street Years* (London: HarperCollins, 1993),
      10.

37   Quoted in Marr, *A History of Modern Britain*, 386.

38   Ibid., 387.

39   Ibid., 411.

40   John Campbell, *Margaret Thatcher, Volume 2: The Iron Lady* (London: Vintage
      Books, 2008), 18.

41   Marr, *A History of Modern Britain*, 423.

42   Harold James, *Europe Reborn: A History, 1914–2000* (London: Longman, 2003),
      351.

43   Marr, *A History of Modern Britain*, 425.

44   Quoted in Roberts and Kynaston, *City State*, 22.

45   Simon Jenkins, *The Sunday Times*, London, 27 October 1987.

46   James, *Europe Reborn*, 355.

47   Marr, *A History of Modern Britain*, 403.

48   Campbell, *The Iron Lady*, 243.

49   Ibid., 253.

50   Thatcher, *The Downing Street Years*, 804.

51   Ibid., 687.

52   Campbell, *The Iron Lady*, 260.

53   Ibid.

54   Thatcher, *The Downing Street Years*, 485.

CHAPTER 3: THE UNITED STATES, 1980:
THE REAGAN REVOLUTION

55   Ronald Reagan, *An American Life* (New York: Simon and Schuster, 1990),
      227.

56   Roger Rosenblatt, 'Man of the Year 1980, Ronald Reagan', *Time*, 2 January
      1981, 3.

57   Reagan wrote in his diary in 1982 that the press were wrong to argue that he
      was taking aim at the New Deal, and that his real target was the Great Society.
      See Dinesh D'Souza, *Ronald Reagan: How an Ordinary Man Became an
      Extraordinary Leader* (New York: Simon and Schuster, 1997), 61.

58   Reagan, *An American Life*, 230.

59   D'Souza, *Ronald Reagan*, 89.

60   Sean Wilentz, *The Age of Reagan: A History, 1974–2008* (New York:
      HarperCollins, 2008), 144. For details on the Tax Reform Act, see 205.

61   Christopher DeMuth, 'Reviving Economic Conservatism', lecture at the
      Legatum Institute, London, 14 May 2009.

62   D'Souza, *Ronald Reagan*, 89.

63   Some see the roots of the Savings and Loans scandal of a decade later in the
      early deregulation of the Reagan years. Niall Ferguson calls it a 'hugely
      expensive lesson in the perils of ill-considered deregulation'. Niall Ferguson,
      The Ascent of Money: A Financial History of the World (London: Allen Lane,
      2008), 253. Wilentz makes the same case in *The Age of Reagan*, 177.

64   Wilentz, *The Age of Reagan*, 143.

65   Ibid., 147.

66   Reagan, *An American Life*, 311.

67   Wilentz, *The Age of Reagan*, 275.

68   Ibid.

69   D'Souza, *Ronald Reagan*, 26.

70   Robert Wade, lecture at 'The Battle of Ideas', London, 31 October 2009.

71   Wilentz, *The Age of Reagan*, 207.

72   Reagan, *An American Life*, 204.

73   Peter Jenkins, *Mrs Thatcher's Revolution: Ending the Socialist Era* (London:
      Jonathan Cape, 1987), 210.

74   Ibid.

75   Alan Greenspan, *The Age of Turbulence: Adventures in a New World* (London:
      Penguin, 2007), 88.

76   Ibid., 87.

77   Ibid., 89.

78   See D'Souza, *Ronald Reagan*, 1.

79   See Michael Reid, *Forgotten Continent: The Battle for Latin America's Soul* (New
      Haven, CT: Yale University Press, 2008), 10.

80   Reagan, *An American Life*, 703.

81   Wilentz, *The Age of Reagan*, 281.

CHAPTER 4: THE EUROPEAN UNION, 1986:
EMBRACING THE MARKET

82   Quoted in John Campbell, *Margaret Thatcher, Volume 2: The Iron Lady*
      (London: Vintage Books, 2008), 303.

83   Tony Judt, *Postwar: A History of Europe Since 1945* (London: Penguin, 2005),
      552.

84   Ibid.

85   Ibid., 553.

86   Harold James, *Europe Reborn: A History, 1914–2000* (London: Longman, 2003),
      362.

87   Ibid., 369.

88   Quoted in Charles Grant, *Delors: Inside the House that Jacques Built* (London:
      Nicholas Brealey Publishing, 1994), 47.

89   Ibid., 50.

90   Ibid., 51.

91   Ibid., 52.

92   Ibid., 59.

93   For a longer account of Thatcher's motives and role see Campbell, *The Iron Lady*, 307.

94   Grant, *Delors*, 80.

95   Ibid., 70.

96   Ibid., 86.

97   Campbell, *The Iron Lady*, 714.

CHAPTER 5: THE SOVIET UNION, 1985–91: GLASNOST, PERESTROIKA AND COLLAPSE

98   Gorbachev gave this account of events to a reunion of university friends in 1990. A fuller version is given in Angus Roxburgh, *The Second Russian Revolution* (London: BBC Books, 1991), 7–8.

99   Alan Greenspan, *The Age of Turbulence: Adventures in a New World* (London: Penguin, 2007), 137.

100 Tony Judt, *Postwar: A History of Europe Since 1945* (London: Penguin, 2005), 595.

101 Mary Elise Sarotte, *1989: The Struggle to Create Post-Cold War Europe* (Princeton, NJ: Princeton University Press, 2009), 13.

102 Harold James, *Europe Reborn: A History, 1914–2000* (London: Longman, 2003), 372.

103 Roxburgh, *The Second Russian Revolution*, 27.

104 Ibid., 25.

105 Ibid., 38.

106 Francis Fukuyama, *The End of History and The Last Man* (London: Penguin, 1992), 29.

107 Roxburgh, *The Second Russian Revolution*, 35.

108 Ibid., 59.

109 Judt, *Postwar*, 596.

110 Quoted in Ibid., 604.

111 The best contemporary journalistic account of the last days of the USSR is David Remnick's *Lenin's Tomb: The Last Days of the Soviet Empire* (New York: Vintage, 1994).

112 Judt, *Postwar*, 657.

113 See David Shambaugh, *China's Communist Party: Atrophy and Adaptation* (Berkeley, CA: University of California Press, 2009).

CHAPTER 6: EUROPE, 1989: THE YEAR OF REVOLUTIONS

114 Quoted in Harold James, *Europe Reborn: A History, 1914–2000* (London: Longman, 2003), 295.

115 See Angus Roxburgh, *The Second Russian Revolution* (London: BBC Books, 1991), 95.

116 Victor Sebestyen, *Revolution 1989: The Fall of the Soviet Empire* (London: Weidenfeld and Nicholson, 2009), 291.

117 There is a good account of Gorbachev's visit to East Germany in Sebestyen, *Revolution 1989*, 322–5. There is a discussion of how close East Germany came to a 'Tiananmen' in October in Mary Elise Sarotte, *1989: The Struggle to Create Post-Cold War Europe* (Princeton, NJ: Princeton University Press, 2009), 19.

118 Ibid., 582.

119 Timothy Garton Ash, *The Magic Lantern: The Revolution of '89 Witnessed in Warsaw, Budapest, Berlin, and Prague* (New York: Random House, 1990), 133.

120 Ibid., 78.

121 Timothy Garton Ash, lecture at Krakow University, 15 May 2009.

122 Tony Judt, *Postwar: A History of Europe Since 1945* (London: Penguin, 2005), 630.

CHAPTER 7: LATIN AMERICA, 1982–91:
THE TRIUMPH OF DEMOCRACY AND MARKETS

123 See Michael Reid, *Forgotten Continent: The Battle for Latin America's Soul* (New Haven, CT: Yale University Press, 2008), 109. This section draws heavily on the work of Michael Reid, a former colleague of mine at *The Economist*.

124 Ibid., 121.

125 Timothy Garton Ash is eloquent on the importance of round-table negotiations as part of the peaceful transition to democracy in Central Europe.

126 Reid, *Forgotten Continent*, 123.

127 Maxwell Cameron and Brian Tomlin, *The Making of NAFTA: How the Deal Was Done* (Ithaca, NY: Cornell University Press, 2000), 2.

128 See Hernando de Soto, *The Mystery of Capital: Why Capitalism Triumphs in the West and Fails Everywhere Else* (London: Black Swan, 2001).

129 The phrase was dreamed up by John Williamson, an economist at the Institute for International Economics in Washington. Williamson's own account of what he meant can be found in John Williamson, 'A Short History of the Washington Consensus', Fundación CIDOB paper, presented at a conference entitled 'From the Washington Consensus towards a New Global Governance', Barcelona, 24 September 2004. Available from

http://www.piie.com/publications/papers/williamson0904-2.pdf.

130   Niall Ferguson, *The Ascent of Money: A Financial History of the World* (London: Allen Lane, 2008), 214.

131   Ibid., 212.

132   See John Campbell, *Margaret Thatcher, Volume 2: The Iron Lady* (London: Vintage Books, 2008), 789.

133   Jeane Kirkpatrick, 'Dictatorship and Double Standards', *Commentary* (November 1979).

134   Campbell, *The Iron Lady*, 142.

135   Reid, *Forgotten Continent*, 135.

136   Dominic Wilson and Roopa Purushothaman, 'Dreaming with Brics: The Path to 2050', Global Economics Paper No.99, Goldman Sachs, 1 October 2003. Available from http://www2.goldmansachs.com/ideas/brics/book/99-dreaming.pdf.

137   Moisés Naím, 'The Washington Consensus: a damaged brand', *Financial Times*, 28 October 2002.

138   Reid, *Forgotten Continent*, 4.

139   Ibid., 194.

Chapter 8: India, 1991:
The Second Asian Giant Awakes

140   Gurchuran Das, *India Unbound: The Social and Economic Revolution from Independence to the Global Information Age* (New York: Anchor Books, 2002), 215.

141   See Edward Luce, *In Spite of the Gods: The Rise of Modern India* (New York: Random House, 2008).

142   Ramachandra Guha, *India After Gandhi: The History of the World's Largest Democracy* (London: Pan Macmillan, 2007), 209.

143   Manmohan Singh, interviewed on *Commanding Heights*, PBS, 6 February 2001.

144   Guha, *India After Gandhi*, 208.

145   Das, *India Unbound*, x.

146   Singh, PBS interview.

147   Ibid.

148   Interview with the author, Delhi, June 1996.

149   Singh, PBS interview.

150   Das, *India Unbound*, 220.

151   Singh, PBS interview.

152   Jeremy Kahn, 'How Singh Blew India's Moment', *Newsweek*, 22 September 2008.

153   Bill Emmott, *Rivals: How the Power Struggle Between China, India and Japan Will Shape Our Next Decade* (London: Allen Lane, 2008), 41.

154   Singh, PBS interview.

155   Gideon Rachman, 'The Bangalore boom revisited', *Financial Times Blog*, 22 September 2008. Available from http://blogs.ft.com/rachmanblog/2008/09/the-bangalore-boom-revisited/.

156   Quoted in C. Raja Mohan, 'Balancing Interests and Values: India's Struggle with Democracy Promotion', *Washington Quarterly* 30:3 (Summer 2007): 99.

Chapter 9: The Gulf War, 1991: The Unipolar Moment

157   George H. W. Bush, State of the Union Address, 29 January 1991.

158   Lawrence Freedman, *A Choice of Enemies: America Confronts the Middle East* (New York: PublicAffairs, 2008), 230.

159   Paul Kennedy, *The Rise and Fall of the Great Powers: Economic Change and Military Conflict from 1500 to 2000* (London: Fontana, 1989), 602.

160   Ibid., 225.

161   Richard Haass, who was working for President Bush on the National Security Council at the time, points out that this exchange was provoked by a disagreement over whether to go to the UN for approval for the enforcement of sanctions, rather than over the principle of the use of force. Richard N. Haass, *War of Necessity, War of Choice: A Memoir of Two Iraq Wars* (New York: Simon and Schuster, 2009), 84.

162   Freedman, *A Choice of Enemies*, 236.

163   Quoted in William Schneider, 'The Vietnam Syndrome Mutates', *The Atlantic* (April 2006).

164   Haass, *War of Necessity*, 230.

Part Two: The Age of Optimism: 1991–2008

Introduction

165   The phrase 'the end of economic history' was actually used in a speech by David Cameron, the leader of Britain's Conservative Party, at the LSE in September 2007.

166   Although, strictly speaking, the word 'Washington' referred to the views of the International Monetary Fund and the World Bank, both headquartered in the American capital.

167   Quoted in Derek Chollet and James Goldgeier, *America Between the Wars: From 11/9 to 9/11* (New York: PublicAffairs, 2008), 195.

CHAPTER 10: DEMOCRACY:
FRANCIS FUKUYAMA AND THE END OF HISTORY

168   Bloom's book was published in 1987. Allan Bloom, *The Closing of the American Mind* (New York: Simon and Schuster, 1987).

169   Interview with the author, Washington DC, 27 May 2009.

170   Francis Fukuyama, 'The End of History', *The National Interest* (June 1989). The article was subsequently turned into a book, *The End of History and the Last Man* (London: Penguin, 1992).

171   Ibid.

172   See, for example, Vince Cable, *The Storm: The World Economic Crisis and What It Means* (London: Atlantic Books, 2009), 3, and Robert Kagan, *The Return of History and the End of Dreams* (London: Atlantic Books, 2008).

173   Fukuyama, *The End of History*, 280.

174   Ibid., 50.

175   Freedom House, *Freedom in the World 2009* (Lanham, MD: Rowman and Littlefield Publishers, 2009).

176   Quoted in Strobe Talbott, *The Great Experiment: The Story of Ancient Empires, Modern States, and the Quest for a Global Nation* (New York: Simon and Schuster 2008), 327.

177   C. Raja Mohan, 'Balancing Interests and Values: India's Struggle with Democracy Promotion', *Washington Quarterly* 30:3 (Summer 2007): 99.

178   Quoted in Derek Chollet and James Goldgeier, *America Between the Wars: From 11/9 to 9/11* (New York: PublicAffairs, 2008), 88.

179   Ibid., 69.

180   Both Bloom and Wolfowitz appear lightly disguised in Saul Bellow's novel *Ravelstein* (New York: Penguin, 2001).

181   Chollet and Goldgeier, *America Between the Wars*, 277.

182   Francis Fukuyama, *America at the Crossroads: Democracy, Power, and the Neoconservative Legacy* (New Haven, CT: Yale University Press, 2006), x and xi.

183   Interview with the author, op. cit.

184   Ibid.

CHAPTER 11: PROSPERITY:
ALAN GREENSPAN AND THE END OF ECONOMIC HISTORY

185   Bob Woodward, *Maestro: Greenspan's Fed and the American Boom* (New York: Simon and Schuster, 2000).

186   Alan Greenspan, *The Age of Turbulence: Adventures in a New World* (London: Penguin, 2007), 97. Greenspan tells this story against himself in his autobiography.

187   Ibid., 40.

188 Ibid., 41.

189 Ibid., 52.

190 Ibid., 15.

191 Ibid., 179.

192 Justin Fox, *The Myth of the Rational Market: A History of Risk, Reward, and Delusion on Wall Street* (New York: HarperCollins, 2009), xii.

193 Greenspan, *The Age of Turbulence*, 370.

194 Ibid., 199.

195 Fox, *The Myth of the Rational Market*, xii.

196 Quoted in Gillian Tett, *Fool's Gold* (London: Little, Brown, 2009), 36.

197 Greenspan, 372.

198 Simon Johnson, 'The Quiet Coup', *The Atlantic* (May 2009).

199 Tett, *Fool's Gold*, 45.

200 Greenspan, *The Age of Turbulence*, 368.

201 Ibid., 367.

202 Fox, *The Myth of the Rational Market*, xii.

203 Sean Wilentz, *The Age of Reagan: A History, 1974–2008* (New York: HarperCollins, 2008), 364.

204 Greenspan, *The Age of Turbulence*, 283.

205 Richard Roberts and David Kynaston, *City State: A Contemporary History of The City of London and How Money Triumphed* (London: Profile Books Ltd, 2001), 33.

206 Quoted in 'India's booming economy', *The Economist*, 2 March 2006, 66.

207 Vince Cable, *The Storm: The World Economic Crisis and What It Means* (London: Atlantic Books, 2009), 90.

208 Derek Chollet and James Goldgeier, *America Between the Wars: From 11/9 to 9/11* (New York: PublicAffairs, 2008), 289.

209 Ben Bernanke, 'The Great Moderation', remarks at the meeting of the Eastern Economic Association, Washington DC, 20 February 2004. The speech is available from www.federalreserve.gov/boarddocs/speeches/ 2004.

210 It would be nice to claim a direct correlation between my joining the paper and its subsequent phenomenal success. But circulation continued to rise steadily, even after the shock of my departure.

211 Michael Mandelbaum, *The Ideas that Conquered the World: Peace, Democracy, and Free Markets in the Twenty-First Century* (New York: PublicAffairs, 2002), 417.

212 Chollet and Goldgeier, *America Between the Wars*, 246–7.

213 Ibid., 246. One such critic was Jagdish Bhagwati of Columbia University, who is quoted in Chollet and Goldgeier.

CHAPTER 12: PROGRESS:
BILL GATES AND THE TRIUMPH OF TECHNOLOGY

214 Alan Greenspan, *The Age of Turbulence: Adventures in a New World* (London: Penguin, 2007), 183.

215 For an account of the hoopla surrounding the launch of Windows 3.0 and the product's significance, see James Wallace and Jim Erickson, *Hard Drive: Bill Gates and the Making of the Microsoft Empire* (New York: Harper Perennial, 1992), 359–63.

216 Greenspan, *The Age of Turbulence*, 167.

217 Tom Friedman, *The World is Flat* (London: Penguin, 2005), 275.

218 Gillian Tett, *Fool's Gold* (London: Little, Brown, 2009), 7.

219 Ibid.

220 Greenspan, *The Age of Turbulence*, 171.

221 Quoted in Robert Wright, *Nonzero: History, Evolution and Human Cooperation* (London: Abacus, 2000), 198.

222 Ibid., 202.

223 Ibid., 7.

224 See Strobe Talbott, *The Great Experiment: The Story of Ancient Empires, Modern States, and the Quest for a Global Nation* (New York: Simon and Schuster, 2008), 311, for a discussion of how Clinton was influenced by Wright's work. The phrase 'win-win world' is, as far as I know, mine.

225 Clinton called the book 'a work of genius' – a quote that duly found its way onto the dustjacket of the paperback edition.

226 George W. Bush, speech at Boeing Integrated Defense Systems Headquarters, St Louis, MO, 16 April 2004.

227 'Plenty of gloom', *The Economist*, 18 December 1997.

228 Talbott, *The Great Experiment*, 461, note 23.

CHAPTER 13: PEACE:
BILL CLINTON AND THE WIN-WIN WORLD

229 Thomas Friedman, 'Foreign Affairs Big Mac I', *New York Times*, 8 December 1996. Friedman was so pleased with his 'Golden arches' theory of war prevention that he later put it in his first book on globalization, *The Lexus and the Olive Tree* (New York: Farrar, Straus and Giroux, 1999).

230 Friedman, *The World Is Flat*, 522.

231 The belief in the peaceable nature of democracies had deep roots in liberal theory. Immanuel Kant, the great eighteenth-century Prussian philosopher, had expounded a theory in which a federation of 'republican' states could establish 'perpetual peace'. Kant was an intellectual hero for Strobe Talbott, Bill Clinton's old college room-mate and deputy secretary of state; see his

book *The Great Experiment: The Story of Ancient Empires, Modern States, and the Quest for a Global Nation* (New York: Simon and Schuster, 2008), 95–100.

232   See, for example, Bruce Russett, *Grasping the Democratic Peace* (Princeton, NJ: Princeton University Press, 1993), and Spencer Weart, *Never at War: Why Democracies Will Not Fight Each Other* (New Haven, CT: Yale University Press, 1998).

233   Quoted in Bill Clinton, *My Life* (London: Arrow, 2004), 365.

234   Quoted in Derek Chollet and James Goldgeier, *America Between the Wars: From 11/9 to 9/11* (New York: PublicAffairs, 2008), 152.

235   Brent Scowcroft, Bush's national security adviser, had travelled to Beijing less than a month after Tiananmen and staged a secret conciliatory dinner with the Chinese leadership. For an account see Zbigniew Brzezinski, *Second Chance: Three Presidents and the Crisis of American Superpower* (New York: Basic Books, 2007), 55.

236   Quoted in Michael Mandelbaum, *The Ideas that Conquered the World: Peace, Democracy, and Free Markets in the Twenty-First Century* (New York: PublicAffairs, 2002), 465. The original reference is to a speech Clinton gave at SAIS Johns Hopkins University on 8 March 2000, quoted in the *New York Times* the following day.

237   Mandelbaum, *The Ideas that Conquered the World*, 268.

238   Gareth Evans, *The Responsibility to Protect: Ending Mass Atrocity Crimes Once and For All* (Washington DC: Brookings Institution Press, 2008), 234.

239   The figures and research methods are spelled out in much more detail in the Human Security Centre, University of British Columbia, *Human Security Report 2005: War and Peace in the 21st Century* (Oxford: Oxford University Press, 2005).

240   Evans, *The Responsibility to Protect*, 224–5.

241   Fareed Zakaria, 'The Secrets of Stability', *Newsweek*, 12 December 2009.

242   Chollet and Goldgeier, *America Between the Wars*, 85.

243   Ibid., 213.

244   Quoted in Martin Jacques, *When China Rules the World: The Rise of the Middle Kingdom and the End of the Western World* (London: Penguin, 2009), 349.

CHAPTER 14: THE OPTIMISTIC EAST:
KISHORE MAHBUBANI AND THE ASIAN CENTURY

245   Quoted in Martin Jacques, *When China Rules the World: The Rise of the Middle Kingdom and the End of the Western World* (London: Penguin, 2009), 348.

246   Gideon Rachman, 'Banquet in Beijing, seminar in Singapore', *Financial Times Blog*, 8 February 2007. Available from http://blogs.ft.com/rachmanblog/2007/02/banquet-in-beijhtml/#more-75. For a discussion of the evolution of the phrase 'peaceful rise', see Robert L.

Suettinger, 'The Rise and Descent of Peaceful Rise', *China Leadership Monitor* No.12 (Fall 2004): 1–10.

247 Quoted in Jim Rohwer, *Asia Rising: Why America Will Prosper as Asia's Economies Boom* (New York: Simon and Schuster, 1996), 333.

248 Political opposition was allowed – but leading figures in the opposition had been financially and politically ruined by costly libel suits.

249 Rohwer, *Asia Rising*, 329.

250 Kishore Mahbubani, *The New Asian Hemisphere: The Irresistible Shift of Global Power to the East* (New York: PublicAffairs, 2008), 14–15.

251 Personal notes from a seminar at the Lee Kuan Yew School in Singapore in February 2007.

252 Ibid.

253 Mahbubani, *The New Asian Hemisphere*, 17.

254 Ibid., 3.

255 Cited in Jacques, *When China Rules the World*, 366.

256 Mahbubani, *The New Asian Hemisphere*, 80.

257 Ibid., 21.

258 Ibid.

259 Gideon Rachman, 'The Bangalore boom revisited', *Financial Times Blog*, 22 September 2008. Available from www.blogs.ft.com/rachmanblog/2008/09/the-bangalore-boom-revisited/.

260 For a good if highly opinionated take on the East Asian crisis, see Joseph Stiglitz, *Globalization and Its Discontents* (London: Penguin, 2002).

CHAPTER 15: EUROPE:
GÜNTER VERHEUGEN AND THE EUROPEAN DREAM

261 Conversation with the author, Warsaw, February 2001.

262 Formally speaking, Verheugen's job was European Union commissioner in charge of enlargement.

263 Quoted in Gideon Rachman, 'A survey of the European Union', *The Economist*, 23 September 2004.

264 See, for example, Christopher Caldwell, *Reflections on the Revolution in Europe: Immigration, Islam and the West* (London: Penguin, 2009).

265 'East, West and the gap between', *The Economist*, 25 November 2005.

266 Quoted in Rachman, 'Survey of the European Union'.

267 Ibid.

268 Conversation with the author, Brussels, March 2003.

269 Rachman, 'Survey of the European Union'.

270 Robert Kagan, *Of Paradise and Power: America and Europe in the New World Order* (New York: Knopf, 2003).

271   Robert Cooper, *The Breaking of Nations: Order and Chaos in the Twenty-First Century* (London: Atlantic Books, 2003), x.

272   Mark Leonard, *Why Europe Will Run the 21st Century* (London: Fourth Estate, 2005), 7.

CHAPTER 16: THE ANTI-GLOBALIZERS:
FROM THE ASIAN CRISIS TO 9/11

273   Philippe Legrain, *Open World: The Truth about Globalization* (London: Abacus, 2002), 17.

274   Quoted in Derek Chollet and James Goldgeier, *America Between the Wars: From 11/9 to 9/11* (New York: PublicAffairs, 2008), 256.

275   Ibid., 257.

276   Naomi Klein, *The Shock Doctrine* (New York: Henry Holt, 2007).

277   Quoted in Legrain, *Open World*, 25.

278   Cited in William Greider, *Come Home America: The Rise and Fall (and Redeeming Promise) of Our Country* (New York: Rodale, 2009), 70.

279   Joseph Stiglitz, *Globalization and Its Discontents* (London: Penguin, 2002), 4.

280   Ibid., 21.

281   Lou Michel and Dan Herbeck, *American Terrorist: Timothy McVeigh and the Oklahoma City Bombing* (New York: Regan Books, 2001), 59.

282   Martin Wolf, *Why Globalization Works* (New Haven, CT: Yale University Press, 2005), 9.

CHAPTER 17: POWER:
CHARLES KRAUTHAMMER AND THE NEOCONSERVATIVES

283   Charles Krauthammer, 'The Unipolar Moment', *Foreign Affairs* 70:1 (Winter 1990/91).

284   Charles Krauthammer, 'The Bush Doctrine', *Time*, 5 March 2001. Some neoconservatives argue that Krauthammer was a latecomer to the party because of his reservations about liberal interventionism in the nineties.

285   Charles Krauthammer, 'Democratic Realism – An American Foreign Policy for a Unipolar World', the Irving Kristol Lecture at the American Enterprise Institute, February 2004. Available from www.aei.org/book/755.

286   Hubert Vedrine, France's foreign minister in the last years of the Mitterrand presidency, had despairingly concluded that the US was more than a mere superpower; it was a 'hyper-power'.

287   See Gillian Tett, *Fool's Gold* (London: Little, Brown, 2009), 99.

288   George W. Bush, address to joint session of Congress, 20 September 2001.

289   Quoted in Derek Chollet and James Goldgeier, *America Between the Wars: From 11/9 to 9/11* (New York: PublicAffairs, 2008), 319.

290 It was a friendly lunch and I was not taking notes on the conversation, so it seems unfair to reveal the identity of the individual involved.

291 Quoted in Andrew Bacevich, *The Limits of Power: The End of American Exceptionalism* (New York: Metropolitan Books, 2008), 126.

292 Francis Fukuyama, *America at the Crossroads: Democracy, Power, and the Neoconservative Legacy* (New Haven, CT: Yale University Press, 2006), xi–xii. Fukuyama was appalled by Krauthammer's speech and dates his explicit break with the neocons from that date.

293 James Miles, 'Balancing act: A survey of China', *The Economist*, 25 March 2006, 4.

294 Ibid.

Part Three: The Age of Anxiety

CHAPTER 18: THE CRISIS OF THE WEST

295 Quoted in Gideon Rachman, 'Is America's new declinism for real?', *Financial Times*, 25 November 2008. I was in the audience for Scowcroft's speech and attended the NIC conference.

296 National Intelligence Council, *Global Trends 2025: A Transformed World* (Washington DC: Government Printing Office, 2008). Also available from http://www.acus.org/files/publication_pdfs/3/Global-Trends-2025.pdf.

297 Ibid.

298 Fareed Zakaria, *The Post-American World* (New York: Norton, 2008), 199.

399 John Plender, 'Decline but not fall', *Financial Times*, 12 November 2009.

300 Francis Fukuyama, 'Thinking About the Future of American Capitalism', *American Interest Magazine Editorial Blog*, 13 March 2009. Available from http://blogs.the-american-interest.com/.

301 Gideon Rachman, 'Asia rides high – for the moment', *Financial Times*, 30 September 2008.

302 Gideon Rachman, 'China makes gains in its bid to be the next top dog', *Financial Times*, 15 September 2009.

303 Ibid.

304 Edward Luce, 'Washington adapts to eastwards power shift', *Financial Times*, 11 November 2009.

305 Stephen S. Cohen and Brad DeLong, *The End of Influence* (New York: Basic Books, 2010), 7.

306 Harold James, *The Creation and Destruction of Value* (Cambridge, MA: Harvard University Press, 2009), 179.

307 Ibid., 222.

308 David Sanger, 'Deficits May Alter US Politics and Global Power', *New York Times*, 1 February 2010.

309   Quoted in Rachman, 'China makes gains'.

310   Quoted in Andrew Bacevich, *The Limits of Power: The End of American Exceptionalism* (New York: Metropolitan Books, 2008), 133.

311   Conversation with the author, Beijing, January 2007.

312   Tania Branigan, 'China's role on world stage is no cause for fear, says Obama', *The Observer*, 15 November 2009.

313   Aaron Friedberg, 'Is China a Military Threat?', *The National Interest* No.103 (September/October 2009).

314   Ibid.

315   Andrew F. Krepinevich, Jr, 'The Pentagon's Wasting Assets', *Foreign Affairs* 88:4 (July/August 2009).

316   Marc Kaufman and Dafna Linzer, 'China Criticized for Anti-Satellite Missile Test', *Washington Post*, 19 January 2007.

317   Conversation with the author, London, March 2009.

318   Conversation with the author, Washington DC, May 2009.

319   Michael Mandelbaum, *The Ideas that Conquered the World: Peace, Democracy, and Free Markets in the Twenty-First Century* (New York: PublicAffairs, 2002), 395.

320   Yukio Hatoyama, 'A New Path for Japan', *New York Times*, 27 August 2009.

321   Quoted in Elitsa Vucheva, 'Laissez-faire capitalism is finished says France', *EUObserver.com*, 26 September 2008.

322   Piergiorgio Alessandri and Andrew Haldane, 'Banking on the State', Bank of England, November 2009. Available from http://www.bankofengland. co.uk/publications/speeches/2009/speech409.pdf.

323   John Reed, 'Back on the road', *Financial Times*, 18 June 2009.

324   Francesco Guerrera, 'Welch condemns shareholder value focus', *Financial Times*, 12 March 2009.

325   Charles Grant, 'Liberalism Retreats in China', Centre for European Reform, London, July 2009.

326   Ian Bremmer, 'State Capitalism Comes of Age: The End of the Free Market?', *Foreign Affairs* 88:3 (May/June 2009).

327   Ibid.

328   Ibid.

329   See 'Madagascar leader axes land deal', *BBC News*, 19 March 2009. Available from http://news.bbc.co.uk/2/hi/africa/7952628.stm.

330   Zakaria, *The Post-American World*, 47.

Chapter 19: A World of Troubles

331   Barack Obama, 'Responsibility for Our Common Future', address to the United Nations General Assembly, 23 September 2009.

332 AIG turned out to be regulated by the state of New York.

333 Geoff Dyer, 'China sets carbon target for 2020', *Financial Times*,
     26 November 2009.

334 Quoted in Global Witness, 'Heads in the Sand: Governments Ignore the Oil
     Supply Crunch and Threaten the Climate', October 2009, 6. Available from
     http://www.globalwitness.org/media_library_detail.php/854/en/heads_in_
     the_sand_governments_ignore_the_oil_suppl.

335 Ibid., 21.

336 Bill Emmott, 'China's accidental empire is a growing danger', *The Times*,
     22 May 2009.

337 Alan Greenspan, *The Age of Turbulence: Adventures in a New World* (London:
     Penguin, 2007), 463.

338 Gideon Rachman, 'The battle for food, oil and water', *Financial Times*,
     29 January 2008.

339 Quoted in Javier Blas, 'Global hunger at the top of the political agenda',
     Financial Times, 9 November 2009.

340 Conversation with the author, Beijing, January 2007.

341 Brahma Chellaney, 'Beware of water wars', *The Times of India*, 24 November
     2008.

342 Jeffrey Sachs, *Common Wealth: Economics for a Crowded Planet* (London: Allen
     Lane, 2008), 124.

343 Paul Collier, *The Bottom Billion: Why the Poorest Countries are Failing and What
     Can Be Done About It* (Oxford: Oxford University Press, 2007), 19.

344 Richard Black, 'Climate "is a major cause" of conflict in Africa', *BBC News*,
     24 November 2009. Available from http://news.bbc.co.uk/2/hi/8375949.stm.

345 Jeffrey Sachs, Letter to the Editor, *Financial Times*, 4 May 2009.

346 Joel Kurtzman, 'Mexico's Instability is a Real Problem', *Wall Street Journal*,
     16 January 2009.

347 Gideon Rachman, 'Mexico's drug war spills over into the US – and Venezuela
     confronts Colombia', *Financial Times Blog*, 3 August 2009. Available from
     http://blogs.ft.com/rachmanblog/2009/08/mexicos-drug-war-spills-over-into-
     the-us-and-venezuela-confront-colombia/.

348 Private information.

349 Quoted in a paper on terrorism and weapons of mass destruction prepared by
     Graham Allison and Joe Costa for the Global Agenda Council of the World
     Economic Forum in Dubai on 17 November 2009.

350 The nuclear powers are the five permanent members of the UN Security
     Council, plus India and Pakistan. Israel is known to have nuclear weapons,
     although it has never acknowledged this in public. North Korea is believed to
     have successfully tested a nuclear bomb.

351 Kishore Mahbubani, *The New Asian Hemisphere: The Irresistible Shift of Global*

Power to the East (New York: PublicAffairs, 2008), 241.

352   Sachs, *Common Wealth*, 7.

353   Ibid., 3.

354   I was a member of the WEF's Global Redesign Initiative.

355   Interview with the author, Washington DC, May 2009.

CHAPTER 20: GLOBAL GOVERNMENT: THE WORLD AS EUROPE

356   I was in Brussels at a European summit on the night that the EU constitution was rewritten as the Lisbon Treaty. A friend who worked for the Union told me, 'If you want to understand what they are doing, you must read Nabokov's novel *Pale Fire*.' The point he was making was that in *Pale Fire* all the really important things are put in the footnotes. This is what the EU did with the Lisbon Treaty, where crucial but controversial measures – such as the supremacy of EU law – were smuggled through in footnotes to the main text. It seems only appropriate to record this fact in a footnote.

357   Quoted in Gideon Rachman, 'Europe's plot to take over the world', *Financial Times*, 5 October 2009.

358   Private information.

359   The Schuman Declaration, 1950.

360   Quoted in Rachman, 'Europe's plot to take over the world'.

361   Anders Aslund, 'G20 must be stopped', *Financial Times*, 26 November 2009.

362   Enter the words 'world government' and 'Gideon Rachman' into Google, and you will see what I mean.

363   The best modern account of the work and powers of the UN is Paul Kennedy, *The Parliament of Man: The Past, Present, and Future of the United Nations* (New York: Random House, 2006).

364   Ibid., xi.

365   Conversation with the author, September 2007.

366   Fiona Harvey, Ed Crooks and Andrew Ward, 'Copenhagen: A discordant accord', *Financial Times*, 20 December 2009.

367   See Tim Harford (The Undercover Economist), 'Political ill wind blows a hole in the climate change debate', *Financial Times Weekend* (magazine), 28–9 November 2009.

368   Moisés Naím, 'Think small to tackle the world's problems', *Financial Times*, 18 June 2009.

369   'Responsibility to protect: An idea whose time has come – and gone?', *The Economist*, 23 July 2009.

370   Richard Gowan and Franziska Brandtner, 'A Global Force for Human Rights?: An Audit of European Power at the UN,' European Council on Foreign Relations, 17 September 2008.

CHAPTER 21: AXIS OF AUTHORITARIANISM:
THE WORLD AS RUSSIA AND CHINA

371 See Gideon Rachman, 'Lunch with the FT, Mikheil Saakashvili,' *Financial Times*, 25 April 2008.

372 Ibid.

373 Press release for Freedom House, *Freedom in the World 2009* (Lanham, MD: Rowman and Littlefield Publishers, 2009).

374 Ibid.

375 There is a longstanding controversy about what exactly western politicians said to the Russians about Nato and Central Europe in the aftermath of the fall of the Berlin Wall. But one of the best recent scholarly accounts, Mary Elise Sarotte's *1989: The Struggle to Create Post-Cold War Europe* (Princeton, NJ: Princeton University Press, 2009), suggests that the Russian complaints have some substance.

376 Quoted in John Kampfner, *Freedom for Sale: How We Made Money and Lost Our Liberty* (London: Simon and Schuster, 2009), 91.

377 Ibid., 99.

378 Quoted in James Mann, *The China Fantasy: How Our Leaders Explain Away Chinese Repression* (New York: Penguin, 2007), 49.

379 Quoted in Gideon Rachman, 'Let us not lose faith in democracy', *Financial Times*, 22 January 2008.

380 Adam Przeworski, Limongi Neto and Fernando Papaterra, 'Modernization: Theories and Facts', *World Politics* 49:2 (January 1997), 155–83.

381 Rachman, 'Let us not lose faith in democracy'.

382 'Clinton: Chinese human rights can't interfere with other crises', *CNN*, 2 February 2009. Available from http://www.cnn.com/2009/POLITICS/02/21/clinton.china.asia/.

383 Robert Kagan, *The Return of History and The End of Dreams* (London: Atlantic Books, 2008), 57–8.

384 Fiona Harvey, Ed Crooks and Andrew Ward, 'Copenhagen: A discordant accord', *Financial Times*, 20 December 2009.

385 Benedict Mander and Jonathan Wheatley, 'Iranian leader's warm embrace in Venezuela stirs US anxiety', *Financial Times*, 26 November 2009.

386 Kagan, *The Return of History*, 98.

387 Ibid..

388 They included Ivo Daalder, Obama's Nato ambassador, and Anne-Marie Slaughter, the head of policy planning at the State Department.

389 Harvey, Crooks and Ward, 'Copenhagen: a discordant accord'.

390 'Whose side is Brazil on?', *The Economist*, 15 August 2009.

391 'South Africa and the world: the see no evil foreign policy', *The Economist*,
     13 November 2008.

Chapter 22: Fractured World:
The World as Pakistan

392 The Pearl Continental itself was the target of a suicide attack in June 2009
     that killed around fifteen people, including Kamal Ahmed, the hotel's popular
     general manager.

393 Gordon later became assistant secretary of state for Europe in the Obama
     administration.

394 See Omar Waraich, 'Peshawar: More and More, A City Under Siege', *Time*,
     11 June 2009.

395 Private information.

396 Obama committed to sending 15,000 more troops shortly after he was elected
     and announced a further surge of 30,000 in December 2009.

397 Barack Obama, 'Remarks by the President in Address to the Nation on the
     Way Forward in Afghanistan and Pakistan', West Point, NY, 1 December
     2009.

398 Some observers, factoring in indirect costs, such as the costs of caring for
     veterans, have argued that the figure is significantly higher. Joseph Stiglitz put
     the cost of the Iraq War at $3 trillion.

399 Paul Collier, *Wars, Guns and Votes: Democracy in Dangerous Places* (London:
     Bodley Head, 2009), 11.

400 'US Seen as Less Important, China as More Powerful: Isolationist Sentiment
     Surges to Four-Decade High', Pew Research Center, Washington DC, 3
     December 2009. Available from http://pewresearch.org/pubs/1428/
     america-seen-less-important-china-more-powerful-isolationist-sentiment-
     surges.

401 Susan E. Rice and Stewart Patrick, 'Index of State Weakness in the
     Developing World', Brookings Institution, 2008. Available from
     http://www.brookings.edu/reports/2008/02_weak_states_index.aspx.

402 'The long arm of America', *The Economist*, 19 September 2009.

403 'Egypt – will the dam burst?', *The Economist*, 11 September 2008.

404 Quoted in Shannon O'Neil, 'The Real War in Mexico', *Foreign Affairs* 88:4
     (July/August 2009), 63.

405 Ibid.

406 See Misha Glenny, 'Drugs cartels open another front in a futile war', *Financial
     Times*, 11 December 2009, and Misha Glenny, *McMafia: Seriously Organized
     Crime* (London: Vintage, 2009).

CHAPTER 23: ZERO-SUM WORLD

407 Tom Friedman, *The World is Flat* (London: Penguin, 2005), 544.

408 Fareed Zakaria, *The Post-American World* (New York: Norton, 2008), 218.

409 See 'Lessons from *The Leopard*,' *The Economist*, 11 December 2009.

410 See, for example, Stewart Brand, *Whole Earth Discipline* (London: Atlantic Books, 2010).

411 Martin Wolf, 'The dangers of living in a zero-sum world economy', *Financial Times*, 18 December 2007.

412 'US Seen as Less Important, China as More Powerful: Isolationist Sentiment Surges to Four-Decade High', Pew Research Center, Washington DC, 3 December 2009. Available from http://pewresearch.org/pubs/1428/america-seen-less-important-china-more-powerful-isolationist-sentiment-surges.

413 Malcolm Moore, 'Timothy Geithner currency manipulation accusation angers China', *Daily Telegraph*, 23 January 2009.

414 Alan Beattie, 'The perception in China is that revaluation ended the Japanese miracle', *Financial Times*, 1 December 2009.

415 Paul Krugman, 'The Chinese Disconnect', *New York Times*, 23 October 2009.

416 Paul Krugman, 'Chinese New Year', *New York Times*, 1 January 2010.

417 Robert Aliber, 'Tariffs can persuade Beijing to free the renminbi', *Financial Times*, 7 December 2009.

418 James Mann, *The China Fantasy: Why Capitalism Will Not Bring Democracy to China* (New York: Penguin, 2008), 26.

419 Greg Muller, 'Right-wing Extremists Seen as Threat,' *Los Angeles Times*, 10 April 2009.

420 Quoted in Robert Kagan, *The Return of History and The End of Dreams* (London: Atlantic Books, 2008), 33.

421 Patti Waldmeir, 'Wen hits out at unfair stance over renminbi', *Financial Times*, 1 December 2009.

422 Richard McGregor, 'Chinese buy into currency war plot', *The Australian*, 27 September 2007.

423 Grace Ng, 'Chinese flip new page in push to be superpower', *Straits Times*, 6 April 2009.

424 Peter David, 'All change, no change: A special report on the Arab world', *The Economist*, 23 July 2009.

425 Harold James, 'The Late, Great Globalization', *Current History* 108:714 (January 2009).

426 Kevin O'Rourke, *Politics and Trade: Lessons from Past Globalizations* (Brussels: Bruegel Essay and Lecture Series, 2009), 5. Electronic version available from http://www.bruegel.org/uploads/tx_btbbreugel/ el_0209_poltrade.pdf.

427 Ibid., 8.

428 Niall Ferguson, '"Chimerica" is Headed for Divorce', *Newsweek*, 15 August
     2009.

429 Jeffrey Ball, 'Summit Is Seen as US Versus China', *Wall Street Journal*, 14
     December 2009.

CHAPTER 24: SAVING THE WORLD

430 Conversation with the author.

431 Andrew Sullivan, 'America wakes up to the shift in global power', *The Sunday
     Times*, 6 December 2009.

432 Francis Fukuyama, *The End of History and The Last Man* (London: Penguin,
     1992), 48.

433 Kishore Mahbubani, *The New Asian Hemisphere: The Irresistible Shift of Global
     Power to the East* (New York: PublicAffairs, 2008), 145.

434 James Miles, 'A wary respect: A special report on China and America', *The
     Economist*, 24 October 2009.

435 'US Seen as Less Important, China as More Powerful: Isolationist Sentiment
     Surges to Four-Decade High', Pew Research Center, Washington DC, 3
     December 2009. Available from http://pewresearch.org/pubs/1428/ america-
     seen-less-important-china-more-powerful-isolationist-sentiment-surges.

436 The poll showed that 44 per cent of the public thought that China was the
     world's leading economic power. Only 27 per cent named the US. In 1989 58
     per cent of the public thought that Japan was the world's leading economic
     power. That was also wrong.

437 'G8: Chinese president flies homes from summit after Xinjiang riots', *Daily
     Telegraph*, 8 July 2009.

438 See Gareth Evans and Yoriko Kawaguchi, 'A plan to eliminate the world's
     nuclear weapons', *Financial Times*, 18 December 2009.

439 Gideon Rachman, 'Why we need a United Nations army', *Financial Times*,
     21 July 2009.

440 Kathrin Hille, 'China seeks reform of UN peacekeeping', *Financial Times*,
     17 November 2009.

441 'Ranking of military and police contribution to UN peacekeeping operations',
     United Nations, November 2009. America's contribution of seventy-six
     personnel, listed in November 2009, was mainly civilian police.

442 J. M. Keynes, 'Open Letter to President Roosevelt', *New York Times*,
     31 December 1933.

Bibliographic Essay

Since *Zero-Sum World* attempts to cover both the recent history and the future of the world – a large topic – it would be futile to attempt a comprehensive bibliography. Most of the works I consulted are already cited in the Notes. But some readers might want to delve further into a particular topic, so here is a guide to some of the books I found especially useful and interesting during the course of my research.

The opening of China under Deng Xiaoping is covered well by a number of histories of the country, including Jonathan Spence's *The Search for Modern China* (Norton, 1999) and Jonathan Fenby's *The Penguin Modern History of China* (Allen Lane, 2008). *Prisoner of the State: The Secret Journal of Chinese Premier Zhao Ziyang* (Simon and Schuster, 2009) is a gripping insider account from a former ally of Deng, who was later purged.

I would particularly recommend two books on the Thatcher era. John Campbell's two-volume biography is marvellously readable, as well as scholarly. The second volume, *Margaret Thatcher: The Iron Lady* (Vintage, 2008) covers the Downing Street years. Andrew Marr's *A History of Modern Britain* (Pan Macmillan, 2007) is an excellent general history. Lady Thatcher's own memoirs are also worth looking at.

Scholarship on Ronald Reagan is still strikingly polarized. Dinesh D'Souza has written a short biography-cum-hagiography, *Ronald Reagan: How an Ordinary Man Became an Extraordinary Leader* (Simon and Schuster, 1997). A longer and more scholarly work, also from a conservative perspective, is Stephen Hayward's *The Age of Reagan: The Conservative Counter-Revolution* (Crown, 2009). Sean Wilentz's similarly titled *The Age of Reagan: A History, 1974–2008* (Harper Collins, 2008) is much less sympathetic, but still argues that Reagan was the central figure defining the politics of the US over the last thirty years.

The history of Europe in the eighties is covered in Tony Judt's magisterial study *Postwar: A History of Europe since 1945* (Penguin, 2005) and Harold James's *Europe Reborn* (Longman, 2003). Charles Grant's *Delors: Inside the House that Jacques Built* (Nicholas Brealey, 1994) is an indispensable account of the transformation of the European Union under Delors.

Judt and James are also good on the Gorbachev era in the Soviet Union. I am very fond of a book written by a former BBC colleague, Angus Roxburgh, and based on extensive interviews with the main players of the Gorbachev period, *The Second Russian Revolution* (BBC Books, 1991). A more recent and academic account is provided by Archie Brown's *The Rise and Fall of Communism* (Ecco, 2009).

The twentieth anniversary of the fall of the Berlin Wall produced several good books on Europe's year of revolutions in 1989. The ones I most enjoyed were Mary Elise Sarotte's *1989: The Struggle to Create Post-Cold War Europe* (Princeton, 2009) and Victor Sebesteyn's *Revolution 1989: The Fall of the Soviet Empire* (Weidenfeld and Nicholson, 2009). Timothy Garton Ash covered these events as a journalist and his *The Magic Lantern: The Revolution of '89 Witnessed in Warsaw, Budapest, Berlin, and Prague* (Random House, 1990) remains a classic.

Michael Reid has produced a brilliant account of the modern history of Latin America, *Forgotten Continent: The Battle for Latin America's Soul*

(Yale, 2008). Maxwell Cameron and Brian Tomlin's *The Making of NAFTA: How the Deal Was Done* (Cornell, 2000) is an important take on a key moment in the history of globalization. Richard Bourne's *Lula of Brazil: The Story So Far* (University of California Press, 2008) portrays one of the region's most charismatic leaders.

There are several good books on the modernization of India. The one for a long plane journey is *In Spite of the Gods: The Rise of Modern India* (Random House, 2008) by Edward Luce, my colleague from the *Financial Times*. Gurchuran Das, *India Unbound* (Anchor, 2002) and Ramachandra Guha, *India after Gandhi: The History of the World's Largest Democracy* (Pan Macmillan, 2007) are also excellent.

Richard Haass has provided an insider's account of the run-up to the first Gulf War in *War of Necessity, War of Choice: A Memoir of Two Iraq Wars* (Simon and Schuster, 2009). Lawrence Freedman's *A Choice of Enemies: America Confronts the Middle East* (PublicAffairs, 2008) offers an insightful, scholarly history of US policy to the Middle East.

The Age of Optimism from 1991 to 2008 was also America's 'unipolar moment'. Derek Chollet and James Goldgeier's *America Between the Wars: From 11/9 to 9/11* (PublicAffairs, 2008) is a superbly researched and written account of US foreign policy during this era. Strobe Talbott's *The Great Experiment: The Story of Ancient Empires, Modern States, and the Quest for a Global Nation* (Simon and Schuster, 2008) goes all the way back to ancient Greece, but also offers some lively insights into the Clinton era and some interesting reflections on the problem of global governance.

Anyone wanting to understand the 'end of history' debate has to go back to Francis Fukuyama's original work, *The End of History and the Last Man* (Penguin, 1992). Fukuyama's later disavowal of neoconservatism, *America at the Crossroads: Democracy, Power, and the Neoconservative Legacy* (Yale, 2006) is also well worth reading. The best thing to read on Alan Greenspan is Greenspan's own surprisingly compulsive memoirs, *The Age of Turbulence: Adventures in a New World* (Penguin, 2007).

There have now been a great many books on the origins of the crash of 2008 and its economic lessons. Two of my favourites are Gillian Tett's *Fool's Gold* (Little, Brown, 2006) and Justin Fox's *The Myth of the Rational Market* (Harper Collins, 2009).

The defining text capturing the optimism generated by the interplay between the technological revolution and globalization is Thomas Friedman's *The World is Flat* (Penguin, 2005). The optimism about the rise of Asia during this period is caught both by Kishore Mahbubani's *The New Asian Hemisphere: The Irresistible Shift of Global Power to the East* (PublicAffairs, 2008) and Martin Jacques's *When China Rules the World: The Rise of the Middle Kingdom and the End of the Western World* (Penguin, 2009). A cooler and more sceptical take, highlighting the rivalries within Asia, is offered by Bill Emmott's *Rivals: How the Power Struggle Between China, India and Japan Will Shape the Next Decade* (Penguin, 2008).

Many European thinkers genuinely believed that the future of the world was being moulded in Brussels rather than Beijing during the Age of Optimism. To understand this view, it is worth turning to Robert Cooper's *The Breaking of Nations: Order and Chaos in the Twenty-First Century* (Atlantic, 2003) – a sophisticated take on the 'post-national' European view of the world by a scholar-diplomat working for the European Union.

The literature for and against globalization is voluminous and often tedious. Anybody wanting to understand the emotions and reasoning of the anti-globalizers has to read Naomi Klein: *The Shock Doctrine* (Henry Holt, 2007) is as good a place as any to start. Joseph Stiglitz's *Globalization and Its Discontents* (Penguin, 2002) is written for the mass market, but still displays some of the scholarly traits that won its author a Nobel Prize for Economics. The best defence of globalization that I know of is Martin Wolf's *Why Globalization Works* (Yale, 2005).

Neoconservatism has been better at producing polemical journalism, by the likes of Bill Kristol and Charles Krauthammer, than books. But

Robert Kagan's *Dangerous Nation* (Vintage, 2007) is a fine, revisionist history of US foreign policy written from a neocon perspective. Andrew Bacevich's *The Limits of Power: The End of American Exceptionalism* (Metropolitan, 2008) is a short, angry and devastating critique of neoconservatism, by a military veteran turned professor who lost his son in the Iraq War.

The third section of my book, The Age of Anxiety, deals with current and emerging trends in global politics, and draws more heavily on my own journalism and on articles in academic journals and newspapers. Books that I found particularly useful in framing my own thinking included Fareed Zakaria's *Post-American World* (Norton, 2008) and Michael Mandelbaum's *The Ideas that Conquered the World* (Public-Affairs, 2002). Paul Collier's *The Bottom Billion* (Oxford, 2007) is a rare book that changed the debate about poverty and development. Jeffrey Sachs's *Common Wealth: Economics for a Crowded Planet* (Penguin, 2007) is a morally impassioned effort to combine the imperatives of development, environmentalism and market economics. James Mann's *The China Fantasy: How Our Leaders Explain Away Chinese Repression* (Penguin, 2007) was a prescient and polemical effort to challenge the official US line that the rise of China was all for the best. Finally, Misha Glenny's *McMafia: Seriously Organized Crime* (Vintage, 2009) is a grimly entertaining study of some of the world's most sinister non-governmental organizations.

Acknowledgements

The period covered by this book more or less coincides with my career as a journalist, which began in the mid-eighties. Thanking everybody who has helped me or shaped my thinking over the course of more than twenty-five years is an impossible task – and I will not attempt it. But I would like to say thanks to some of the people who have been particularly important to me, both in the writing of this book and during my career.

When I left *The Economist* after a fifteen-year stint, it struck me that there was an alarming overlap between my closest colleagues and my closest friends. It would be invidious to single out any individuals. Nonetheless, I will do it. For their friendship and intellectual support, I would particularly like to thank Emma Duncan, Christopher Lockwood, Andrew Miller, Sophie Pedder, Simon Long, Matt Ridley (who hired me), Johnny Grimond (the best editor I've ever worked with), Ed Lucas and Peter David. Bill Emmott, who was editor-in-chief during most of my time at the paper, was the ideal boss: remote, vague, but always supportive and intelligent when it mattered. John Micklethwait and Adrian Wooldridge have inspired me in ways that only they truly understand.

In 2006 Lionel Barber, the editor of the *Financial Times*, offered me the best job I could ever have hoped for – chief foreign affairs commentator for the *FT*. At my new paper, Martin Wolf, my fellow columnist, has been a fantastic source of ideas and stimulation. John Thornhill, Lucy Kellaway, Phillip Stephens and Caroline Daniel have all been generous and helpful colleagues. On my travels, I have benefited hugely from the *FT*'s unrivalled network of correspondents. For their expertise and hospitality, I would like to thank Ed Luce in Washington, Neil Buckley and Arkady Ostrovsky in Moscow, Jon Boone in Kabul, Farhan Bokhari in Islamabad, Geoff Dyer and Richard McGregor in Beijing, Patti Waldmeir in Shanghai, Victor Mallet in Madrid, James Lamont in Delhi, David Pilling in Hong Kong, Bertrand Benoit in Berlin, Vincent Boland in Istanbul, Richard Lapper in Johannesburg, Gwen Robinson and the Tokyo team, Ben Hall in Paris and Adam Thomson in Mexico City. In the slightly less remote reaches of the *FT*'s research department, Peter Cheek and Bhavna Patel were also a great help.

I would also like to thank three other editors who published my work and helped me in other ways: David Goodhart of *Prospect*, Moisés Naím of *Foreign Policy* and Alex Lennon of the *Washington Quarterly*.

The Brookings Institution in Washington DC was generous enough to let me tag along on fascinating study trips to China, Ukraine and Georgia. I would particularly like to thank my fellow strategic tourist, Phil Gordon, the former head of US foreign policy studies at Brookings, who was a congenial companion on trips to China, India and Pakistan. I much appreciated his un-American willingness to reschedule the most important meetings in favour of watching the soccer on television.

I owe particular thanks to Daniel Dombey of the *FT*, who read the whole of this book in draft and made a number of devastating, but accurate, comments that I am certain have improved the end-product. Charles Grant of the Centre for European Reform also read an early draft and saved me from numerous errors of fact and interpretation. Mike Reid, Christopher Hum and Harold James (my former teacher at

Cambridge and Princeton) have all read and commented upon parts of the book.

Long before I became a journalist, my ability to think and write was honed by three years studying history at Caius College, Cambridge, where I was fortunate to be taught by, among others, Noel Malcom, Neil McKendrick and Vic Gatrell. In 1987–8 Princeton University made me a visiting fellow at the Centre for International Studies, where I was lucky enough to follow an extraordinary course on Cold War history taught by John Lewis Gaddis.

I owe huge thanks to Sarah Chalfant, my literary agent in London, and to Scott Moyers, her colleague at the Wylie Agency in New York. I have been both astonished and grateful by how much time and energy they have been prepared to devote to me. Partly thanks to their efforts, I ended up with outstanding publishers in the UK and the US. Toby Mundy at Atlantic Books in London was enthusiastic about this project from the off and his comments were invariably helpful and to the point. Alice Mayhew at Simon and Schuster in New York knew when to intervene and when to leave things alone, which is just what you want in an editor. Margaret Stead at Atlantic and Roger Labrie at Simon and Schuster were also encouraging and professional throughout.

Finally, I would like to thank my family. My sister Carla, my brother Tom, my sister Emily and both sets of parents: Dawn and John, and Jack and Clare. Together they provided love, and an education in how to win an argument over dinner. My children Natasha, Joe, Nathaniel and Adam seem to have inherited the family interest in debate and discussion, for which I am (largely) grateful. Above all, I thank Olivia, for her love, patience and sense of humour – and for keeping the show on the road. This book is dedicated to her.

INDEX